S0-ATR-508

In the Sky
Copy Right © 2019 Jerry Farquhar
ISBN: 978-1-970153-09-5
Library of Congress Control Number:2019911538

Cover Art: Image is Actual Photo taken by the Author
Printed in the United States of America

La Maison Publishing, Inc.
Vero Beach, Florida
The Hibiscus City
lamaisonpublishing@gmail.com

Maison

In the Sky

A Retired Captain Looks Back over Fifty-nine Years
(Over Twenty-six-thousand Hours of Flying Time)

By Captain Jerry L. Farquhar

Dedication

I am dedicating this book to my late wife, Captain Dorothy (Dotty) Westby. She pushed me to write it. She also triggered the Flight Safety Division of the FAA to research my flying record. This resulted in the award, given at 2014 Sun-n-Fun, of the Wright Brothers Master Pilot Award plaque. Mine was one of nine given that year for fifty plus years of flying with no violations or accidents. Dotty engineered the whole thing, and I had no idea about it until the morning of the awards show.

I want to share the memory of my Dotty with the reader. She was one of those very rare women who was not only knockout beautiful, but widely talented. As a girl, she won trophies for swimming, diving, and riding (both dressage and jumping). She also played polo and quarterbacked a girls' football team. At the same time, she was a National Merit Scholar and straight A student.

After graduating from Sweetbriar College, she did post grad studies at Rhode Island School of Design. Married, she had a son and daughter while enjoying a successful career in art in the Boston and Hartford areas.

Divorced from a cheating husband in 1978, she moved to Fort Lauderdale to be near a sick mother and her stepfather. Here she started a new career in aviation. While holding a full-time job, and paying for training, she soloed in nine hours. In one more year, she added Commercial, Multi-Engine, and Instrument ratings. She then began working charter flights around Florida, Bahamas, and the Caribbean.

She flew King Airs with Capt. Gustavo Ponzoa. The Castro brothers put a price on Gustavo's head because he led the B-26 bombing raid on the Cuban Air Force prior to the Bay of Pigs fiasco.

After my first wife, Joyce, and I rode back from the Bahamas with Dotty, she went on to fly as Flight Engineer on the Boeing 727 with Miami Air. There, she moved up to co-pilot and then, captain.

Dotty loved to challenge herself with new things. Once she saw, or read, or was told some new thing, I could almost see her organize it in her mind and then, she owned it. I taught her to shoot. I started by showing her how to clear and then take apart, clean and re-assemble a semi-auto pistol. I showed her how to do it once! She reached across the table for the pistol. She cleared it, stripped it, put it back together, put it on the table and pushed it toward me with one finger and a mischievous grin.

Dotty was always interested in things which required mental effort or the demonstration of her terrific athletic ability. I think she knew she was beautiful, but it was just not important to her, because it was not something she had accomplished.

Proof of this came many years after we were married with the visit by Ed Wheeler and his wife. Ed was a high school classmate of Dotty's at Tulsa Central High. He and I have become friends and have in common that we both lost a first wife.

Sitting in our living room, Ed spoke of his high school days. He admitted to being in love with Dotty, but was too shy to ask for a date. To this admission, Dotty replied, "Ed, you were such a sweet guy, I would have gone out with you in a minute." Ed answered, "Well, I was just too shy back then." He asked her if she was aware that the boys referred to her as "Dotty the Body." She said she did not know that. He said that nearly all the boys voted for her to be Homecoming Queen, and that when she was elected he went around to the home rooms to tally the voting. He said it was about ninety-percent of the boys and, surprisingly, over seventy-percent of the girls voted for her.

At this point, I said, "She never told me about this." Ed asked, "She never showed you her yearbook?" When I answered no, he asked her to go get the yearbook. There, for the first time, I saw the spectacular full-page photo of the beauty I married. Ed went on to make the point that Dotty was the most popular girl in their class of nine-hundred-seventy-six students, because she was friends with *everybody*.

Yes, she was movie star beautiful, but it was just not important to her, and she was too honest ever to use it for any advantage. She took pride in *doing* things well and was one of those *natural* pilots who don't get into an airplane. They put it *on* and *wear* it.

I miss her terribly, so this book is for her... because she asked me to write it.

Foreword

This book is an attempt to paint a picture of the airline world from fifty plus years ago through my career. There are 8,760 hours in a year. My title derives from the three [flying] years I have spent at the controls of many different aircraft. Many pilots who have flown the airlines will have had similar experiences. I make no attempt to be exclusive or comprehensive, but rather to offer a flavor of what this world was like. Most names here are true. Some have been changed or omitted to preserve the sensitivities of those involved. In a few cases, I must plead Winston Churchill's excuse, "that a gentleman never insults someone by accident."

The airline world has changed dramatically in the fifty-six years since I entered it. Some changes are for the better, but some are not so good. I hope you enjoy my story.

Sincerely,
Captain Jerry L. Farquhar

A Brief Biography of Capt. Jerry L. Farquhar

My friends, Jim and Ruth Jacobs, suggested I should include a brief bio in this work, so here it is.

I was born August 19, 1938, in Hollywood, CA. My father, James, was a graduate of the University of California, Berkeley. Dad was quite an athlete. For three years, he held the Pacific Coast Championship in diving off the ten-meter tower and three-meter springboard. A dislocated shoulder, when diving off the tower, ended his career. His teammate, Dutch Smith, went on to join in the 1936 Olympic Team.

Dad and my mom, Agnes, owned a service station and store near Huntington Beach. Dad had been Army ROTC and wanted to fly. He was nearly blind in one eye as a result of a BB gun accident as a boy and had successfully passed "casual" ROTC physicals by memorizing eye charts. A pre-flight training physical was more thorough, however. It detected the bad eye and he lost his Army Commission, DQed (disqualified) for any service.

After Pearl Harbor, he became a junior executive at North American Aviation in Long Beach. We lived on 7th Street, in Huntington Beach during the early part of the war and then, moved to L. A. to put Dad closer to work.

I was probably about five years old, but clearly remember being led down our street a block-and-a-half to Coast Highway (now, the Pacific Coast Hwy, or PCH) and the beach. A crowd stood in the night, looking in awe up the beach at the burning oil refinery at Signal Hill. A Japanese sub had lobbed shells into the refinery and set it ablaze. After that experience, the ration stamps and blackout curtains in our house took on new meaning. The war was real. They really were out there in our ocean and might come ashore on our beach one night.

I did not understand it, but can remember the wild cheering in our local theater when *Movie Tone News* showed clips of Jimmy Doolittle's B-25s lifting off the deck of the carrier, Hornet. Of course, we all now know the heroic story of the Tokyo Raiders. I later briefly met Jimmy Doolittle on one of his visits to the Air Force Academy. Recalling this now gives me pause. Just how young was I when the flying bug bit me? I don't know. I knew, early on, that it could be dangerous.

My Dad and uncles were regular surfers. The Huntington Beach Pier offered an easy way to get out past big surf. You simply walked out past the breaker line and dropped the board over the rail and, then, made a thirty-foot jump. Dad did fancy dives off this rail. I learned to swim early on. By age three, my uncles would drop me off to ride the surf on Dad's back. By age four, I was jumping off on my own.

I recall a sunny surfing day on the wide beach. Sitting on a big towel, we watched a Lockheed P-38 Lightning make roaring low passes out over the surf line. He would aim at the pier, lift just over it, and then drop down on the other side. We watched four or five passes in breathless awe, each one getting lower. The shiny fighter lifted to clear the pier and then, dipped again. I recall clearly the loud *Boom!* and a huge splash as it disappeared. I remember my Dad yelling, "Stay here!" as he and the other lifeguards dashed into the surf and swam madly to the spot. The words "died instantly" did not fully register at my age, but the comment that he had "done something really stupid" somehow, did register.

I recall the backbone-tingling thrill I felt when Dad took me to watch a Japanese Zero fighter being towed through the streets of Long Beach. This was *it*, one of the planes that had bombed Pearl Harbor! Somehow it had been captured in perfect condition. I think it was going to North American Aviation to be studied.

Post War saw a move to Santa Ana and Dad's entry to the home building business. I had begun to swim competitively by then and won my first medals by age ten. In the summer of 1952, we moved to Newport Beach. Dad's success led him to build a new home there and put me in a four-year high school system. I won my school letter in my freshman year and began to set school and California records in butterfly and breaststroke events.

Dad worked me hard at swimming and even harder at good grades. These were the years before the current school philosophy of "every student is equal" and the "dumbing down" of curricula to the lowest common denominator. At Harbor High, if you wanted to learn math, you needed to be in Webster Jones's class and you needed to maintain a B grade to stay in his class. Web Jones did not suffer fools or slackers.

He had a cheerful ability to coax excellence from students willing to work! How un-P. C.! How many lazy students suffered self-esteem "issues" by being booted from his class? I don't know and I don't care. He sure as hell taught me! I would never have survived the engineering courses at the Air Force Academy had I not been exposed to Webster Jones. God bless that bowlegged, red-haired, happy dynamo!

My high school days were a ball. I had two younger sisters who were (and are) on another planet. I loved them, but learned early that understanding them was never going to happen. Dad set the example that girls were wonderful creatures, who should be pretty much allowed to go their own way. One should value them, protect them, never abuse them, but never expect fully to understand them. My sisters were treated as equals, but were *very* different. I have grown to appreciate smart, capable, thinking women. I do not claim really to understand them, but I am attracted to "can-do" women. My wife, Dotty, was a champion swimmer, a rider, a shooter, an artist, and an airline captain! That just tickles me to death!

By my junior year, I was a BMOC (Big Man on Campus), with lots of pretty girls to date and a beautiful 1924 Cadillac in which to take them out. Yes, it was an antique even then, but was in mint condition and ran like a fine watch! It rode on tall, hickory-spoked wheels. Its klaxon (*Aaaooooga!*) horn, compression whistle (*tweet tweet*), carriage bell (*ding-dong*), loud pipes, and a huge set of Grover air trumpets hidden under the hood, would loudly announce my arrival!

It carried six of us to Lake Arrowhead one winter weekend. We were the only ones at the Lodge, because my old Caddy was the only car the Highway Patrol would allow to proceed up a snow packed, un-plowed road. A smiling trooper waved us on after I promised to turn around if he blew his horn. I watched him in my rear view window, laughing and waving us on as the old car steamed easily over two feet of snow.

As noted in my story later on, my exposure to Paul Mantz and his airplanes solidified my desire to fly. Toward the end of my senior year, I had to face some realities and examine some choices. I had a record of very good grades and could probably have gotten a swimming scholarship, which would have helped with the college costs, but college costs would still be a hurdle and what about flying? Dad could not afford private lessons.

We learned that the new Air Force Academy was open to applicants. Through letters from Paul Mantz and others, I secured a nomination to take the competitive exams. I submitted my SAT scores and reported to March Air Force Base for a weekend of work. Interviews, written tests, a thorough medical examination and physical competitions filled our days. We were sent home with only the promise that an Air Force board would use the accumulated data to select ten high school grads to attend the new academy. They would accept no Congressional appointments. I went home and put any possibility that I would be one of the ten out of my mind. As the school year ended, it appeared that some scholarship help might be available to attend Stanford and join their great swim team. Money would be somewhat tight, however, and I would have to work.

A few weeks before graduation day, my father found me on the school lawn eating lunch with classmates. He carried a telegram which he handed to me. As I read it, I was stunned. The message was from the Air Force. It offered me an appointment. They also wanted a reply... *today*.

"What should I do?" I asked Dad.

"It's your choice," He answered. You'll get a great education and you will fly. "So what should I tell them?" he asked.

I stood still for some moments and then said, "Tell them yes."

He nodded and walked away. I noted tears in his eyes as he turned to leave.

Instructions soon followed. Among other things, they told me to purchase a pair of black, military, low quarter shoes. One evening, an old friend of my Dad's showed up. This old friend, Vern Bager, had flown B-17s over Germany. He handed me a box. I opened it to find a shiny pair of French Shriner shoes from the El Toro Marine Station BX. After I stuttered my thanks for these top-of-the-line shoes, Vern handed me a coin, a silver dollar with most of its markings polished off. Vern explained that it was his lucky piece and that it was worn because he had polished it with his thumb through all of his missions over Germany. He figured it had brought him home safe from twenty-five missions and now wanted it to protect me. I was truly speechless. I still have that coin. Perhaps it truly *is* lucky.

Around mid-June, I boarded a flight to Denver. No summer vacation that year. I would turn eighteen in two more months. A night in a motel full of new classmates was followed by a string of Air Force busses delivering us to Lowry Air Force Base the next morning.

There, we trooped into a room to sign papers and take an oath to protect and defend the Constitution of the United States of America. Sobering. We marched out, carrying a motley assortment of suitcase and bags and were herded into groups and yelled at to line up and stand at attention. First Lieutenant John D. Bowser yelled at us, "Drop your bags!" We leaned over and set our bags down. Bowser yelled, "Pick up your bags!" We did. Again, he yelled, "Drop your bags!"

I think it took me two tries to realize that his command to "drop your bags" meant for me to remain at attention and release the handle. Half-dozen repetitions finally had everyone performing to his satisfaction. Lt. Bowser once more commanded, "Pick up your bags! Right turn, forward march, follow me!" We marched to our new home in WWII wooden barracks, remodeled with Spartan, two-man rooms.

We were rapidly paired off with a roomie, told to deposit bags and then reassemble to be marched to a clothing issue building. Loaded with boots, fatigues, poncho, helmet, M-1 Garand rifle (a real one, complete with sharpened bayonet), we were herded back to barracks. We were allowed a whole ten minutes to don our new wardrobe and line up for inspection. The look on Bowser's face made it clear that we had failed to impress him.

Succeeding days were filled with marching, bayonet drill, memorizing lore, and endless inspections. We had time only to learn, eat, and sleep. My memory recalls it was about two weeks before we were finally given a Sunday off and allowed to visit among ourselves and read a Sunday paper. I finally learned that my roomie, Tony, had a last name. It was Jones and he was from Hartsville, South Carolina.

The summer was spent learning military discipline and such things as how to disassemble and reassemble a Garand rifle rapidly while blindfolded and, later, how to hit a distant target with it. We learned the same drill with the Colt M-1911 .45-caliber semi-automatic pistol.

In addition, we began induction into the mysteries of the "Honor Code." The Code states that, "We will not lie, steal, or cheat, nor tolerate among us those who do." It is important to understand that this Code has nothing to do with any command or administrative function. Command cannot dismiss any cadet for violation of this Code. The Code belongs to the cadets and functions through an Honor Committee of Representatives selected *by* the cadets. A violator may be convicted only by the *unanimous vote* of cadet reps. He would then be asked to resign. Should he refuse, he would then be silenced. He would have no roommate and no words would be spoken to him except on official business. I have never witnessed the necessity for silence.

The point of the Code is to develop a habit of absolute integrity. There would come a time when lives would depend upon the truthfulness and accuracy of a report, or upon a promise to perform some act. Failure to log an aircraft hard landing, or accidentally over-temping an engine, could cost the life of the next pilot to fly it. We would learn to accept the word of a classmate as if written in stone. My class will celebrate our 60th reunion next year. I still think of every one of them as brothers whose word is solid gold. That is what integrity means.

We also learned another valuable lesson. A classmate, who was not such a great athlete, or rifle shot, might be a whiz at history or math. If one expected a bit of math tutoring it might be a good idea to give him some coaching through the obstacle course, or on the rifle range. Thus, we developed the saying "cooperate and graduate." Such an attitude serves to weld diverse talents into a whole greater than its parts.

Our life was not all work and no play. A collection of bright minds can devise some serious mischief. One classic example involved some aircraft which had been donated for purposes of static display. One plane, which is still on display, was a test version of the F-100, tail number FW-754, flown to Lowry Air Force Base and parked on the ramp. There was also a tiny red X-plane. Early one morning, Academy Superintendent General Briggs arrived for work and could not open the door to enter his office. The nose of FW-754 was parked some six inches from his door, blocking its opening. The red X-plane was parked nearby. How these planes were removed from the flight line and moved clear across an Air Force Base to our area on the east side remains a secret even today.

As an aside, I would mention a bit of lore about the F-100. FW-754 has a tail to which some 18 inches has been added to make it taller. The F-100 had a nasty adverse yaw characteristic which killed test pilot George Welch. The slightly different color of the added-on tail height on FW-754 can be seen today. The added rudder did not entirely cure the adverse yaw problem. It was improved, but still there and it later killed one of my roommates, Jim Fey.

Training toward the wings of a Rated Air Force Navigator began in our first year. We flew regularly on our Convair T-29 Nav Trainers. They were a version of the piston powered twin-engine airliner I later flew at Delta. The art of navigation was totally intriguing to me. To locate your position on Earth and proceed accurately to a destination by observation of the sun, moon, stars, and planets, is a hugely rewarding art to master. Today's use of a GPS receiver offers no such thrill.

Solving for a position based upon star sightings involves the math of spherical trigonometry, not an easy art to learn. Early navigators solved these equations on a slide rule, since the pocket calculator was still in the future. We learned these methods, but an easier method had been devised by some very bright minds. In the late 1930s, the Army and Navy were searching for a way to simplify and speed up the training process to mass-produce navigators.

The Army and Navy detailed two young officers to solve this. Their work resulted in the HO-229 (Navy) and HO-249 (Air Navigation) tables. These tomes offer multi-thousands of pre-solved answers, based upon "assumed positions," rather than "'dead-reckoning" positions. These tables remain available today to those who wish to learn the art. Today, a GPS is easier and more accurate, but the stars do not blow fuses, get dead batteries, or fail in other ways.

Nav training was hard work, but still left room for pranks. I recall a classmate deplaning after a flight looking like a one-eyed raccoon. Someone had applied Kiwi boot polish to the rubber eyepiece of his sextant.

After two years at Lowry, we packed up and boarded busses in the summer of 1958 for our move to the new campus north of Colorado Springs. The facility was, and is, spectacular. We continued to work hard and play hard, too much to mention at length here. I would, however, like to answer a question about the place. I have, over the years, been asked (or challenged) whether we got a good education or not. Good question.

The answer is that we carried almost double the semester hours of most universities and in solid subjects. Toward the end of the 1959 school year, the Academy still lacked the credentials to award a Bachelor of Science degree. The class of 1959 was to graduate in a few months. Our Dean of Faculty,

Brigadier General Robert McDermott, was a very bright man. He had been the first (and I believe the only) West Point Cadet to amass a grade point average higher than General Douglas MacArthur. McDermott decided to put the icing on the cake by having the class of '59 take the extensive Princeton College Record Exams and, while he was at it, he decided that he might as well have my class of 1960 take the exams, too. We were nearing the end of our third year, so he might as well see how we were coming along.

The '59ers did very well and gained credentials for a B. S. degree. At the end of our third year, the two-hundred-thirty-one cadets in my class handily outscored every graduating class in the country, including CalTech *and* M. I. T. That's fairly good evidence that General McDermott's program was working!

I graduated from the Academy in 1960 with a B. S. degree and the wings of an Air Force Rated Navigator. Off to Pilot Training.

Assigned to Military Air Transport Service (MATS), I flew C-118s and then C-135s. Leaving the USAF in 1963, I briefly flew the Lockheed L-1049 Constellation (Connie) for Capitol Airways. Delta Air Lines hired me in August of that year. I spent 33½ years at Delta, flying pistons, turbo-props and jets. I spent three-and-a-half years in Delta's Flight Training Department. Twenty-nine years at Delta were spent in the left seat as Captain on seven different aircraft. During the Delta years, I also flew light planes for fun and, sometimes, for pay. A list of the aircraft I have flown includes the:

North American T-28 Trojan

Lockheed L-100 (C-130)

Beech T-34 Mentor

Boeing B-727

Cessna T-37

Lockheed L-1011 (Tri-Star)

Lockheed T-33

Boeing Stearman

Douglas C-118 (DC-6B)

Cessna 150, 172, 310

Boeing C-135 (B-707)

Mooney M-20

Lockheed L-1049 'Connie'

Beech Bonanza

Curtis C-46 Commando

Beech Baron

Douglas DC-6, -7,-8,-9

Piper Aztec

Convair CV-440

Piper Navajo

Convair CV-880

...And probably a couple I have forgotten.

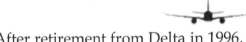

After retirement from Delta in 1996, my wife Dotty and I flew Piper Navajos for a college and helped get a new charter company off the ground. Dotty already owned a beautiful J-3 Cub, and, in 1998, we bought a very nice Piper Aztec. The Aztec, a six-place twin was our "freedom machine," It carried us and loads of "stuff" comfortably on dozens of flights to the Bahamas, from Florida to Canada and Oregon and it made an annual flight to Colorado for visits with our kids and Academy classmates.

My flying now spans some fifty-nine years and twenty-six-thousand-plus hours. Gas is getting expensive, but I'm only eighty and not ready to give up yet. So far, I can claim no bruised passengers, no scraped paint and no violations!

In 2014, I was one of nine pilots to receive the FAA Flight Safety, "Wright Brothers Master Pilot Award" for fifty-plus years with no accidents and I have delivered over 2.5 million passengers without a scratch or bruise.

I've had plenty of chances to "score" on all three. Did dumb luck account for my record or was some skill involved? Well, read my book and then, you decide. I hope you'll enjoy it.

Sincerely,
Capt. Jerry L. Farquhar

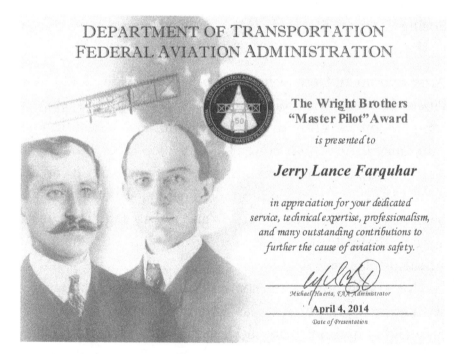

DEPARTMENT OF TRANSPORTATION
FEDERAL AVIATION ADMINISTRATION

The Wright Brothers
"Master Pilot" Award

is presented to

Jerry Lance Farquhar

in appreciation for your dedicated service, technical expertise, professionalism, and many outstanding contributions to further the cause of aviation safety.

Michael Huerta, FAA Administrator

April 4, 2014

Date of Presentation

Preface

I have now been retired from the airlines for 23 years. My wife, also a retired Captain, and others have urged me to tell my story.   My tale logically begins with the awakening of my thirst to fly and why. This consuming interest dates from my days at Newport Harbor High School in Southern California in the early 1950s.

My best pal was Paul Mantz, Junior, who lived on an elegant motor sailing yacht called the Pez Espada at the Balboa Bay Club. He was called Paulie by his famous aviator father, Paul Mantz. Mantz was the most well-known movie pilot, racer, and stunt pilot of the '50s. When someone called him a stunt pilot, he would growl, "I'm a *precision* pilot. All the stunt pilots are dead."

Mantz taught (or tried to teach) Amelia Earhart to fly instruments and he was the only pilot to win the Bendix Race from Burbank, California, to Cleveland, Ohio, three times in a row. His flying work included such classics as *12 O'clock High*, *The Court Martial of Billy Mitchell*, *The Spirit of St. Louis*, and all three Cinerama productions.

His great hangar at Santa Ana Airport (now called John Wayne Airport) housed a large collection of World War I and World War II aircraft, all flyable. This collection of fighters and bombers included his big red Bendix Trophy-winning P-51 Mustang, #46. This Mustang was an early 'B' model with the faired-back canopy. The entire wing had been sealed as a fuel tank. Its Rolls Royce Merlin V-12 engine had been hopped-up and wore beefier Canadian Transport Heads that had been developed to allow longer periods of high-power flying in such applications as the DC-4 transport. Nobody knew how much horsepower that engine produced, but it was probably in the two-thousand horsepower range. It swung an oversized four-bladed prop (from a DC-7, as I recall). That prop had such minimal ground clearance that takeoffs were made with partial power and the tail held low.

In 1953, Paulie and I helped Simonize Wax this beast for a special run. Mantz had a contract to fly to New York and pick up films of Queen Elizabeth's Coronation. He was to race the films back to be shown on West Coast TV. Fueling took a long time. Wings were covered by bags of ice to shrink the fuel and every last pint was squeezed in. The airplane staggered into the air tail-low. Mantz circled, then flashed over the field at full power and headed east. He set transcontinental speed records each way. Film was picked up in New York and raced back to LA, where a West Coast TV station was able to show the Coronation only a day after the event.

The goings-on at Mantz's hangar were irresistible to a couple of high school boys.

The Court Martial of Billy Mitchell, The Spirit of St. Louis, and the Cinerama series were filmed during my high school years. Paulie and I watched the process and worked as "go fors" and general errand boys. It was high excitement for us.

I recalled the day they filmed the scene where General Billy Mitchell's pilots dropped bombs on the captured German battleship *Ostfriesland.* Mantz had one DH-4

DeHavilland (with its big 12-cylinder Liberty engine), two Curtis JN-4 "Jennys" and a Canadian Orenco that had dummy radiators to make them look like DH-4s. The four planes each carried two sheet-metal 'bombs.' They were just finned cans drilled full of holes and loaded with sandbags. Mantz flew the Stearman camera plane and Stan Reaver flew the DH-4 followed by the other three planes. They all took off to film the bomb drop scene over water off Newport Beach.

When they landed later, Mantz climbed down scowling. Reaver and the other pilots were dancing around in hysterical laughter. The scene had been difficult to coordinate, since the mail plane DH-4 was faster than the other three planes and they only had the eight sheet metal 'bombs' to use. The DH-4 was the lead, and all the others were concentrating on Stan to achieve the echelon formation with the right sun angle and so on.

When they set everything up, Mantz gave the signal and the "bombs" dropped in sequence, two by two. Their fall was followed by the cameraman all the way to splash down. (The scenes of hits on the *Ostfriesland* were done in a tank with a miniature ship.) As the 'bombs' splashed into the ocean, it was seen that they were closely bracketing a large mahogany speedboat, now engaged in frantic evasive maneuvers! With everyone concentrating on holding positions on Stan, he was the only one aware of the speedboat chasing them, five-hundred feet below. Stan was elated over the incredible 'gag' he had engineered. Stan had a weird sense of humor and Mantz was not amused. It turned out okay and Mantz got a great 'outtake' strip of film to entertain guests on the Pez Espada.

I remember watching Mantz's crew building the two replica Ryan NYP aircraft for *The Spirit of St. Louis*. The "NYP" stood for New York to Paris. He had first located a 1929 Ryan mail plane to convert into the 'Spirit.' Charles Lindbergh dropped in for a look-see. Yes, we met him. He apparently had control over the movie rights, because he nixed the 1929 Ryan. He said people would recognize the differences between his 'Spirit,' built in 1927, and the later mail plane, so Mantz obtained blueprints of the original from archives in San Diego. Two identical replicas were built from scratch. The movie includes scenes of their construction. They truly were identical to the original. Lindbergh even caused them to change the bezel mount for an instrument which had the wrong number of screws.

Because the replicas would need to make so many takeoffs and landings during filming, the lack of forward visibility in the original was a real concern for safety. The solution was to eliminate the three hundred gallon gas tank in front of the instrument panel and under the wing. In its place was a second cockpit for the wild-man pilot Stan Reaver. They made the swirl-brushed cowlings (Paulie and I worked on them) removable. They made Plexiglas panels to replace the panel which would be away from the cameras. This gave Stan good forward visibility for takeoffs and landings. Lots of fill-in scenes were filmed over the Pacific. For alongside shots, Jimmy Stewart (a pilot and USAF Brigadier General) took the controls to fly in formation with Mantz in his camera plane. Their work made a movie which is still a classic. No computer-generated fakes in this one; just a lot of terrific flying.

All of the above is my way of trying to explain how I contracted the 'bug' to fly. Mantz was an incredibly charismatic character and superb pilot. He was my inspiration, and he encouraged me, writing one of the letters which led to a nomination for me to compete in the exams for the new United States Air Force Academy. The Air Force would not accept a political appointment to the new Academy, but would select from a field of tested candidates. Thus, I was lucky enough to become one of the ten high school graduates from California, in 1956, to enter for the second class in history to graduate in 1960 from the USAFA.

I'm going to skip over my Academy days in this story. The experience was very difficult, but incredibly rewarding. I formed much of my character and personality there. The original Academy course of study included four years of navigation training. Our Convair T-29 Nav trainer was a military version of the Convair 440 twin-engine airliner. Beginning in 1956, we learned all the ways to find our position on Earth. LORAN, DECCA, and CONSOLAN are now out of use, but I loved using a sextant and the stars to solve the mystery of finding a position.

In 1960, we shipped off to pilot training, already wearing the wings of a Rated Navigator and carrying a Bachelor of Science degree.

Table of Contents

In the Sky

Chapter 1 | USAF Primary Pilot Training

In August of 1960, a fresh batch of young recruits gathered at Graham Air Base just north of the little town of Marianna in the Florida Panhandle. We were fresh faced and young. Mostly bachelors recently freed from confining campuses, we filled the parking lot with new Corvettes and other sports cars. The excitement and energy level was off the charts. We paired up into two man rooms in the neat, cinderblock BOQ (Bachelor Officers Quarters), sited among large oaks draped with Spanish moss.

After a couple of days spent in briefings and drawing our equipment and books, we reported to the flight line. Three trainees were assigned to each instructor. These instructors were experienced men, mostly World War II vets. Now civilians, they were paid as contract instructors. The fellow I was assigned to was Andrew B. Bray. At the time, I had no clue how much "dust" the Luck Fairy had sprinkled on my head that morning by seating me at Andy's table.

Andy was a rather ordinary looking fellow with a round face and a quiet manner. When he spoke, he betrayed a bit of a tongue-tied speech impediment. He spoke quietly to us that morning as he laid out the program for us. Andy was not our imagined vision of a dashing pilot, but we listened anyhow.

An opening briefing by the Training Squadron Commander had advised us of the new realities. We learned that Graham Air Base was not an aircraft dealership, willing to sell us an airplane, and then spend forever teaching us to fly it. He reminded us of all the predictive exams and tests we had passed. These exams, he said, predicted that we would all be fast learners. It was expected that we would solo after nine or ten hours. If we had not done so after twelve hours, a panel of instructors would assemble to decide if we were worth any further efforts, or whether we should be shipped off to learn to inventory warehouse material.

We are expected to *know* the aircraft and all of its systems, in addition to normal and emergency procedures, by heart. Instructors would begin each session with oral quizzes. Failure there would be rewarded by study time, while our flying time for that day would be shared by our two training partners. Gulp! A slightly more subdued cadre filed out of that room. It was our first introduction to the strange concept that a pilot was expected to know more than which way to push stick and rudder. Divided into two groups, we would fly half days and attend ground school the other half. Morning and afternoon schedules would rotate weekly.

A summer orientation exercise back in 1957 had given me five hours of flying time in the Beech T-34 and seven in the North American T-28, but three years had passed since then. On the morning of August 30, 1960, I climbed aboard a T-34 with Andy Bray. The Beechcraft-built T-34 was a two-man, seated fore and aft, little beauty, powered by a 220 hp Continental engine. With retractable landing gear, variable pitch prop and strong wings, it was fully aerobatic. I recall feeling very excited and confident, finally able to be starting the process.

Part of my good feeling that first day flowed from newfound information about my soft-spoken instructor, Andy Bray. Another instructor had informed a classmate that Andy had a very distinguished record escorting bombers over Germany in the P-47 Thunderbolt. I had also been informed that the gentleman now climbing into the back seat of the little T-34 was, in fact, an Ace. Wow, heady stuff! I was both thrilled and intimidated. I realized that I had an instructor who surely knew what the hell flying was all about. I was, at the same time, concerned about my own upcoming performance. I was determined that such a man, who had actually shot down Luftwaffe fighters, should *not* think I was a klutz!

I had a huge level of admiration for Andy and total confidence that Andy could manage to remove us from whatever mess I created. In six flights with Andy, he

3

demonstrated—and then talked me through—spins, stalls, aerobatics, takeoffs and landings. I paid attention and did my damnedest to please him. He indicated his approval by a slight narrowing of the eyes and a small uplift of one corner of his mouth. That was enough for me.

On our seventh flight, Andy told me to do touch-and-go landings. After two, he said to make the third landing a full stop. Instructing me to pull over in front of a line shack, he climbed out. *Both* corners of his mouth just slightly turned up.

"Go do some landings, have some fun," he said. "I gotta get a cuppa coffee."

He waved and walked toward the shack. I sat, stunned. Did he really mean go alone? He turned at the doorway, cocked his head, and then clearly waved me away.

This was *it*! I was so excited I was almost bouncing in the seat. I recall no sense of doubts. If Andy said it was okay, then it was okay. I remember telling myself to slow down and be sure of my checklist items. I shot four landings. It went by in a blur, but I do remember frequent glances at the back seat to recheck that Andy really wasn't there. As soon as I parked, classmates grabbed me and heaved me into a nearby and very muddy pond. That first solo is the most exciting event you can ever experience while still wearing clothes and it may top the other contender.

My brand-new logbook showed a grand total of seven hours and 21 minutes, with 32 landings, at the time Andy walked off for coffee. As more of the class successfully soloed, the party and rowdiness levels grew. We had no time for much contemplation over those who washed out for various reasons. A few simply could not conquer motion sickness. I'm one of the blessed few who have never been touched by this affliction, either flying or sailing.

After three more weeks of polish in the little T-34, we faced the next step... *jets*! The Cessna T-37 was a compact little beast with two small jets buried in the wing roots. It sported side-by-side seating, allowing the instructor to scowl directly in his student's face. The outward beauty of this little machine disguised some vile habits. It truly was not suited to be a primary trainer. We were introduced to this sneaky little trickster with all of about 27 hours of experience.

The first nasty bit about the T-37 had to do with its jet engines. These were designed with *centrifugal* compressors, meaning that the compressor section operated like the blower on a vacuum cleaner. A cone shaped single unit compressed air by drawing in at the center and flinging air outward by the centrifugal force of the spinning cone. It looked okay on paper, but the problem was that these tiny engines had to spin at some hellacious RPMs, up into the twenty thousand rpm range. This meant that it took a long time to spin one up from a low power setting. This fault would present no problem to a pilot experienced in jet aircraft. Students, however, were repeatedly warned never to allow the engine to unwind during an approach. Should you discover at five-hundred feet at idle power that your glide angle was aimed at the weeds short of the runway, it was too late to correct the forthcoming grass landing. It simply took too long for the engines to wind back up and produce any power.

This engine was also cause for the appellation "Flying Dog Whistle," because it made noises only a dog could hear... and drove them mad. The power lag problem was eventually solved by placing small panels in the exhaust stream, called "thrust attenuators." They popped out and spoiled thrust when throttles were retarded below eighty-percent, while allowing the engine to remain "spooled up."

The other fault with this engine was its tendency to flame out. That's right... *quit!* No big thing. The cure was to hammer the air-start procedure into each of us trainees until we could recite it even while drunk or asleep. A classmate, Ace Holman, was chased through the woods by fire trucks as he disappeared behind some trees, while yelling a garbled string of curses about flamed out engines over the radio. The firemen found him sitting on the wing of an undamaged plane, parked in a pasture. He had the logbook on his lap, still muttering curses as he wrote up both faulty engine fuel control units.

Incredibly, after taking off over the woods, he had made three air starts on alternately failing engines. He related that, when the pasture popped up in front of him as he kissed the last row of trees, he just thought, *screw it,* and plopped her down in the grass. The instructors couldn't fault him. He'd had the presence of mind to lower the gear, so the airplane only had to be raised in slings and trucked back to base. He even filled out the logbook correctly, including the three minutes of flying time.

The T-37's other fault was a real grizzly bear. If allowed to proceed beyond about two turns in a spin, it would raise its nose to a flat attitude. In this attitude, it would wind up like a Chinese pinwheel, while falling out of the sky at a rate in excess of twenty-thousand feet per minute. The only escape from this wild gyration was to apply opposite rudder to slow the spin somewhat. After rotation slowed, you drew the stick back slowly and then slammed it violently to the forward stops. This was supposed to force the nose down, allowing you to fly out of the spin. Since even this somewhat eccentric recovery technique did not always work on the first, or even the second try, a developed spin in the T-37 was truly hairy.

This small fault in manners was cause for a hard and fast rule that, *No student shall enter spins intentionally.* They warned us all that, if you ever observed an altimeter rapidly unwinding below ten-thousand feet while simultaneously observing spinning farmland and structures, you were to apply the following procedure immediately: Release controls. Grasp handles on left and right of seat. Raise left and then right handle. Squeeze trigger found on right handle. This would fire the ejection seat, and you would then descend quietly beneath the shade of your "nylon elevator." Thus, warned of the "gotchas" concealed beneath her shiny skin, we approached the T-37 with an "approach-avoid" emotion akin to meeting a really beautiful streetwalker.

This airplane imparted another bit of required pilot lore. It began to dawn on us young "immortals" that airplanes may not always be merely great fun toys. It began to soak in that they could also kill us if they so decided.

In four flights, Andy quietly taught me to control the aircraft, while respecting and avoiding its faults. Using a truck-mounted control cab, a remote airstrip at Bascom was one of our facilities. On October 20, 1960, Andy told me to head for Bascom on our fifth flight in the little jet. After three landings, which I felt were fairly decent, Andy growled. "Pull over by the grass there, I gotta pee." I waited with parking brakes set while he unstrapped. Before he unplugged his headset, he said, "I'm gonna take a long pee and then stretch my legs a bit. You go do some landings and don't you forget to come back for me. I don't wanna walk back." He walked into the tall grass and unzipped, then looked over his shoulder with the first grin I had ever seen on his face and waved me away.

After five hours and fifty-nine minutes and twenty-four landings, I was up in a jet… *solo*! I felt ten feet tall! I made four more landings and really worked hard to make the last one a squeaker. Andy climbed back in and buckled up. As soon as he plugged in, he mumbled, "That last landing wasn't too bad. Think you can find your way back to base?"

When we logged in our times, the squadron secretary pointed out that Andy's math was a bit off. Six hours was supposed to be the absolute minimum to solo the jet. Andy just shrugged and said, "What's a minute matter?"

During the next two months, we trainees logged another fifty-plus hours, polishing our new skills. Close across the Chattahoochee River, there was a sister training base located at Bainbridge, Georgia. Weekend parties offered the chance to select supposedly unused radio frequencies, which could be employed during impromptu "dogfights" over the Chattahoochee. This was, of course, verboten. It was known that instructors often scanned radio frequencies in search of culprits. So, of course, fake call signs were adopted. An instructor, having discovered the frequency, once broke in, demanding to know the real call signs of the guilty. Hearing a response of, "Oops, we are f--ked," he demanded, "Who said that?" The response, "Well, I'm not *that* f--ked up."

Other hilarities occurred. The two bases were close enough to require the use of different frequencies as traffic over one could be clearly heard by the other. A classmate once found himself lost on a night cross-country navigation flight. He circled, trying to sort things out until he spotted a string of running lights passing in the distance. Aha! Just tag on and follow! The tower at Graham responded to his call with clearance to land. He felt proud of his problem-solving skills as he taxied in and parked. It all evaporated as he walked into a totally unfamiliar squadron room... at Bainbridge! Oh what fun we had, ribbing our very own incarnation of Wrong Way Corrigan!

You see, in the early 1930s, a pilot named Corrigan planned a flight from New York to Europe. The Civil Aeronautics Board nixed his flight plan, so he re-filed for a flight from New York to California, which they approved. Corrigan took off and flew to Europe. Upon landing, he claimed that his compass must have been "off." This stunt earned him fame as "Wrong Way Corrigan."

It was not all hilarity, however. While luck held for our group at Graham, we were sobered by the deaths of three classmates at Bainbridge. Yes, it was the nasty spin manners of the T-37 that got all three.

Chapter 2 | Basic Flight Training

In January of 1961, I reported to Webb Air Force Base, located on the flat prairie outside of Big Springs, Texas. The next eight months there would be spent learning to fly formation, instrument flying, aerobatics and more navigation. We would use the venerable Lockheed T-33. The "T-Bird" was a two-seat version of the first USAF jet fighter, the P-80. This old girl looks like ancient technology today, but was exciting enough to us back then.

The plane's J-33 engine produced only some forty-seven-hundred pounds of thrust and had no modern "fuel control unit." The modern fuel control unit gets inputs such as RPMs and EGT (Exhaust Gas Temperature). It allows fuel to accelerate the engine at a rate the engine can digest, regardless of how fast a throttle is pushed forward. On this engine, the throttle *was* the fuel control unit and it was entirely possible to melt the ass end off the engine with injudicious forward motion of that lever. For that reason, the instrument cluster included a LARGE tailpipe temperature gauge and a LARGE tachometer. Students were admonished to observe those two closely when applying throttle in order to avoid the dreaded meltdown.

There was yet another way a "fumble fingers" might achieve such a meltdown. Three simple toggle switches on the left side panel served to engage an electric starter motor, turn on the ignition spark plugs, and open a valve to inject fuel. Proper sequence was to engage starter and allow the engine to spin up to a certain rpm. At this point, you turned on the ignition switch, followed—after a count of two or three—by the starting fuel switch. You then looked for ignition to be reported on the LARGE tailpipe temperature gauge. Seeing such evidence, you watched the RPMs rise to another point and, then, moved the throttle from its *off* detent into the *idle* position and, then, promptly turned the starting fuel switch back to *off*. Done in proper sequence, things went reliably well. A fuel switch left on, would cause that LARGE temperature gauge to climb ever higher. An even more spectacular show resulted if you should happen to turn on the starting fuel toggle, count to three, and then engage the ignition switch. This sequence would result in a loud *boom!*— followed by some forty feet of flame shooting out the tailpipe—accompanied by many voices in your earphones chanting, "Ignition, *then* fuel. Ignition, *then* fuel," along with a lot of nasty laughter. This was a very humiliating event, because it called for a complete shutdown and a thorough inspection of the tailpipe.

Lieutenant Floyd Hester was my instructor at Webb and I was his first student. Floyd was a 1959 Academy grad, a year ahead of me, and this was his first assignment. It sounds a bit scary, but it worked out well. Floyd was a real gentleman to deal with. He had the good sense to explain that, since I was his first "project," we were going to have to cooperate and look after each other, but he knew his stuff and had a knack for explaining what I needed. I liked Floyd, so we got along well. He "soloed" me after some 14 hours, which was about par for the T-33. Things rolled along smoothly. I was getting good grades and enjoying the hell out of the whole experience.

However, good things don't last forever. A very unnecessary event killed an instructor and put a classmate in the hospital for many months. The hot section (exhaust) turbine blades (buckets) of a jet engine are subjected to intense heat in a direct flame. The process of hardening these buckets was to subject them to a blasting with small shot. This "shot-peening" pounded the surfaces and hardened them.

Some unknown people convinced some unknown Air Force officers to test a new chemical hardening process for these highly stressed buckets... on training aircraft and dozens of T-33s bore a placard in the cockpit, which advised the pilot that chemically hardened buckets were installed and requested that he enter a list of temperatures and other parameters in the logbook. We all flew these aircraft without suspicion.

I was on close final approach behind one of these aircraft, flown by instructor Danny and student John. They were doing a touch-and-go (landing and takeoff). They lifted off just as I touched down behind them. Puffs of spark and flames first grabbed my attention and then a long torch of flame from their tailpipe. An immediate call from the tower advised them that they were "torching." As they staggered over the end of the runway, we could hear Danny yelling to John, "Get out! Get out!" As I rolled to a stop on the runway, too stunned to turn off, the canopy flew off their plane and a seat popped out, followed by the other seat. The first seat separated from the man. A chute popped out and filled, going sideways. The figure swung, then hit. The second seat arced up, then fell and hit. Someone never separated from the second seat.

A very quiet squadron room soon learned that John was alive with multiple broken bones. His chute had slowed him just enough to save his life. Danny hit before he could get out of the seat. His few seconds of delay, to make sure John got out, cost him his life.

It was clear from examination of the engine and the numerous witnesses that a set of the test buckets had melted and robbed the engine of all power. They were immediately removed from service. The ultimate, heartbreaking irony was that the plane glided to a landing in the flat sandy terrain with only some sheet-metal damage to its belly. It was soon repaired and returned to service.

Accidents like that one spurred development of better ejection seats. Today, seats can lift a pilot clear, open his chute, and float him down from a parked aircraft. Many of us began to realize that progress in aviation usually comes at a pretty high price.

During that period, one morning I had an experience, which fortunately went undetected. We were mostly bachelors at this time and living in the BOQ. We adopted the philosophy prevalent in the military of our time: "Work hard, play hard (meaning drink hard)." During a week when I had been on the morning flying schedule, a mid-week holiday of some sort occurred. No class, no flying. A large group put on a pretty good bash in the BOQ, which lasted far later than it should have.

Somehow, I got the idea that our schedule was rotating to the classroom in the morning. After very little sleep, the alarm clock went off. Upon leaving my bedroom, my roommate asked why I was dressed for class. Observing my puzzled look, he explained that we were still scheduled for morning flying. I quickly suited up in flying gear and boots and off we all went. On our way to the flight line, I heard my roommate telling me I was in no shape to fly. I was praying for a cross-country flight and for a second period slot. No such luck. The board showed me out for solo stage landings... for a grade and first period, too. There was no way out. Back then, a trip to the Flight Surgeon's office was out of the question.

I conned my skeptical roomie into helping me get the engine started and off I went. I flew round and round, making spot landings for a grading team. Taxiing in, I wrote up the oxygen system for a suspected leak. Of course, I had sucked it empty. I still don't recall much of that flight, but I did score one of the highest grades for my landings... while in no condition to fly. My roommate later gave me one hell of a Dutch uncle talk. That episode did grab my attention. The fact that I could not recall details of the flight scared me.

My "solution" was clearly to separate drinking and flying by a good night's sleep and I rigidly followed this prescription for the next thirty-three years. There is more to this story, but I'll leave it to the appropriate point in time to tell it.

As previously mentioned, there was a lot of high-spirited activity among us. I had a brief association with a rather colorful young woman. This association would later have a profound effect on my career. She was a bit wild and that's a modest description. An active rodeo rider, she drove a pickup with loud pipes, which usually carried a bale of hay and a couple of saddles. She was a few levels removed from what one thinks of as a debutante.

I don't clearly recall the incident that somehow caused offense to the Base Commander's wife. For all I know, the rodeo rider may have parked her fancy pick-up in his wife's parking spot. Who knew? Suffice it to say, it caused me to receive a good chewing out from the Webb Base Commander. This officer was not in my chain of command. He ran the base, but not the training command on it. I did not learn until much later that he had also written a rather scathing letter, the results to be revealed later.

As the end of our Basic Training neared, and receipt of our silver wings grew closer, anticipation mounted. Everyone wanted to be a fighter pilot. What else? The Thunderbirds demonstration team was flying the F-100 Super Sabre, also called the "Hun." It was the first fighter capable of straight and level supersonic flight. Wow! We all drooled. Per tradition, the list of possible assignments was posted a few days before graduation. There were many groans heard when the list revealed only three fighter slots. Oh well, bombers are jets, too. They chose slots by order of class rank, determined by cumulative grades received. Everyone knew the three fighter slots would go to the first three in class rank.

On the morning that the slots were chosen, a full Colonel and his entourage marched into the squadron room and ordered, "All Academy grads come across the hall." Half of our class were ROTC and we had devoted months making friends among them. We all assumed the system was fair. Slots would be spoken for by order of class standing. An embarrassed group followed the Colonel across the hall. We found a slide projector set up and other displays up on walls. The Colonel and his entourage were from SAC (Strategic Air

Command). We sat through a dog and pony show about bombers.

The Colonel finished the show by announcing that, "You can name your airplane and name your base."

In other words, we were encouraged to bypass the process and choose SAC, before the selection process opened for our ROTC classmates across the hall.

I had a classmate from Syracuse University who shared the same instructor with me. He wanted to fly a B-52 in the worst way and outranked me in class standing. Yet, he agreed that the SAC offer was clearly unfair and didn't bite.

The Colonel was astonished and, then, angered when his offer produced *no takers*. Apparently, I was not alone in feeling this offer was a slam against classmates who had worked hard. He angrily dismissed us. To my knowledge, this was the last time SAC tried to bypass the system.

We went back to our squadron room amid the curious stares from our mates and got on with the selection process. I opted for a slot flying the C-118 (DC-6) at Maguire Air Force Base. A disappointment at the time, which later turned out to be a blessing in disguise.

We later received our wings in a nice ceremony with some wives and families attending. I recall comments by our Squadron Commander prior to the ceremony. He warned that if we lived long enough to accumulate a thousand hours in our logbooks, we *might* be on our way to becoming *pilots*. We all had about two-hundred-sixty-five hours at that point. The next morning saw me off for California on leave.

At the age of twenty-three, I was still too immature to philosophize very deeply about the plateau I had just attained. Looking back, I can make some observations. Most pilots, who are good at it, are Type A personalities and being an athlete with good hand-eye coordination is a great help. Flying an airplane solo is in no way related to driving a car. The car can be stopped and one can step out. Taking an aircraft off solo requires the aggressive confidence that you can control it in flight and, then, set it back down in one piece on a narrow strip of pavement. Doing this on instruments in weather requires that you approach the runway without seeing it until the last few hundred feet. An aggressive and self-confident personality is an absolute requirement for success. If you're afraid of the machine or your abilities, you will never master flying.

A fearful pilot may resolve to apply super caution, but that is no solution to the problem. Flying often presents events which require aggressive action. The fearful pilot who cannot act quickly will, if he persists long enough, eventually allow the machine to take over... and kill him, but the aggressive Type A also faces a dangerous hurdle. Two-hundred-plus hours is enough flying time for a pilot to start feeling very comfortable in a jet aircraft and therein lies the trap. Such a flyer is really at the stage of a baby who has just learned to toddle across the floor standing up. The baby gains confidence even through setbacks. He can be expected to stumble and bang his head on the coffee table. Such stumbles for the new pilot can have far more draconian consequences, thus, the admonition from our squadron commander about that one thousand hour mark. Even that is only a beginning.

Flying as a professional is a unique business. One can attend a university and attain a doctorate in medicine or the law, but not so for the aspiring pilot. These skills are attained only by OJT (On-the-Job Training). The Type-A, newly minted pilot will need, if he expects to live very long, to rein in his enthusiasm with some judgment and caution. Just because the Thunderbirds do rolls over the crowd at two-hundred feet does not mean you are ready for that stunt.

The problem is perhaps best stated in a claim by old pilots, usually heard after some pilot has killed himself in a manner suitable for entry into the "Darwin Awards." "If you have enough patience and a large enough truckload of bananas, you can teach a chimpanzee to fly, but you will *never* teach him when *not* to do some things."

Chapter 3 | Military Flying

Reporting for Duty

During my post-training period of leave, I received a phone call in which I was advised that my assignment was to be converted to fly the C-135. The Military Air Transport Service (MATS) squadron to which I would report at Maguire Air Force Base, New Jersey, was transitioning into flying that military version of the Boeing 707, an exciting development.

Actually a B-720, the first aircraft they received was a converted SAC tanker. Upper deck fuel tanks and a refueling boom were removed and the boom hydraulic power was used to provide a powered rudder. Upon reporting in, I learned that I would actually fly on the C-118 for a short period. Squadron officers would transition into the C-135 through training at Castle Air Force Base near Merced,

California. Groups would be sent in order of rank in the squadron.

My brief experience in the C-118 was a lot of fun. That military version of the Douglas DC-6B was powered by four Pratt and Whitney R-2800 radial piston engines. I have been captivated by machinery since childhood and have tinkered with engines for as long as I can remember.

At this time, I was living with two other bachelor pilots in a rented house. In the living room, I was building a new 327 engine for my Corvette, so rumbling along through Argentia, Newfoundland, or Goose Bay, Labrador on the way to Thule, Greenland in that grand old lady of the skies was truly thrilling. I loved it! I got to fly and, since I had a navigator rating, I got to spell a navigator in a challenging high latitude area in which to work.

One evening, a group of young pilots talked me into going along to a newly discovered dance hall in Camden, NJ. With a live band, it was a popular spot to meet young ladies. I soon spotted a raven-haired beauty sitting with three older girls. I learned that this was the first time her parents had allowed her to attend, but with the three chaperones. It was only about nine o'clock and they were about to leave. She was clearly bemused by my tooled cowboy boots and finally gave in to my smooth pitch for "Just one dance." I concentrated on being smooth and not crushing her toes. Before they departed, I was rewarded with a slip of paper with her phone number on it. I later learned that she had just been named runner up to Mary Ann Mobley in the Miss New Jersey

Pageant. (Mary Ann went on became Miss America that year.) Her name was Joyce and she was a spectacular beauty.

There is more to this story, but I did not see her for a while, because it was time for my roomies and me to proceed to Merced, California, for our introduction to the C-135.

The Big Jet:
Check out on the C-135 began with weeks of ground school and intense study. It was my first exposure to the complicated systems and procedures we had to learn before flying a large aircraft. We still enjoyed happy hours at the O'Club (Officer's Club) bar to unwind, but I primarily recall hours of study. There were also lots of cram sessions, where we quizzed each other on systems and checklist items.

The C-135 was a big four-engine jet with a takeoff weight in excess of two-hundred-seventy-five thousand pounds. The idea of flying it as a copilot, with less than three-hundred hours in my logbook, was a bit daunting. Therefore, I worked hard and was rewarded with good grades.

An interesting feature of this aircraft, at least the A model, was its water injection system. As a SAC tanker, in order to boost takeoff weight of this aircraft to well over three-hundred thousand pounds, water injection was used. The four Pratt and Whitney jet engines produced the equivalent of having a fifth engine when water was injected during takeoff. The water turned into steam and produced some twenty-five-percent more thrust per engine.

The design of the system that pumped that water could cause some problems, especially in the aircraft's coming transport role with MATS. Two very large pumps, powered by large electric motors, dumped hundreds of gallons of water through the engines. During a takeoff, they emptied the tank in about two minutes while boosting a heavy plane into the air.

The first little "oops" in this setup was in the plumbing. One pump supplied the left engines and the other the right engines. The loss of a pump not only caused a loss of some eight-thousand pounds of thrust, but the loss was all on one side. Well, I guess that's what a hydraulically boosted rudder was designed to do. Many years later, this plumbing was finally changed to an inboard-outboard configuration that maintained even thrust if a pump failed.

The second part of this "oops" in design was the fact that the plane only had three engine-powered generators. The number four engine carried, instead, a cartridge-powered self-starter. The electrically driven pumps created a huge load for the three generators, so a tripped off pump on takeoff would *never* be reset. Resetting it could cause starting loads to trip off the generators. Anybody got a flashlight handy? Likewise, the loss of a generator could result in either tripping a pump, or *pumps*, or the loss of the remaining two generators.

Lest you think the above s like undue criticism, I must point out that this was a magnificent airplane to fly. It was fast, handled beautifully and had a huge range with a heavy payload. This was a design reflecting fairly early technology for a large jet transport, but the engineers got most of it right. However, nothing built by man is perfect.

Ground school only touched lightly on some of these little foibles. My training in aeronautical engineering caused some of these things to tickle my curiosity and there was some discussion among trainees with "What if?" questions, but the program pace left little time for deep probing of those questions.

Ground school was followed by further training in a flight simulator at Loring Air Force Base, near Presque Isle, Maine. Some of us junior officers stopped off on the way back to Maguire to check another box. Stead Air Force Base, outside Reno, Nevada, was the home for Survival School training. That program was a non-flying experience, so I'll skip over it, noting only that I got a very good report from it.

Simulators are designed to provide experience and practice in flying without the cost and hazard of handling emergencies in a real airplane. We practiced dealing with fires, hydraulic failures, electric failures, making landings with one, or two, failed engines and other exciting contingencies. Three trainees took turns in the pilot's, copilot's and engineer's seats. Events often became somewhat farcical, with newbies trying to play all the roles of a coordinated crew. None of us was aware at the time that airlines trained a new crewmember with qualified people in the other positions, a far more reasonable and productive approach, but we slogged our fumbling away through and were eventually signed off and sent back to our squadron.

MATS:

My roomies and I reported back. We now carried the endorsement claiming as "Pilot, Military Transport, Jet, Heavy." Well, sort of. Flights carrying cargo and troops followed to such places as Greenland, England, Germany, North Africa, Turkey, etc. The flying was hard work and *fun* at the same time. We flew a lot.

About this time, I relocated that slip of paper with the phone number from the night at Camden and I decided to try for a date. Joyce agreed to my offer for dinner and a movie, but explained that I would need to come and meet her family and secure her father's permission.

Somehow, I passed inspection. We had three more dates, and I knew I was a goner. She was, not only drop-dead beautiful, but smart and sweet as well. I could not help myself and popped the question. To my astonishment, she immediately said yes. She also revealed that she had been accepted for training as a stewardess by TWA. We made plans for an engagement of at least one year. Upon completion of her training, she was based in Los Angeles. I got to see her on New York layovers, but my parents in Newport Beach, California saw her more than I did. My father, a great connoisseur of beauty, finagled a day at the beach in order to get a look at her in a bathing suit. He called one night to confess his scheme.

The *Huntington Beach News* was owned and operated by both my grandfather and my dad's older brother, George. As an avid surfer, Uncle George had built a large shower room facility in the newspaper building on Main Street. Uncle George, also a recognized expert on the female figure, was a regular judge at the annual Fourth of July beauty contest. The two schemed to get her to change at the *News* building and then escort her to the beach. Dad reported that when she stepped out in a modest two-piece bathing suit, they were both stunned. His normally laconic and laid-back elder brother lost his cool when his mouth gaped open and his ever-present cigar hit the floor. He reported that at five-foot seven, one-hundred eighteen pounds, distributed in a conformation of 36-19-35, she existed in a totally new class from any girl ever seen at the Fourth of July pageant. Poor Dad, he was a goner, too. He reported in amazed tones that she had great poise, but seemed totally unaware of her impact on the male eye. What the hell, Dad. You taught me how to pick 'em! Well, back to flying and learning.

One of our regular runs was delivering supplies to the base at Thule, Greenland. These runs revealed another of the C-135 foibles. We were receiving B-Model aircraft at the time. These had bypass-fan engines with thrust reversers. The older A-Model "water-wagon" had no reversers. This was no problem in its role as a SAC tanker. They operated from ten-thousand- and twelve-thousand-foot runways. Thule had only an eighty-three-hundred foot runway with a high glacier on one end. Thus, regardless of wind, landings were made from over the water toward the glacier. Takeoffs were in the opposite direction. The problem there was that the A-Model had only brakes and no reversers for stopping. This runway often had alternating patches of ice and pavement. This condition, coupled with early anti-skid technology, presented a problem. The slow cycling anti-skid brakes could be fooled. Sensing pavement, they would allow pressure to the brakes. The next ice patch would be met with brakes applied, resulting in a wheel lockup. The next patch of pavement would be encountered with wheels locked. Resulting *Boom-boom!* sounds allowed the crew to count how many tires were blown and radio in how many wheel changes to order. The Air Force solution was to include a pallet of mounted main tires in the needed cargo load. This compromised the load which could be delivered, but assured that Thule had a supply of wheels and tires to change out for blown ones. An added problem was that Thule was usually too cold to allow use of water injection for takeoff, so we couldn't carry as much weight returning.

The obvious solution was to use B-Models for Thule flights. Too obvious. Morning flights posted from Maguire often showed departures for Thule and Frankfurt, Germany. When it was noted, one morning, that an A-Model "water-wagon" was slated for Thule, while a newer B-Model was departing to test its stopping power on the two miles of runway at Frankfurt, a question arose. Why can't the two aircraft be swapped, thus carrying more cargo while increasing safety? Well, any new officer had heard of RHIP (Rank Hath Its Privileges). No one was surprised that senior officers would opt for a flight to Frankfurt over an icebound Thule. That they were spoiled enough to compromise the mission by also insisting on getting the new B-model toy did grate a bit. Oh, well, "leadership" in action. Therefore, we continued to blow perfectly good tires and replace them at taxpayer expense.

Flights offered time in Germany, Spain, Turkey, and other fun and educational places. I got to fly my first complicated instrument departure from Frankfurt, Germany, one early a.m. — by surprise. The "work hard, play hard" ethic resulted in a rather rocky looking aircraft commander showing up that morning. Because he was a Lieutenant Colonel, and I a Second Lieutenant, I opted to keep my mouth shut. As the gear and flaps were tucked away and power had been set for climb, I noted that we did not appear to be climbing at a rate to make an upcoming crossing point. A glance to the left revealed the "Light" Colonel in a very comfortable-looking, chin-on-chest repose. This was no time to play the valet waking the master, so I grabbed the controls. He woke up as we leveled off at cruise altitude and said nothing.

Another interesting and learning experience occurred on a flight from Adana, Turkey. Flying from Maguire through Madrid, we arrived at night in Adana. We were tired, out of crew duty time, and ready for a bed in the BOQ (Bachelor

Officer's Quarters). On arrival, we were met by the base commander, a "Full Bird" Colonel (his insignia an eagle with wings outspread, rather than a Lieutenant Colonel's silver oak leaf insignia). He related a problem. The wife and 12-year-old daughter of an officer based at Adana needed to be spirited out of the country *tonight*.

While browsing in the base bookstore near closing time, she had been assaulted by the clerk, a Turkish national. The ruckus brought help as she and her daughter fought off the attempted rape. The man was fired and thrown off the base. The husband, a Captain, returned from his day flying an F-100 and heard the story. He was intercepted as he tried to leave the base armed with his .45 Colt, on his errand to kill the SOB. Stopping him was probably the first mistake, as shooting the bastard would have been okay under Turkish law, since the NATO agreement put the base and its people under Turkish law. Women had *no rights* under this law. We soon learned that the man had filed suit against the wife for the loss of his job. The coming of morning would see a demand for the wife and daughter to be turned over to Turkish authorities, pending resolution of the suit. That would entail housing accommodations in a Turkish women's prison.

The Colonel put the question simply. "Can you take her and her daughter to Torrejon Air Base (near Madrid) tonight?" Someone made a phone call to MATS HQ, waived duty time limits and our tired crew departed for Madrid — with two passengers.

I don't recall whether I had yet become a fan of the great aviation writer Ernest Gann, but this flight produced an event worthy of his book *Fate Is the Hunter*. Our tired crew worked to keep each other awake, as we cruised through a clear night westward over the Mediterranean, toward Spain. The empty aircraft continued to gain speed as it burned off fuel, so our flight engineer, a Master Sergeant, occupied himself by reducing power in fractional bits to keep our cruise speed constant. I was looking down at a chart in my lap and writing clearance instructions from Barcelona Control, when my upper peripheral vision caught a red flash moving from right to left. Then, *crash!*

A violent jolt threw stuff all over the cockpit. We all sat stunned for seconds, until it finally registered that we had not actually *hit* whatever it was! Our Sergeant, with eyes the size of wagon wheels, swallowed a couple of times and then whispered, "It was a B-52. I saw the tail go past our windshield." The wake turbulence behind the huge eight-engine aircraft caused the jolt. A call to Barcelona Control produced adamant denial that any other planes were in our area.

Well, we certainly were awake now! Soon the question arose of 'where would we have been if our engineer had not been easing off power?' Our discussion produced no answer for the simple reason that there *was* no answer. *Fate Is The Hunter.* We had escaped him... that time.

31

As my flying experience grew, my fiancée neared the end of her year of working for TWA. Airline policy at the time required stewardesses to remain single. She resigned as our wedding date neared.

It was about this time that some controversy arose in regard to a MATS policy in dispatching our flights. I must digress here to explain the concept of a "balanced field length," which has to do with the length of a runway. To conduct a safe takeoff, it is necessary to have enough runway for the aircraft to accelerate to a speed at which the loss of an engine (in a multi-engine aircraft) will leave the crew with two viable options. The first option, to abort the takeoff and *stop*, obviously requires that enough runway remain to accomplish this maneuver. The second option, to continue the takeoff with reduced power, likewise depends upon having enough pavement left to result in a happy outcome. A very light aircraft on a long runway will allow the crew some seconds of time to mull over these options. The weight of an aircraft, and the temperature of the day, determines how well it will perform. As these two parameters rise, performance suffers. A so-called "balanced field" condition exists when these two parameters have risen to the point where the pilot must decide his go-*no-go* options in a split-second. Allowing weight or temperature parameters to exceed this condition means that neither of the two options remains viable. A decision to push beyond this envelope on purpose is evidence of pure stupidity, but that's exactly what MATS commanders encouraged.

You must understand that a high "tonnage hauled" score reflected well on a commander's O E. R. (Officer Efficiency Report). Of course, no commander would openly order a junior crew to attempt an overweight takeoff. That might leave him exposed to criticism in the event of a mishap. Inevitably, *Fate Is The Hunter* did catch up. More later. They employed a more roundabout CYA (Cover Your Ass) tactic.

The Boeing performance charts were very accurate. The airplane would do what they predicted, no more, no less. Thus, the dispatch department would use these charts to establish how much cargo they could load to reach a "balanced field" condition. The problem was that calculations might be done at 0500 hours (in the morning). Temperature is a major factor in aircraft performance. By the time the outbound crew sat down to calculate takeoff numbers, it might be 0900 hours and the temperature could be twelve-to-fifteen degrees warmer. This regularly resulted in the crew discovering that they were seriously overweight. Complaints brought by a junior crew to the head of dispatch, usually a Major, would be met with a question: "Are you refusing the trip, Lieutenant?" or "Are you going to force us to offload priority cargo?" Suitably intimidated, the crew would usually depart. So, the practice continued.

This is, most likely, the appropriate point to relate the inevitable results. The event is out of order in my tale, as it occurred some six months after my employment by Delta Air

Lines, but it will bring continuity to my story about this foolish practice to relate it here.

A pilot training classmate, Bill Cordelle, was the aircraft commander on a flight from El Toro, California, to Guantánamo Bay, Cuba. His aircraft was loaded with supplies, ammo and a large number of Marines. El Toro Marine Air Station has a nearby geographical oddity known as Red Hill. This mound lies off the departure end of the main runway. It is known that Bill made a phone call from California to MATS headquarters in New Jersey — the subject his takeoff weight. What they said, and with whom he spoke, remain unknown. What *is* known is that there was a big push on to reinforce Guantánamo Bay defenses. Whatever they said led Bill, a junior aircraft commander, to climb aboard and take off. His aircraft impacted some forty feet from the crest of Red Hill, killing all aboard. As usual, with nobody living to argue the point, they found the cause to be "pilot error."

Back to the timeline. I was now married, living in a tiny, one-bedroom apartment, and flying my ass off. I was in love with my new bride and with flying. Everything was perfect. Well... not entirely. Certain events began to occur, which prompted some slight uneasiness about my chosen career.

One such event was a phone call at about 0130 hours. I had only arrived home around eleven the previous evening, returning from a round trip to Frankfurt, Germany and back. The ringing phone failed to stir me, so my new bride answered. I only heard one side of the conversation, so what follows is what she reported after I was finally awake.

"Hello?"

"Hello, this is Mrs. Colonel Mattress calling about the Officers' Wives upcoming dance."

"Yes?"

"I have been working on the project and have decided to put you on the entertainment committee. So let me explain what you will be doing."

"Wait a minute, *Mrs. Colonel*. You have assigned me to a committee?"

"Yes, dear, so let me continue."

"Wait a minute, *lady*. I have two questions. I'm not sure how all this stuff works, so you may be a Colonel, but I'm a civilian. I have a full-time job, for which I have to get up only a few hours from now. So in the future you could call at a civilized hour and request my help. I don't think you can assign me to anything. Good night."

Now fully awake, I asked, "Who was that?"

"Some Mrs. Colonel Mattress."

Oh dear God, my squadron commander's wife! There was absolutely nothing I could say to my bride. She was right, but this was surely not going to promote my standing in his eyes! This was but one example of how out of control the wives of senior officers had become on this headquarters base. Their influence had proscribed crews in flying gear from eating in the very nice Transient Cafeteria or in the Officers Club. Heaven forbid that ladies enjoying lunch should have their sensitivities disturbed by brutes wearing "coveralls" — on an Air Force Base yet! Do I sound too critical? Well, it wasn't all bad. There was some great flying, fine friendships, and pretty high morale, but a few nagging "command failures" did occur.

One such failure was the decision that MATS should establish an "Alert Crew" capability. Strategic Air Command had alert crews on tap to man their bombers. So, wouldn't it be great if MATS had such crews to scramble transports at the ring of a bell? Boy, this was going make some commanders look really good!

As implemented, the MATS procedure bore no resemblance to the SAC system. First of all, SAC assigned its alert crew an *airplane*, one they could go and touch and prepare for flight. Most of the time, our alert crew was informed that the aircraft they *might* use was in the maintenance hangar. It *might* be available "some time tonight." MATS aircraft were heavily used. None sat idle to cover an alert capability. When this problem first popped up, we queried Colonel Mattress as to whether his alert crew might be allowed to stand by the phone at home until such time as an *airplane* might become available. Well, no, because then, he would not be able to show an available alert crew, so they laid on an obvious paper shuffle on top of crews often flying over one-hundred hours per month. To top it off, they added insult to injury. SAC crews were provided a station wagon. They were allowed to go anywhere on base, so long as they did so together. They could eat dinner, in flying gear, at the O'Club with their wives. We, as MATS crews, could not go there. Since the Bachelor Officers Quarters had no space to accommodate alert crews, they decided to house them in open bay, transient, enlisted barracks. Thus, banned from the O'Club and Transient Cafeteria, alert crews fed on hot dogs from a cart in the barrack's lobby. What a fun two-day duty this was! Needless to say, morale suffered.

The glaring phoniness of this paper shuffle became impossible to hide or defend one sad morning. The crew I was on reported to our squadron room to be relieved of our stint in the barracks by the replacement alert crew. Gloomy silence, and a room full of long faces, greeted our entry. What happened? Major Barney (not his real name) crashed at Guantánamo with a planeload of Marines. The approach to "Gitmo" required that flights remained within the boundaries of the Naval Air Station and not transgress over Cuban territory. Compliance with this directive required that the final turn to the runway be kept close and tight. A steeply banked and tricky maneuver for a large aircraft, it called for a very alert crew. The aircraft had apparently caught a wingtip and spun into the bay. No survivors.

A glance at the schedule chalkboard revealed that this crew had flown a round trip to Frankfurt, Germany. Arriving home in New Jersey, they had been off duty only some half dozen hours. They had then been called back out to cover a surprise assignment. Thus, they flew across the country to El Toro, loaded the Marines and then, flew back from California to Cuba. Realization of the root cause for this tragedy dawned on most of us at about the same time. I remarked to someone on my crew, "Well, I guess we know what our f--king alert crews are for now. Whoever sent them out without a decent rest just killed a bunch of people." Everyone in the room knew that our rested alert crew should have flown that trip. Unfortunately, Lieutenant Colonel Mattress had just walked in and heard my remark.

I was commanded to follow him to his office, where I got a good ass chewing, including threats of a court-martial. The night Duty Officer had already let the cat out of the bag. When a request for the flight had come in the previous night, it was Lieutenant Colonel Mattress who instructed that crew be called to cover it. Angry and sick at the stupid loss of friends and disgusted over the alert crew bullshit, I answered rashly. I challenged him to court-martial me and air the whole farce.

"Get out of my office!" he yelled and I fled.

Hoo Boy! My career was really soaring! The whole squadron room heard it, but nothing more surfaced and our illustrious boss was never called to account. "Pilot error" struck again.

I knew things were not going so swimmingly when, right on time, the other shoe dropped. All my contemporaries received papers promoting them to First Lieutenant. Except me. I was summoned by the Wing Commander, a Bird Colonel. He advised me that there was probably some paperwork glitch in the Pentagon. He said that a review of my training and other reports had convinced him that I was performing at a high level. He had therefore decided to exercise his discretion to grant me the promotion. He also advised that I should promptly motor down to the Pentagon to sort out the cause of this glitch, so I did.

Upon finally locating the records storage area and having the file placed in my hand, I got a huge surprise. There was a letter among my pilot training records, which was *highly* uncomplimentary. Hoo Boy! The Base Commander back there at Webb had really vented all his life's frustrations. The before-mentioned problem with his wife and his subsequent anger over it, prompted him to write that terrible letter which affected my career. I knew I had been no sweet pink angel, but had I been that bad?

I was allowed to read, but not to copy. So I memorized. On advice, I located the Judge Advocate General's office and was introduced to a helpful Major. This gentleman, a military lawyer, patiently explained that Catch 22 was not just a book title. It really existed. First, he explained that regulations *prohibited* such a letter — generated during a training situation and especially coming from an officer not in my chain of command — from ever being included in my permanent file.

"Well, that's great," I answered. "If regs say it's not allowed in the file, you can just pull it out."

"Well, no. You see, it's already part of the permanent file, so it can't be removed."

There really *is* a Catch-22!

I followed his advice and prepared an application to the Board for Correction of Military Records. A rather shaken and disappointed young pilot motored back to base and began seeking counsel from more senior officers. Eventually, these conversations led to a difficult but clearly necessary decision. Get out. A phone call and visit with my Congressman resulted in an Honorable Discharge within a few weeks.

Well, now what?

Chapter 4 | My Search for a Job

The "crash" of my Air Force career had been rather abrupt. It shocked my family and my wife. Yet, strangely, as I reflected on events, I began to realize that I was not as disappointed as everyone expected me to be. I recalled the advice from an officer I respected, which had great weight on my decision. He said that the sort of records mess I had suffered could happen anytime and that I might not even know about it. He had challenged me to answer whether I was really happy there. I could not truthfully say yes, as I had pretty much lost respect for my commander, and his controlling wife. He had also hammered me with my own obsession to fly, observing that the Air Force was going to command its officers to occupy many roles unrelated to flying.

I was surprised by how eager I was to get on with flying. Presenting my records, Air Force Form-5, to the FAA resulted in issuance of a Commercial, Multi-Engine, Instrument license. A small surprise came when they declined to issue an Air Transport Type Rating on the Boeing 707. It seems that one of the requirements for a Type Rating is the conducting of a V_1 cut, the abrupt failure of an engine just at the critical decision speed on a takeoff. The Air Force deemed this maneuver too dangerous to practice, even though it could happen. No box checked. No Type Rating. Hmmm! It was the first inkling that, maybe, those civilian fliers knew some stuff the Air Force didn't.

My new wife, being a talented typist, went to work assembling a slick looking bio and copies went out to all the major airlines. Meanwhile, I scored a job with Capitol Airways, flying out of New Castle, Delaware. I was to be a copilot on the venerable, Lockheed L-1049 Constellation. The "Connie" was a beautiful old girl, designed by the famous Lockheed Skunk Works, run by the genius, Kelly Johnson. Ordered for TWA (Trans World Airlines) by Howard Hughes, it was given its distinctive tripletail rudder configuration because Hughes refused to raise the height of hangar doors to accommodate a single tall rudder. The Connie was a queen, well past her prime, but still a queen.

On reporting for a single day of ground school, I was issued two books. One, about the size of a Reader's Digest, was the Pilot Handbook on the Constellation. The second, about double the thickness, was the Differences Book. The Capitol fleet of seventeen of those aircraft had been purchased from wherever they could find one. They all had different layouts, as ordered by many different airlines. Some had Curtis Electric prop controls. Some had Hamilton Standard prop controls. Well, you get the idea. You had to sit in the seat a few minutes to adjust your approach to the personality of a different queen.

Ground school proceeded apace. All were admonished to "do some reading." The new class, hired to staff a heavy summer tourist charter season, had some real characters in it. One Captain, whose real name I recall—but decline to mention— was the subject of a hilarious story. I'll call this resourceful fellow Garfinkle as that's as far from his real name as my imagination allows. The story, as related by a fellow in our class, who knew the captain, follows:

Captain Garfinkle had recently flown as Captain of a DC-4, employed by a fly-by-night company in the Middle East. Alerted that the company was issuing I. O. U.s in lieu of three months' pay, he made a plan. He and his crew were in a hotel in Athens, Greece, for a few days, while awaiting their next assignment.

When the assignment finally came, the crew could not find Garfinkle. The hotel desk said he had checked out a few days back, leaving only a sealed letter. When they opened it, the note said, essentially, "I quit," and named a hotel in Switzerland where his pay could be sent. The crew waited another day for a substitute Captain to arrive.

When this crew finally assembled and proceeded to Athens airport, days after Garfinkle had quit, they couldn't find a DC-4 airplane. Certain that Garfinkle had stolen the airplane, and probably sold it somewhere in North Africa, the owners mounted an investigation. All they learned was that someone bought an airline ticket and rode on Garfinkle's passport from Athens to Switzerland. They never found the aircraft.

In the parking lot that afternoon, a couple of us approached Garfinkle. When asked whether he had really "disposed" of the DC-4, Garfinkle just smiled and shook his head. "I'd never do a thing like that," he said, he twisted the key in the ignition and drove off—in a brand new Lincoln.

Three landings qualified us to fly the Connie. Professional Flight Engineers knew all the nuts and bolts stuff, so all we needed to know was how to fly. The four big Wright R-3350 radial engines on the Connie fascinated me. The management of a jet engine is simple. Push forward to go faster, pull back to slow down. Controls for this three-thousand horsepower, eighteen cylinder, fire-breather included throttle, propeller governor, fuel mixture, and "under cowl" intake air heat. Modern writers today often refer to this engine as turbocharged. Not so. It had a mechanically driven two-speed (high or low) supercharger. What confuses those unfamiliar with such an engine is its description as a turbo-compound engine. A brief description of this configuration follows.

Three exhaust driven turbines, roughly a foot in diameter, were mounted, spaced about the rear of the engine. At takeoff power those turbines, spinning at extremely high rpms, each poured some three-hundred horsepower through a shaft-and-fluid coupling directly into the main crankshaft. All that could be seen externally were the three titanium shrapnel shrouds, which looked like the bottom of a big iron skillet. For a night takeoff it was a good idea to pre-brief passengers that the white-hot skillets they were about to see were normal.

Working for Capitol Airlines was a real eye-opener on my road to learning the flying business. One of the largest of the non-scheduled airlines of the day, they still paid peanuts. Captains received a flat thousand dollars per month and I was hauling in a whopping four-hundred dollars. Pay was also delayed for a couple of weeks past the end of each month because it took some time for the office (in Nashville) to calculate the flight pay. We quickly learned a way around this problem.

Since the company had no credit anywhere, Captains were sent out with a wad of ten to fifteen thousand dollars to pay for gas, landing fees, etc. Thus, one could wait until arrival in some far off spot—such as Prestwick, Scotland—to inform the Captain about a shortage of funds and sign for a one-hundred-dollar advance. Playing this scam resulted in a zero-zero washout on the late arriving pay stub.

A flight across the North Atlantic could take thirteen hours with a fuel stop in Keflavick, Iceland, or Gander or Argentia, Newfoundland. This provided more time for me to read a good novel than the previous eight hours I was used to on a jet. Set up for long range cruise, our big R-3350s would be running at wide open throttle and deeply leaned out with props pulled back to take deep bites at sixteen-hundred-fifty to seventeen-hundred rpms. The prop governors could not always maintain synchronization at such low rpms, so you would continue to hear the out-of-sync beat through the next night's sleep.

I flew a couple of these trips with a great old-timer, Captain Hank Dodson. How old? Well, Hank had instructed Lufthansa pilots on their newly purchased Constellations right after the war. A landing at Keflavick, Iceland, demonstrated how well he knew the Connie and also what a pilot with tens of thousands of hours could do.

As we neared Iceland that day, weather reports indicated "zero-zero in heavy snow." A fast moving Arctic front had surprised everybody. The closest alternate, Stornoway, Ireland, was way beyond our remaining fuel. Zero-zero means no reported ceiling and no forward visibility. We were going to land. Wondering just how cold the ocean below us might be, I sat up to pay close attention to the coming event. Puffing idly on his cigarette, Hank appeared totally unconcerned. With our gear and flaps extended and the engines set at twenty-four-hundred rpms, Hank gently rolled the Connie into alignment with the ILS. (Instrument Landing System) localizer course.

A transmitter sends two beams. One beam, the Localizer, provides left-right alignment. The other, the Glide Slope, provides a sloped "ramp" down to the runway. The cockpit display is a gauge with a vertical bar and a horizontal bar. When these two bars form a centered plus (+) sign, you are on-course and on-glide-slope. The trick, of course, is to keep them centered.

Now lined up with the invisible runway with snow flashing past the windshield, we watched for the first movement of the glide slope indicator. As the glide slope bar began to slide down from the top of the instrument, toward alignment in the center, I was introduced to a new technique. Hank began to chant power settings to our engineer who was handling throttles at his side console.

"Manifold twenty-four. Manifold twenty-five. Take a half-inch off."

As he settled in and trimmed to slide down the glide slope he held the airspeed at a steady one-hundred-thirty knots. Localizer and glide slope bars remained glued to the center of Hank's instrument. Hank called small power corrections as we continued down towards the invisible ground. Minimums for a Class I ILS system are generally at two-hundred feet above the runway.

I called, "Two-hundred feet above minimums, no contact. One-hundred feet above minimums, no contact. At minimums, no contact."

Hank continued to descend.

"One-hundred feet above the runway, no contact. Fifty-feet, no... *yes*, I'm getting some glow from the runway lights."

Hank eased off throttles as we gently kissed the snow-covered pavement. The props blasted in reverse pitch as we slowed. Turning onto the taxiway, we followed a truck to parking.

I had previously believed that I knew how to fly on instruments. This demonstration soundly drove home the realization that there was a *hell* of a lot more to learn. Yes, the approach was illegal, but there was no warm cuddly option.

Flying for Capitol was a real learning, shall I say, *adventure*. Upon reporting in one morning, I heard an incredible tale, which, as it was now over, was also hilarious. Capitol owned three British Argosy freighters. With a high wing, four turboprop engines, and twin booms supporting the tail, it looked like a big brother version of the C-119 Flying Boxcar. A crowd stood awed as the just returned crew told their tale.

Returning from Africa, they carried a cargo which included two baby elephants. The babies had been set up in two pens, fabricated of wood, and shackled to prevent them from walking around in them. They were provided with tubs of water and lots of hay. Everything proceeded smoothly as the long flight neared New York in the early pre-dawn hours, until a violent wing rock shattered the peace for the tired crew. While one grabbed the controls and tripped off the autopilot, the other radioed New York to ask if they might have sailed through the wake of another aircraft. New York assured them that they had not and the thought apparently popped into three heads simultaneously. *The elephants!* With cigar still firmly clamped in his teeth, Roy, the large, bald flight engineer, jumped from his seat and dashed aft to investigate. Seconds later, following another violent left-right roll, he reappeared, minus cigar, muttering, "Oh, shit, oh, shit, oh, shit."

A shaken captain and copilot watched as Roy still muttering "Oh, shit," grabbed a CO_2 fire extinguisher and again dashed aft. The two pilots snapped their heads toward each other with round eyes. The next thought hit them both: *He's dropped his cigar in the hay!*

"We're on fire!" yelled the Captain as his Copilot leaped from his seat. Grabbing another fire bottle, he dashed after Roy. Bursting into the cargo bay, he was stunned to discover Roy yelling curses at Dumbo and hosing bursts of CO_2 at the elephant. Seeing no fire, he thought, *Roy has gone 'round the bend!*

It all came clear to him, when he saw Dumbo lift his trunk to reach overhead and Roy, cursing, fired another foggy shot. The cargo bay was clad with quilted fabric insulation. Dumbo had picked at this quilting until his little trunk could explore what might be hidden behind it. Feeling a wire-like "thingy," Dumbo latched on and pulled, until it snapped, like a banjo string, free of his grasp. You guessed it. Dumbo had found the aileron control cable and had decided that the wild lurch produced by his pulling on it was great fun. Somewhat concerned that Dumbo's new game might actually break the cable, the crew was *not* enjoying Dumbo's entertainment.

They declared an emergency and aimed directly for Idlewild Airport. By the time the scared Captain, flying solo, had lurched onto the runway, the other two had emptied all the fire extinguishers and were playing a desperate game of "bat the broom" with Dumbo.

Having survived, the crew now found the whole thing very funny.

"Goddam elephant thought batting brooms back at us was great fun," Roy muttered around his cigar, "He loved the attention, but my arms were really getting tired. The little shit nearly killed us all! Haw, haw, haw… ain't that a hoot?"

New info byte: "Animals can present unforeseen adventures."

My last trip for Capitol was with "Gentleman" Hank. I enjoyed flying with him. Most of the captains at Capitol used their copilots alternately as a seat-warming device and ballast. Hank taught me to fly the Connie and shared landings. I learned a lot about flying from this very patient old-timer.

It started out as a round trip to Chateroux, France, a charter for tourists. After landing at Dover, Delaware, we flew through Gander, Newfoundland, and on to Shannon, Ireland. A lumpy bed at the Royal George seemed quite luxurious after twelve-and-a-half hours of flying time. Two days later, our three-hour hop to Chateroux met with news of a change in schedule. We refueled and departed with military cargo for Adana, Turkey.

Weaving through a pass in the Alps at sixteen-thousand feet, following a wobbly ADF (Automatic Direction Finder) needle in clouds is guaranteed to keep you from dozing off. Hank appeared at ease as quick glimpses of gray rock peeked through cloud breaks from alternate sides. I reminded myself that Hank had flown this route many times and it helped. Our safari continued over the coming days: Adana, Turkey, Port Lyautey Naval Air Station, North Africa, the Azores, Bermuda, Charleston, Norfolk Naval Air Station and, finally, home to Wilmington, Delaware. By that time, twenty-eight days had elapsed.

I called my wife at work to announce my arrival and asked her to come and fetch me after work. She had our only car, an old Porsche.

"Where have you been?" she asked. I began to relate our safari and reminded her of our discussion about the uncertain schedule of my job.

"I got a postcard from some place in North Africa," she said, "so I called Capitol to ask where you were. They didn't seem too sure, but thought you were in the Azores and would be home before much longer, so I didn't worry, but I missed you. Oh, a letter from Delta came a few days after you left."

"Oh-my-gawd! What did it say? Did you open it?"

"Yes. It says they would like you to come to Atlanta for an interview."

In near panic, I asked, "Did it have a name or phone number?"

"Yes, it was signed by a Joe Mangum and here's his number."

My watch read just past three thirty. After a hasty, "I love you. I'll wait for you outside," I scrambled to trade bills for coins from a break room coffee collection and dashed for the pay phone.

"Hello. Joe Mangum here."

"Oh, yes sir, this is Jerry Farquhar calling about the letter you sent."

I heard a pause and sounds of paper shuffling.

"Yes, I see it here. That was sent over three weeks ago. I was beginning to think you weren't interested."

"Oh, no sir... er, *yes* sir... I mean I'm very interested, but I was gone for four weeks. I'm flying for Capitol Airways and I just got home."

"I see. Well, would you like to come down and speak with me?"

"Yes sir, I really would."

"Would tomorrow (a Friday) be convenient, or would you prefer next week?"

"Tomorrow is fine, sir. I'll start driving tonight."

"That's not necessary. One of our flights will depart from Philadelphia at oh-eight-thirty tomorrow and there will be a pass for you at the ticket counter. See you tomorrow."

I'm not sure if my feet met the floor as I dashed to scheduling to see how many days off lay ahead.

"We need you here at 0730 tomorrow for a trip to Ireland. Pack for about four days."

"*What?* Wait, I just got back an hour ago. I was gone four weeks. Don't I get a couple of days off?"

"No. We need you here tomorrow morning."

"Oh, *rats* (substitution of words here), this is awful!" I dashed for the office of our Chief Pilot, Captain Fox. *Maybe he can fix this*, I thought. I blurted out my appeal for, "Just one day off."

"Well, if they say they need you, there's nothing I can do."

Shit! "Well, okay, Captain Fox, I guess I quit."

"I see," he said. "Got an airline interview do you? Well, best of luck. Call me if it doesn't work out." Hi paw came across the desk and we shook goodbye.

I'm elated *and* scared, as Joyce and I drive the hour-and-a-half back to our tiny apartment.

"You quit?" she said.

"Yeah, I had to. They wouldn't give me a day to go talk to Delta and there's no career with Capitol anyhow."

A hasty repack of my suitcase and not much sleep later, early a. m. found us battling morning traffic to Philly.

Chapter 5 | Introduction to Delta

Arriving in Atlanta in my best (and only) suit, I followed the directions to Joe Mangum's office. The gentleman who greeted me limped on half-crutches as he led me back into his office. I later learned that Captain Mangum was a survivor of polio, contracted as an adult. Management, considering him to be a valuable asset, placed him in Personnel.

My interview seemed to be going well as he skillfully posed questions and eased my nervousness, followed by the expected question. "So, you're flying now for Capitol?"

"Ah, no sir. I quit yesterday to come down here."

His eyebrows arched. "You understand, we only offered an interview, not necessarily a job?"

"Yes sir. My wife was a stewardess with TWA. Their pilots told her that Delta was the best place to be, so when Capitol wouldn't give me a day off to come talk to you, I quit."

Another long stare with raised eyebrows. "You really rolled the dice, didn't you?"

"Yes sir. I want to work for this airline."

He gave me another long stare before he picked up his phone. When he finished, he scribbled on a pad and handed me the paper. "Go see this doctor and then, come back here."

"Yes sir!"

I took a shuttle bus to the terminal, located a cab and proceeded to address on the paper. A plaque on the door read, Dr. Janus, and further informed any who read it that he was a psychiatrist. A series of exams followed and then, a lot of strange questions from a strange little man. My memory fails to recall details, but I finally stepped back out into the sunshine and climbed into a cab, summoned by his secretary and traveled back to the Delta offices.

"Come in," greeted my knock on the open door of Mangum's office. "Well, Dr. Janus reports that you appear to be reasonably sane, for a pilot, so I'm gonna offer you a job."

I managed to refrain from whooping and leaping about his office. "Yes sir, thank you sir!"

"You're welcome. Now, we have a class starting on Monday and another starting in six weeks. I expect you will need some time to get organized, so Monday is probably too soon."

"No, sir. Monday would be fine."

His eyebrows flew up again. "You're sure?"

"Yes sir, I'm ready now."

"Very well."

I noted the first smile that I had seen from him as he scribbled on some papers. He handed me another piece of paper. "Call this man. He'll set you up with a place to live. Be at the Training Department at eight on Monday. Come here on your lunch break to do some paperwork. Good luck," he said followed by his hand across his desk. I was dismissed.

Holy shit! I thought. *I can't grasp the reality. They hired me! I can't believe it's real! Holy shit! Holy shit! I've got a real job now! Oh-my-gawd, I've gotta call Joyce! No, I've gotta call the man on the paper, first. Get a place to sleep first. Oh man, oh man! This is real!*

The rest of that afternoon passed in a blur. I cannot recall the order of things now, but I made a call and was picked up by a Captain Dana Jones. He was a tall, handsome man who greeted me warmly in an elegant Southern drawl. He introduced me to three of my new classmates. We would share a two-bedroom unit in an apartment building he owned in College Park. Set amid grass, tall trees, and with a small pool, it looked beautiful to me. Dana filled his units with young Delta people. No lease was required and weekly rates were very generous.

Dana was the first Captain I met, and we later became good friends. Dana had been a World War II B-24 bomber pilot. The man I came to know and admire was a movie version of the soft spoken, elegant, Southern gentleman. He would become known later as "Mister Delta." The care and time he devoted to seeing me settled in that first day left an

57

incredible first impression on me. He is gone now, but was loved by many and shall never be forgotten.

The weekend passed quickly. After getting introduced to classmates, I made a phone call to my wife. She was wildly elated. We arranged for shipping some clothing to me via the airline. There were excited meetings with other classmates in the building. Of the four of us in our unit, Bobby Haggard had the only car, a beat-up Volkswagen, so transport agreements were worked out among the group.

The first day of class and start of our new lives finally dawned.

Chapter 6 | Plumber's University

Why Teach a Pilot to be a Plumber?
This may be a good place to explain why a group of thirty-plus, newly hired pilots were reporting to a class to learn how to be Flight Engineers, sometimes referred to as Plumbers. Most airliners today, even large ones, are flown by a two pilot crew. This has resulted from design changes to simplify and automate many of the aircraft systems. Delta was the first to operate the DC9, one of the first aircraft designed to eliminate the Flight Engineer.

Back in 1963, all the airliners of any size required a Flight Engineer. Also referred to as the Second Officer, or S. O., he was needed to manage engines, fuel, electrical, hydraulic, pressurization, and other systems, especially when some system took a dump. Some airlines of the day still maintained Engineers on a separate seniority list. They were basically flying mechanics and were not required to have a pilot's license. One of the problems with this approach from management's view was higher pay for those with lots of seniority. Another was a crew function source of friction. A senior, old-timer engineer, paired with a couple of junior pilots, tended to become "Daddy," and take over decisions which properly belonged to the captain. Another inherent pitfall was that pilots were seduced into relying on their Engineer for knowledge of systems nuts and bolts. Falling into this trap through laziness, pilots were forced to rely on their engineer for knowledge of steps to take when a system failed. Thus, critical emergency decisions might be abdicated by a captain, whose knowledge of some system was fuzzy, not a good situation for the decision-making process.

Delta was a leader among the majority of airline companies to adopt a new approach. Entering the bottom of the seniority list, newly hired pilots would serve as flight engineers (second officers) until seniority allowed their progression to a first officer (copilot) slot. This philosophy solves many problems. The Engineer (S. O.) would always be the junior crewmember and receive the lowest pay. Because he was usually a newbie, the pilots he served were driven to keep themselves up to snuff on their knowledge of systems. A long-term benefit was that a newly promoted captain would have had the experience of serving in the other two-crew positions, perhaps on the same aircraft. In my opinion, this broader experience did generally produce captains with a better understanding of the functions of their other crewmembers. This broader understanding also allowed better decision-making, better coordination, and a smoother running cockpit.

These simple principles of respectful and efficient interaction between three people, all working toward the common purpose of producing a safe operation, would later be given a name. Cockpit Resource Management (CRM) would later become a major subject of dedicated training classes. You, the reader, may think, "Well, *duh*, that all seems obvious," but not so at the time. There were still old-timer captains who had learned their skills on aircraft which had no engineer or on WWII bombers where that position was filled by an enlisted man.

It's almost universal today for a captain to split landings with his copilot. Not so when I started. While most captains gave away landings, a few did not. A humorous result of such stinginess was the case of a copilot who reported, after signing in one morning, that he was not legal to fly anymore. His statement was received by the crew schedulers with an incredulous, "*What?*" He explained that he had not made the legally required three landings in three months and was therefore non-current to fly. The Captain was hastily called into the Chief Pilot's office for a chat. His lack of consideration had resulted in the necessity for an instructor pilot to take an empty aircraft out and give the Copilot his required three landings!

We were about to enter the program where pilots would learn all the nuts and bolts of the DC-6 and DC-7. We were guaranteed that the coming training would result in the issuance of a ticket proclaiming us to be a Flight Engineer, Reciprocating Power. Such a rating has also been referred to by the more irreverent as a "Baptized Plumber." Such ribbing would later be characterized by the wry description of seating arrangements on the Boeing 727. It had only four seats which faced sideways, and three were toilets.

And so… off to class.

Plumbers University:
The class which gathered that morning back in August of 1963 was a diverse group of eager young pilots. Seniority had been pre-determined. Thus, we were free to coach and help each other, rather than competing. Whether this was the intended outcome, I don't know, but it did quickly result in a class bonding, which made the learning easier and more fun.

Our ground school instructor introduced himself as Frost Ward. A tall, lanky, handsome gent, he quickly showed a confident manner and a great sense of humor. "Frosty," as we soon began to call him, had been an aircraft mechanic. Rising through supervisory positions, he had finally been tagged to be a ground school instructor. We soon learned why. Frosty not only knew the DC-6 and DC-7 inside and out, he possessed great patience and a very unique and rare ability to explain the function of a system so that everyone got it. If a student had trouble grasping the flow of some electrical system, for example, Frosty would back up and present the circuit as a garden hose with valves controlling a flow of water.

I won't attempt to teach the DC-6 and -7 systems here, but some detail is needed to fill out the story. The two aircraft were look-a-likes to the casual observer, but were really two different aircraft. The DC-6 was powered by four Pratt and Whitney R-2800 radial engines. Two rows of nine cylinders, with a displacement of twenty-eight-hundred cubic inches (i. e. six Corvette engines), were fed fuel through a huge Stromberg Carlson carburetor and a two-speed supercharger. They could pump out twenty-four-hundred horsepower and could turn a three bladed, thirteen-and-a-half foot, Hamilton Standard prop at twenty-nine-hundred RPMs.

The DC-7 represented the next step up from its older brother and it was the final example of a long line of piston-powered airliners. Like its competitor, the Lockheed Constellation, it was powered by Wright Turbo-Compound R-3350 engines. These brutes represented the peak of piston engine development. Displacing thirty-three-hundred-fifty cubic inches (i.e. ten Corvette engines), these turbine boosted, supercharged, fuel injected monsters cranked out three-thousand-fifty horsepower. This power required a larger prop with four blades to harness it.

The proper care and feeding of these beasts was far from the simple matter of lighting a fire in a jet and pushing the throttle forward. We were to learn their innards like a watchmaker knows a fine timepiece.

It's difficult to describe to a non-pilot, or even a pilot, who has only known engines that whine, the vast gulf between jets and these big radial "recips" (reciprocating engines), but I shall try by giving an example of response to an engine fire.

R-2800 or 3350:
1. Feather the propeller.
2. Shut off the fuel mixture.
3. Pull firewall shutoff T-handle. (which isolates fuel, oil, hydraulics, shuts off the generator, and opens a valve for the CO_2 gas.)
4. Check gear and flaps are up.
5. Set cowl flap selector to plus four degrees.
6. Put oxygen masks on. (Two banks of three CO_2 cylinders, located in the nose-wheel well, are plumbed through the pressurized cabin area. Should there be a leak in this plumbing, the crew would be gassed by CO_2 and rendered unconscious.)
7. Pull T-handle to discharge a bank of CO_2.

If the fire goes out, continue with:

8. Close cowl flaps.
9. Switch Generator off.
10. Turn fuel boost pump off.
11. Close oil cooler door and shut off oil cooler.
12. Turn magneto switch off.
13. Turn fuel tank selector off.
14. Push that engine's throttle full forward. (Yes, wide open. Should the prop un-feather, it would be slowed by forcing

it to turn against the compression pressure of eighteen cylinders, essentially making the engine a large "air compressor.")

15. Toggle the prop governor to full-low rpm and select a new "master engine" if the previous synchronization "master" has been shut down.

16. Turn carburetor heat off.

Jet:

1. Shut off the fuel (by various methods and that's it—no more, no less).

We would learn such procedures by heart and I just wrote this example from memory over fifty-three years after my last flight on a DC-6. Of course, the best way to memorize anything is simply to *understand it* and Frosty's mission was to ensure that we did!

The process was not all grinding study. There was an ongoing level of humor. Frosty had a very effective means of driving home important lessons. At the conclusion of study on each area, or system, he would conduct an oral quiz. Pointing to students at random, he would pose questions. His questions fully covered the "foot-stompers," those key things to know. We helped each other by whispering answers, should a classmate hesitate.

This presented some irresistible opportunities for mischief. I sat next to a fellow I'll call Harry, who had a rather dour personality. A smaller man, he displayed a bit of suspicious attitude toward his classmates. I couldn't resist the temptation. Whispering correct answers produced no smile of thanks and wrong ones produced a scowl. The whole room, along with Frosty, caught on to my game right away.

An example of such mischief requires an explanation of the system used on both aircraft for the purpose of feathering a prop. It involved an electrically driven oil pump. This feathering pump used engine oil to do its job. They had cleverly provided each pump's engine oil tank with a standpipe to preserve the last bit of oil in the event of a leak. The DC-7, having a larger four bladed prop, also had a higher volume in its hub, where blade pitch is controlled, requiring more oil.

The stage is now set:

Frosty, pointing to Harry: "How much oil is below the standpipe on a DC 6?"

Harry: "Two-and-a-half gallons."

Frosty: "Right. How much on a DC-7?"

Harry: "Three gallons."

Frosty: "Right. Why does the DC-7 need more oil?"

Harry: (long silence, a frown of concentration, a perfect chance for me to whisper a "helpful" answer, so I do)

Harry: "Because it has one more blade to fill up."

Pandemonium! People fell out of chairs and rolled on the floor holding their stomachs. Frosty stood, trying mightily to keep a straight face—and failed.

"Okay, you people, ten minute coffee break. Try to get a grip."

Harry scowled darkly at me, as whooping classmates bounced off each other and the walls on our exodus to the break room.

While learning our new jobs, we were also getting an introduction to our new employer. At the time, Ground Training was housed in a single story cement block building behind a Gulf gas station on Virginia Avenue. A group gathered in the break room following lunch one day. A half-dozen stewardess trainees entered, and each had a big orchid pinned to her blouse. Someone asked, "Where did you get the beautiful orchids?"

"We have been going over to the office building in groups to get our pictures taken for I.D. cards," one young lady answered. While we were there, just a little while ago, a nice old man came out of an office, talked with us and he gave us each an orchid. Isn't that sweet?"

An instructor, hearing her comments, asked, "Did he tell you his name?"

The group looked at each other questioningly. "Yes, I think so," one said,

"Was it Woolman?" he asked.

"Oh, yes," chimed a couple other ladies.

"Congratulations," he said. "You have just met Mister C. E. Woolman. He's the President of the company and he now knows your names."

"How can that be?" someone asked.

The instructor looked around at the little crowd. "C. E. knows every name on our payroll."

I thought about his claim as I walked back to class and decided to file it with a grain of salt. Other bits of lore popped up from time to time. In the break room one day, an older pilot asked me to slide an ashtray over to him. Curiosity popped up as I did so. "Where did these cheap aluminum ashtrays come from," I asked idly. They seem to be everywhere?"

He looked at me with a friendly grin and asked, "You're new, aren't you?"

"Yes sir, I'm in new-hire training."

"Well," he said, "I'll explain. Some years ago, the airlines were all going through a bad slowdown. Companies were firing people, or putting them on furlough. Mister Woolman refused to let our people go. He found at least part-time work for them. Those ashtrays were stamped out by men in the sheet metal shop from scrap aluminum. If you look around, you'll find a lot of stuff made by people C. E. kept working so they could feed their families. You see, C. E. considers the people who work here to be the company's most important asset and he says so often."

I thanked him and, as he left, I sat thinking. *Everybody I talk to seems to love this man, Woolman. There has to be something good behind this.* I was very encouraged by so much enthusiasm. A thought came into the open. *People here seem* happy! I would come to know more about this incredible man, but I'll save it for where it fits in later.

All my classmates successfully passed the Flight Engineer written exams, and were passed on to the Flight Training Department for our hands-on introduction to the DC-6.

Chapter 7 | Flying the DC-6

On to the "Big Six":

Things were moving fast now. We had three flights in three days. Every normal and emergency procedure from a walk-around to engine fires was practiced. During this period we were also scheduled for some evening sessions in the old-fashioned Link Trainer to practice instrument flying.

While driving to a session with a classmate named Buddy one evening, he posed a question.

"What's a Link Trainer like?"

I answered that I had been in some simulators, but had never been in the old Link.

He thought for a few minutes and then asked, "If I tell you somethin', will ya promise not to tell anybody?"

"Sure, Buddy," I answered.

"Waal, I ain't never been in any sorta trainer in mah life," he said.

Surprised, I asked, "But you've got a multi-engine instrument license, don't you?"

"Waal, I do, but I had to teach mahself."

"What?"

The whole story poured out. Buddy was married with kids and driving a milk truck in a small southern town. He decided that he wanted to fly, so he begged and borrowed and bought time when he could afford it. He eventually earned a Private Pilot, Single Engine rating. A flying friend, who had helped Buddy, got a job with Southern Airways. This friend told Buddy that he should take over his old job flying an old Piper Apache. This sturdy twin was owned by a chicken farmer. It had only one seat and was set up to fly trays of newly hatched chicks.

Buddy was introduced to the crusty old farmer, who asked, "You recon' you kin fly this thang?"

Buddy gulped and said, "Yes, sir. Get in."

The old man looked at him as if here were crazy. "Son, I ain't never flown, he said, "an' I ain't never gonna. Ah just wanna see you do it."

Buddy got the old Apache started, took off, landed and got the job. He learned instrument flying by reading and then doing it. I was amazed.

"Buddy, what if the FAA had found out you were flying a multi in instrument conditions for pay on a private ticket?" I asked,

"Waal," he laughed, "They couldn't fine me. I was broke. Ah guess I'd a' been back on that milk truck."

The next day, after our first ride on the DC-6, Buddy expressed serious doubts as to whether he could pass the course. He was worried that the biggest plane on which he had experience was the old Apache. We went out for our second ride together. I took a chance to speak with the Captain about Buddy's doubts. I had a feeling that this Captain, Beau Morgan, was a "good guy." Beau started our session by putting Buddy in the right seat with me starting in the engineer's spot. As we lined up on the runway, Beau slid his seat back and opened a *Playboy* magazine. When the Tower gave us a "Cleared for takeoff," Beau looked over at Buddy and drawled, "You got it."

Buddy looked stunned and stammered, "I ain't never flown anything bigger than an Apache."

Beau drawled, "This is just another airplane."

Buddy gulped and asked, "Where do you want me to go?"

"I don't care. It's VFR," Beau answered, as he pushed up the throttles. "Go anywhere you want to."

Beau read his *Playboy* while Buddy flew around south of Atlanta and I got my training session on the panel. On our way home, Buddy was grinning. "I think I can do this thang," he mused. Buddy went on to become one of our excellent captains. God Bless Beau Morgan, one of the coolest captains I ever knew.

We took oral exams—first by the company instructor, followed by another with the FAA—and passed. Then a company check-ride went by. The fifth flight was it! As to the

FAA check ride, I felt confident, but there was a degree of concern, because the whole job rode on this flight.

The FAA flight check went by in an easy breeze, much easier than the Company check ride. I was elated and patting myself on the back. I was still unaware of the policy, dictated by the Flight Training Chief Pilot, Captain Walter Lee MacBride. His policy was basically that the FAA will not set standards for Delta. Our standards will be higher, and *we* will control them. A company check-ride was to be far tougher than FAA standards and nobody was to be seen by the FAA until they clearly passed company standards.

I had purchased my uniforms and had them fitted. I leased a little one-bedroom apartment. Joyce was on the road to Atlanta in our old Porsche. Everything we owned fit into it. I now belonged to the Atlanta Line Chief Pilot.

On The Line:
Within days, I was called to work my first line rotation. That was it, the real deal. Somehow, I sensed a subtle difference at Delta from my Air Force experience, since my time with Capitol fled by too fast for much contemplation. We were not carrying cargo or troops anymore. They were paying passengers.

The center quadrant on the DC-6 and -7 sprouted two sets of throttles. Four on the left belonged to the Captain. The right set belonged to me. I would do all engine starts and the run-up to test prop controls, magnetos, and feathering pumps. On takeoff, the captain would set his throttles a bit shy of full power as he started the roll. He would then call for "takeoff power" and, then, keep his right hand loosely over his throttles. He could now pull them off in the event he needs to abort the takeoff, but, if all went well, the throttles were now mine to fine tune for takeoff power.

A large bank of gauges reported on the "health" of each engine. The first is the B. M. E. P (Brake Mean Effective Pressure), a torque meter that directly measures how much power is delivered to turn the big propeller. This would be the first indicator of any 'hiccup' during the first critical minutes, while those beasts hammered out all the thousands of horsepower of which they were capable. I also had gauges reporting manifold pressure, RPMs, cylinder head temperatures, oil pressure and temperature and carburetor air temperature. My job was to assess what those all reported and to inform the captain that "power is good," before we reached the V_1 critical decision speed.

After liftoff, the Captain would first call for reductions to METO (Max Except Takeoff) power, and then climb power as gear and flaps are retracted. If we are climbing to a higher cruise altitude, there will be a call to shift superchargers to high blower as we pass through about sixteen-thousand feet. Here, the throttles are wide open, and we are running out of manifold pressure. This tricky bit must be handled quickly to keep from losing too much airspeed. Inboard throttles, two and three, are reduced to twenty-inches of manifold, and their propeller governors toggled back from twenty-four-hundred to sixteen-hundred RPMs. Their "blowers" are quickly shifted to *high*, and then RPMs and throttles are pushed back up to climb power.

These steps are then repeated for the outboards, one and four. Done smoothly, it sounds like a big diesel rig going through a couple of double clutch gearshifts. An engineer who can run both shifts smoothly and without costing much loss of climb speed will earn a nod of approval from his grateful captain. Thus begins a reputation for competence.

One morning, during my early months, there came my first occasion for an engine shutdown. We had just lifted off in a DC-7, and the Captain had called for METO power. As I eased back on the throttles and props, the number three engine began surging RPMs. Attempts to toggle its governor back produced no help. It repeatedly wound up, with an accompanying howl, toward three-thousand RPMs. I asked the captain if I could pull off some throttle. He nodded yes. Still no help. I told him I thought we should shut it down before something let go.

He eased the throttle back some more and asked the copilot, "What do you think?"

A calm copilot nodded. "Yeah, I guess we're gonna have to to go back in."

Nodding at his copilot, the captain said, "Yeah. I agree. Go ahead and punch her out."

The copilot responded, looked at me and said, "He's fresh out of school, so let him do it."

The captain looked my way, "Go ahead."

I feathered number three. He rolled around the pattern, slid her onto the runway, and taxied back to the gate, no muss, no fuss. Mechanics swapped out the failed prop governor, and we departed about an hour later.

Pilots experienced only in jets may fly through a whole career without ever having to shut one down. Not so with the big radials. While they had a good level of reliability, they were just far more complicated than a jet. Most shutdowns were of the precautionary nature to prevent further damage from a suspected fault, but shutdowns were a regular event.

In fact, there was one memorable night when every DC-7 we owned was in the air at once. Our dispatchers in Flight Control, logging calls from crews on the company radio net, suddenly realized that not one of them had all four engines running! Sounds like a shaky sort of operation, but the decision by Delta to stick with its old recips, while transitioning into jets, proved a wise one.

Delta was the first to operate two of the new four engine jets, the Convair CV-880 and the Douglas DC-8. These jets opened new markets or expanded existing ones, while the older recips filled in. A number of competitors replaced their old recips with fleets of turboprop aircraft. The jets were coming rapidly, so these turboprop fleets were only a short-term bridge into jets. This move turned out to be a costly mistake for many.

As jets took over the longer routes, the recips filled in on shorter, feeder routes. While turboprops were somewhat faster, they lost any real edge over the DC-6s and DC-7s on shorter runs. A passenger might spend three-and-a-half hours from home to destination with the actual flight requiring only an hour. A DC-6, flying an hour leg, might be beaten by a turboprop by ten or fifteen minutes. So, what's fifteen minutes out of three-and-a-half hours? We would have to wait for jets to see any meaningful drop in total travel times.

An example at this point might illustrate this competition. It also added one more brick to my growing pile of proof that a lot of our captains were real characters. I came to realize that this individualism wasn't just tolerated, it was pretty much a company trademark.

I was on a DC-7 operating one night from Chicago through Cincinnati and Knoxville to Atlanta. Descending into Cincinnati, my ignition analyzer scope reported a double-shorted secondary on one of the eighteen cylinders of the number two engine. A shorted secondary simply meant that the high-voltage current to a sparkplug is shorting directly to ground. With no spark, the plug would not fire. A benign cause can be fouling of the tip by a carbon buildup from burned oil. Such fouling is either self-curing or can be burned out by leaning the fuel mixture. The second possible cause is not so good. A small bit of metal, a broken off piece of piston, or ring, or valve, may be bouncing around in the cylinder. The rising and falling piston could be causing this bit of metal to peen (hammer) the tip of the sparkplug closed.

While *two* failed plugs may still be caused by carbon, the not-so-good possibility trumps any benign assumptions. It's time to feather the prop and shut down the engine before any really un-good stuff happens. Alerted by our radio call, our Cincinnati mechanics immediately swarmed over the engine. While they unbuttoned the cowling and unscrewed the offending sparkplugs, we placated the passengers with drinks.

Our captain, watching the mechanics from atop the boarding stairs, was approached by a passenger.

"How long do you think it will take?" he asked.

"Not too long, I hope," answered the Captain. "I think they are only going to have to change some fouled plugs," he added.

The man looked thoughtful a moment then said, "You know, I've been loyal to Delta for years. I fly to and from Chicago and my home in Knoxville every week for my business. United operates a Viscount (turboprop) on this route and I see it over there boarding now. I think I'm going to have to start riding with them because your planes are getting a bit old."

Our leader responded politely, "Well, sir, I'm sorry to hear that, but our agent right there at the fence can handle your ticket change for you."

As soon as the man was out of sight, he dashed to the agent, ordering, "Load 'em up!" and sent me to urge our sweating mechanics to 'button it up.'

The Viscount was rolling from its gate as the Captain told me, "Start number three and four!" With the main door closed and boarding steps moving away, he called, "Spin two and one."

I was doing my best imitation of Van Cliburn on the switches as the copilot called for taxi and informed the controller, "We'll take it out VFR," he said, since our Operations Specifications allowed for Visual Flight Rules departures for non-jet flights.

Rolling at NASCAR speed toward runway 18, the Captain ordered, "Get your mag checks done and gimme the BCT (Before Takeoff Checklist) and tell 'em we're ready," he ordered the copilot.

With a prompt response, the tower controller radioed "You're cleared for takeoff, do ya think you can catch him?"

As we rolled directly into our takeoff with throttles already coming up, our captain picked up his mike and answered, "Watch."

Liftoff. Gear-up. Flaps up. Our four 3350s still howled at full roar. I glanced nervously at my watch. Full power carries a two-minute time limit. As the second minute ticked past, he called, "Gimme METO power! Get her cowl flaps closed a bit, but watch your head temperatures." No call for "climb power" followed.

The big Wrights are now bellowing at twenty-seven-hundred RPMs and churning at their maximum continuous rating. The old "queen" had hiked up her skirts and begun to sprint. Now aimed directly for Knoxville, we peered ahead. There he was, a bit high, directly ahead. We slid under, still gaining on him, about thirty miles from Knoxville. The

Viscount, flying on an IFR flight plan, would be handed off to Approach Control soon. Flying VFR, our captain had cleverly bypassed that step.

Our copilot called Knoxville Tower and announced, "We have the field in sight, request visual approach, straight in."

"You're cleared to land," came the response. We spotted the Viscount's landing lights as we cleared the runway and headed for the parking area, which was by a low, open-air chain link fence. I was standing, with my small jump seat folded out of the way, as we rolled to a stop and shut down.

The Captain jumped out of his seat and sprinted aft. The copilot and I peered out the windshield as the Viscount rolled toward the gate ahead of us. We spotted the Captain hustling along the fence toward the inbound Viscount. He pulled a cigarette from his shirt pocket, tore it in half and lit the stub as the door swung open and a stream of passengers begin leaving the Viscount.

We watched as they filed past our Captain, who was now leaning against a post with his cigarette. He reached out and tapped a man on the shoulder. The man looked at him and, then, did a classic double take. We could see his mouth form a large O as he turned and stared directly at us. We could hear our cooling engines ping occasionally as he stood and stared. They exchanged a few more words and, then, the man turned and walked slowly away, shaking his head.

Joining our Captain at the gate, I had to ask, "What did you say to that man?"

"Oh, nothing much, jest asked him how he liked his ride on a Viscount."

While flying as a new Engineer on the DC-6, a classmate T. P. O'Mahoney got a Passenger Service "Feather in Your Cap" award. He took a lot of ribbing about how he got it. While doing his walk-around inspection, T. P. noticed a large dog in a kennel box which was going aboard in the forward baggage hold. T. P. petted the friendly critter and refilled his water bowl.

Later, during final approach to land in Knoxville, the crew was roused by a fire alarm in the forward hold. It turned out to be a false alarm, but T. P. had already discharged a bank of CO_2 before he remembered the dog. The Captain hurriedly taxied to the gate and T. P. rushed off to open the hold and get the dog out. Baggage handlers helped carry the unconscious dog out of his kennel and some pushing on his chest got him breathing, but he was very dopey. T. P. borrowed a piece of rope for a leash and began slowly walking the animal to revive him. As the dog came alert, a lady walked up to the open chain link fence boarding area and spotted T. P. walking her dog. She thanked T. P. profusely. She also wrote a letter praising T.P. for taking time out of his busy schedule to walk her dog. T. P. accepted the *Feather in Your Cap* award and told only close friends how grateful he was that the dog could not talk!

This same classmate later won a second Feather in Your Cap award. The DC-6 and -7 had a toilet tank under a four-foot-wide, polished, stainless steel counter, which had an "outhouse" hole and a fold-down toilet seat. Under the counter, a quarter-inch hole in the fuselage provided a flow of air, down and outside to vent fumes.

A stewardess rushed breathlessly into the cockpit seeking help for a drastic problem. She related that a very overweight woman had sat on the counter without folding the seat down. Air going out the vent hole and the pressurized cabin had quickly formed a vacuum, which "glued" her to the counter—an eight p. s. i. cabin pressure had her truly "vacuum sealed."

T. P. had to work his hand under her (ahem) rump to break the seal. Problem solved. Of course, the stewardess just "had" to send in a nomination for the "Feather" award, which he won, but he adamantly and indignantly refused to answer any questions about his "heroic save."

Chapter 8 | Instructor Pilot

I had been on the line some four and a half months when I answered a call one evening. "Hello?"

"Hello, am I speaking to Jerry?" The deep voice and slow speech pattern sounded somehow familiar.

"Yes sir."

"This is Lee McBride calling. Your name has been brought to my attention."

"Yes sir?" *What have I done*, I thought, to bring on a call from the head of Flight Training?

The voice continued. "I have been informed that you're pretty sharp on the DC-6."

"Thank you, sir."

"How would you like to come over here and instruct on it? We pay seventy-five hours of flying, plus a hundred bucks override, and we'll get you a Captain's Type Rating on it."

Holy cow! Think fast! A full month's pay plus a hundred bucks and a captain's rating on the DC-6? "Uh, Yes sir," I stammered, "I'd be very interested."

"Very well. I'll be in my office tomorrow morning. Good night."

Joyce thought I was setting up a gag when I reported on the call. I'm often surprised when I have to go through my "Boy Scout's honor, swear on a stack of Bibles" routine to convince someone I'm not pulling their leg, I'm such a straight-laced sort of fellow.

I stood as Captain McBride strode into his Training Department the next morning. A tall, lean man with square chin, wearing a white Errol Flynn mustache, he looked like a casting director's version of what he was—a pioneer of aviation.

Ice blue eyes crinkled as he smiled and rumbled, "C'mon in."

He led me into his office and nodded toward a chair. We talked about his offer. He explained that the ATR (Airline Transport Rating) would come sometime after I had instructed engineers for a while. He laid out the working conditions and I eagerly accepted his offer. He said that the program was ramping up as increased hiring was planned and asked if I would care to suggest names of others he might consider as instructors. I offered some names and a couple were subsequently brought in. As our interview wound to a close, I asked when he would like me to start.

"Well, if you're gonna work here, you may as well start today," he drawled. "Go find some training manuals and look up Captain Gillette. We'll set you up with him for a while to break you in."

One last question popped into my head. "How will I know when it's okay with you to sign somebody off?"

"Well, Dick Gillette will help you on that, but it's a good question. My answer is that when you would feel comfortable about putting your wife, on a flight with a fellow on the nastiest night of weather you've ever seen. You can sign him off."

That was it! The standard he expected had been explained in a single simple sentence. *How incredible,* I thought, as I walked out of his office.

I soon came to learn a lot more about my new boss. Captain McBride held number *two* on the Delta seniority list. He had been a contemporary and friend of Charles Lindberg, flying the early airmail planes. Those open cockpit, DeHavilland DH-4 biplanes were powered by a four-hundred-fifty horsepower, twelve-cylinder Liberty engine. The airmail pilot flew solo.

In 1929, Mister C. E. Woolman owned a crop dusting company in Monroe, Louisiana, called Delta Air Service. That year, he succeeded in his efforts to gain an airmail contract. With this award of a route, serving cities between Dallas and Atlanta, he advertised for pilots. Walter McBride and his flying pal, Charles Beebe, drove to Monroe to apply. Both were hired. They chose to flip a coin for the first spot on the new seniority list. Beebe won and McBride settled for number two.

The new Stinson-T aircraft carried two pilots. Thus, these two Captains had never flown as copilots with anybody — and never would.

The Training Department back then was an exciting place. It was a small operation, bearing no resemblance to the enormous facility of today. A couple of dozen instructors were a colorful cast of characters and were superb pilots. That's why they were there. There were no simulators. We flew.

The half-dozen of us assigned to the New Hire Program on the DC-6 were very busy as hiring was steady. We needed an airplane for at least four hours per session and they were all needed on the line as well, so we had to be flexible. We set up shop wherever the line schedule showed a plane available and at whatever hour. If Atlanta wasn't possible, we got hotel rooms and set up shop. Detroit, Chicago, Memphis, Dallas, and Houston became second homes. We rotated, working four or five days on the road and, then, three days home.

The Captains we paired with were all great guys and freely passed on their years of experience. Nearly all were certified characters. I recall such names as Dick Gillette, Beau Morgan, Louie Smith, Roy Layton, Bob Studer, Charley Rarick, Hank Summers, Charlie Green, Dick Tidwell, Bob Davis, Jack Champion, Sam Bass, and John Ellers. There are others whose names deserve mention for their great work. I can only apologize for omissions and plead holes in my memories of forty-plus years ago as the cause.

All these Captains were generous about finagling training time to give us Instructor Engineers lots of stick time. One of our interesting side jobs was flying three-engine ferry flights. We generally stood available for these during our first day home from being on the road. As previously noted, shutdowns on the recips was not uncommon. If the fault required an engine change, the plane needed to be ferried empty to Atlanta on three engines. We generally started with an early AM departure to deliver a healthy airplane and then return with the sick one.

The Pratt & Whitney R-2800s on the DC-6 were nearly bulletproof. Wright R-3350s on the DC-7 were far more complicated and delicate. They were more susceptible to damage from "miss-leaning" the fuel or other accidental abuses and from simple wear and tear. Intended for long-haul use, they were now making far more full-power takeoffs on shorter routes. Whatever the cause, we ferried DC-7s about three times more often than the DC-6. In fact, my logbook shows I have about twelve hours more DC-7 time on three engines than on four!

Some special training was needed to conduct these flights. For one thing, they were flown without a flight engineer. The two pilots had to cover his duties. The obvious hazard here was getting off the ground. With an engine already out and its prop feathered and "roped," the loss of another on the same side would be cause for more than minor concern. Roping an engine brings visions of a spider web of rope around a propeller, but roping actually meant that the mechanics pulled a spark plug from a master cylinder. The feathered prop was then turned by hand to bring the piston to the bottom of its stroke. A mechanic then patiently stuffed about forty feet of clothesline into the spark plug hole, sort of like stuffing toothpaste back in the tube. The purpose was to build a cushion for the piston to prevent the engine from turning.

Back to our coming takeoff, with two engines out on one side, the airplane had a V_{MCA} (Velocity Minimum Control, Air) of one-hundred-twenty-five knots, which simply means that below this speed there is not enough rudder authority to keep the airplane in a straight line—not a good place to be. At ferry weights with no cargo, no passengers and minimum fuel, the airplane wanted to leap off the runway at about ninety-five knots. If this were allowed, the crew would be in a thirty-knot no-man's land until they reached a hundred-twenty-five knots. Very bad things could happen in this speed range if the remaining engine on the dead side should quit pulling its share of the load.

Mechanics would have prepared the aircraft with a thorough inspection of the three remaining engines, including a careful check of their oil screens for any telltale metal debris. The two pilots would conduct a thorough engine run-up. A primary preparation was careful adjustment of our seat.

The DC-6 and DC-7 had no powered flight controls. They had cables and loads were *heavy*. A strong man would quickly find his leg shaking while trying to hold full rudder against two engines on one side. The only way you could prepare for this possibility was with a properly adjusted seat. You adjusted fore-and-aft travel with your butt firmly planted against the seat back. You tuned the seat location until your knee was locked-out at full rudder deflection. Smart pilots soon learned to give this adjustment priority over a comfortable arm position during *all* takeoffs and landings.

On the runway, the pilot not flying would set the two symmetric engines to takeoff power. If, for instance, number four was the dead engine, then numbers two and three would be powered up. The pilot flying the takeoff would bring up the odd engine, number one in this example. He would feed in power against his ability to control direction with rudder and nose-wheel steering. Forward elevator pressure and a firmly planted nose-wheel gave added control. As speed climbed and the rudder became effective, his odd throttle would eventually match the other two. He would then turn all three over to his copilot to be evened up. The nose-wheel remained planted until reaching a hundred-twenty-five knots or the pavement ran out. Lifting off, the plane would be held flat to gain speed, while landing gear and flaps were quickly snatched up. A reading of a hundred-forty knots on the airspeed dial was indication of the appropriate time to exhale and take another breath. Lots of fun — and good experience!

John Sargent was my copilot on a three-engine DC-7 flight from St. Louis one fine day with the number four engine feathered. As we gained speed, I fed in more throttle to the number one engine. At around ninety knots, I could feel that the number one throttle knob was now matching the other two.

"Your throttles, even 'em up," I told John as we headed for the right edge of the runway.

With my left leg locked out on the rudder, I lifted off early as we passed over the right edge and, then, flattened out for speed.

"Gear up," I called to John.

"You guys okay?" the tower called.

As we got up to flap retraction speed and back under control, we realized what had happened. John was watching power, while my eyes were outside on the runway. We discovered that the number one throttle was about two knob widths out of rig. When I told John to "Even 'em up," he pushed up number one to give even power. I had thought the power was even when the knobs matched on my side. John had evened them on the *gauges* before I had enough rudder to handle it.

Another of our duties called for a couple of us to brief a class of new hires being handed off from Ground Training to Flight Training. In another recent example of "fast hands'" a trainee had managed to shut down *two* engines in his response to a simulated engine fire. I have detailed the procedure on a previous page and the reader may see, upon review of it, how easily this might happen. While we pushed for prompt responses, we cautioned against allowing fingers to outrun brains. Yet, multiple engine shutdowns remained a regular event.

The Instructor group put our heads together and came up with an idea. During our briefing of each class of thirty to thirty five trainees, we offered a challenge. For cases of beer, the bet was that "Out of your class of more than thirty people, at least *three* of you will manage to shut down *more than one engine*, and at least *one* of you will do it without realizing he has done so." This challenge was always accepted with shaking heads and voices claiming, "No way!" During the period of more than three years I worked in this program, first as Engineer Instructor and later as Captain, we *never* lost that bet.

On one memorable occasion, while I was flying as Captain, we saw one "Speedy Gonzales" Marine ex-fighter pilot manage to shut down all *four* engines. At about seven-thousand feet over the Mississippi River, a stunned trainee and his training partner in the Copilots' seat contemplated the sudden silence produced by two feathered props and two dead "windmilling" engines. Previous attempts to coach this hotshot to slow his hands to match his brain-speed had failed. At that moment, I realized that the situation called for a more serious approach.

Telling "Speedy" to get out of the way, I unbuckled and climbed out of the left seat. I told his buddy in the right seat,

"You've got it. Keep it above one-hundred-forty knots and don't stall it; it's a glider now. Keep it over the river and see if you two can get something running before you splash into the water. We're going for some coffee."

The instructor and I both headed down the aisle to the galley. As we doctored our lousy airline coffee with cream and sugar, we heard first one, then the other windmilling engine rumble to life and surge toward climb power. Pouring our seconds cups, we watched one of the feathered props begin to spin and join the chorus.

As we walked back into the cockpit, "Speedy" and his copilot were working diligently together to un-feather the fourth engine. I took my seat.

"Good recovery," I told them but you, "Speedy," are buying all the beer while we're in Memphis."

He slowed down his hands and passed all his training and check rides with flying colors. Who says you can't train a Marine?

One morning, a very startling event happened to me. I was on the sidewalk in front of the General Offices a little before noon, on my way to Flight Training. Mister C. E. Woolman came out of the building with three other men, walking toward a limo at the curb.

"Good morning, Mister Woolman," I said as they passed in front of me in busy conversation.

He turned and stepped toward me with his big paw extended to shake and boomed, "Good morning, Jerry. How are you enjoying the Flight Training work?" I stammered an answer and he then asked, "Did you get that Corvette you were working on painted yet and how's Joyce enjoying her job at the YMCA offices?"

Again, I somehow found answers. We chatted some more, before he graciously excused himself to rejoin his group. I stood stunned, rooted to the sidewalk as his limo pulled away. My thoughts spun. *This was a chance meeting. This wasn't an appointment, where his secretary could have briefed him. Our only other meeting had been just a couple of minutes on a flight to Chicago almost a year ago and I don't remember what I told him then.* I stood dazed as the only explanation sank in. *He really does know who I am. The only way he could possibly have such instant recall is that... he* cares!

What an incredible revelation! I could not have been more amazed if a cloud had opened and God had spoken. It was suddenly crystal clear why everyone loved this man.

My day passed in a light-headed haze. When I told Joyce about it that evening, she was incredulous that he knew her name, since she had not yet met him. I later heard Mister Woolman introduce a Captain to someone and describe him as, "One of the fellows I work for."

Training was expanding rapidly and Captain McBride decided to lay on another duty on top of DC-6 work, so I went to school on the Convair CV-880. This incredible four-engine jet was ordered for TWA by Howard Hughes. Hughes was pulling a scam on Convair. As 880s rolled off the line, he had inspectors finding faults and refusing to accept them. As new airplanes piled up on the ramp with no payments coming in, Convair stock fell. Hughes was busily buying up the depressed stock with the aim of taking over that company. Delta rescued Convair for a while by purchasing seventeen of the fast jets. It wasn't enough, however and Convair later closed its doors.

The CV-880 was an incredible airplane for its time. It was faster than anything today except the SST, which no longer flies. Its General Electric CJ-805 engines were a commercial version of the J-79, which powered the supersonic F-104 Starfighter. To my knowledge, these were the only engines produced with variable pitch stator blades. The compressor section of a jet engine is comprised of rows of wheels carrying blades around their outer rims. These spinning blades alternate with rows of fixed (stator) blades mounted inside the drum of the engine case. To give the F-104 rapid throttle response, GE developed the idea of mounting these 'stators' with linkage to allow their pitch (or angle) to vary. The result was a real eye-opener! The engine could accelerate from idle to full power in a count of *one … two*. This feature allowed the CV-880 to do some interesting things, some good, some not so good. More later.

Flight controls were another interesting 880 feature. The first large swept wing jet was the B-47. It's necessarily flexible wing displayed one nasty "gotcha." At certain high speeds, a deflection of its outboard mounted ailerons for a turn produced a rather unsettling reaction. Acting like flying trim tabs, the ailerons simply warped the flexible wing and caused the airplane to roll in the *opposite* direction! Oops!

Engineers took notice and scrambled to devise solutions. Convair engineers gave its wing two sets of ailerons, inboard and outboard. To prevent the dreaded wing warp at high speeds, the outboard ailerons were locked (faired) upon retraction of the wing flaps. Having solved the warp problem, engineers were faced with a new one.

At slower speeds, with flaps retracted, the small inboard ailerons were not enough to produce crisp role response. The wing had inboard and outboard sets of speed brakes. These panels, mounted atop the wing, could be raised to spoil lift and slow down. Engineers decided to make these panels full-flying controls. Thus, a roll left control input would raise the left aileron *and* the left spoilers, and lower the right aileron. Response was certainly crisp then. In fact, the resulting roll rate of eighy-seven-degrees per second was quicker than an F-86 fighter! Convair test pilots, thrilled by the idea of a *four-second* aileron roll, tried it. The airplane did a nice crisp roll. The crew was mildly surprised to discover that the crisp centrifugal forces had flung the outboard engines off their pylons into the Pacific Ocean!

The CV-880 wing had no leading edge devices or slats, and this resulted in a very fast wing. Approach speeds in landing configuration "over the fence" at one-hundred-eighty knots were common. Instant responding engines, combined with speed brakes, very high landing gear and flap extension speeds, allowed for some startling performance.

In the days before the current speed limit of two-hundred-fifty knots below ten-thousand feet, it was common to have a little fun. A CV-880 pilot could pass over the outer marker (about five miles from the runway) with the over speed warning clacker chattering and showing four-hundred-twenty knots on the Indicated Air speed—and *land the airplane*! High landing speeds, combined with a rapid roll and a yaw produced by spoilers popping up made the Convair 880 a real handful to tame. Getting out of phase trying to tame the rapid roll-yaw "couple" would just aggravate it, small wonder that senior Captains, who had flown recips like the DC-6 and DC-7 for decades, found their first transition to a jet a *major* hurdle. Having flown the Boeing C-135, B-727, DC-8 and -9, and the Lockheed L-1011, I can judge them all rather tame compared to the CV-880.

One of my first run-ins with the FAA involved that airplane. I had been working with the superb Captain Jack MacMahan as he checked out a senior Captain, transitioning from the DC-7. I had served as Engineer on the DC-7 with this Captain. I'll call him George. He was a fine pilot, an old-fashioned Southern gentleman. I liked him and held him in great respect.

At this time, the Captain was expected to call for his landing numbers from his Engineer. The Engineer would look up the required speeds, which varied with weight and aircraft configuration, write them on a tear-off pad, and pass the data forward. Maneuvers on a check ride came fast. A takeoff with a V_1 cut, followed by three engine ILS, a go-around on three engines, a second failed engine, a two engine circling landing, and all required different numbers.

George was a skilled pilot and soon tamed the CV-880, but its speed and the rapid sequence of maneuvers tended to get ahead of him and result in late calls for the numbers. On that check ride morning, I steeled myself to suggest some help. George listened as I explained that the coming evolution pretty much followed a script, with which I was familiar. I suggested that, when he needed new numbers, I could clue him by ripping the needed page off my pad. He thought that a great idea and, ever a gentleman, thanked me.

Off we went with an FAA inspector I'll call Gary Reynolds. A rather self-important fellow, he delighted in creating situations which would allow him to catch someone in a mistake. George was doing well, when Reynolds tumbled to my ripping off a page. I feigned total innocence to his accusation that I was coaching George. The ride was mostly finished, with only an ILS approach to be flown.

George flew a flawless ILS, wearing a headband and hood. Approaching Minimums, Jack reached across to raise the hood to indicate a runway in sight at two-hundred feet. As his hand distracted George only a few feet before his call, "Runway in sight," Reynolds pulled the circuit breaker for the ILS Glide Slope receiver. The ILS indicator on the CV-880 had a major fault, since corrected on today's jets. Failure mode left the indicator bars *centered* instead of biased off the dial. A tiny one eighth of an inch tall yellow OFF flag superimposed over the orange glide slope bar. George did not see it as he went on to a nice landing. A triumphant Reynolds pointed out that George had "busted minimums" by continuing to the runway.

A wrung out George slumped in his seat. I was embarrassed for him and angry as hell, both with Reynolds and with myself for not catching what he was up to. Jack began diplomatically to smooth things over. Observing that George was exhausted, he suggested that Reynolds fly back from Augusta to Atlanta, where George might redo the ILS. Reynolds climbed into the seat wearing a very satisfied smile. Arriving in the Atlanta area, Jack handed him the headband and hood and suggested he make an ILS approach. Reynolds fumbled with the hood a bit, and then put it aside, claiming he couldn't get it comfortable. "I'll just keep my head down," he said.

Watching a beaten George trying to maintain his dignity on the return flight just made me madder. As we were radar-vectored toward the Outer Marker for the coming ILS, a pompous Reynolds announced that Outer Marker passage should always be verified *three ways*. One should observe the needle swing around, the blinking blue light, *and* hear the *beep-beep-beep* radio signal in one's headset. As he reached to adjust a little volume knob for the Marker Beacon as he pronounced this wisdom, a light bulb flashed on in my head!

Waiting until he was looking away, I reached over and dialed the little knob to *Full Volume*. Approaching the Marker, he called for "Gear down" as the glide slope bar slid down toward the center. At the first blink of the blue light, a *beep-beep* blasted from his headset that you could have heard back in the galley. A startled Reynolds fumbled to relocate the tiny volume knob. While his head was down to find the offending knob, I popped the glide slope circuit breaker. Jack spotted the OFF flag at once and casually looked around at me with a questioning eyebrow raised. I smiled. His eyes crinkled and the corners of his mouth twitched up a fraction as he turned back forward.

All the way down the glide slope, I watched Reynolds eyebrows lift as he snuck peeks from his head down pose. George sat in the jump seat behind him watching. I got his attention and with hand signals and mouthing silent words, got him to stretch up and look over Reynolds's shoulder. Spotting the tiny OFF flag, George sat back, beaming a huge grin. Reynolds managed a landing from which we could at least walk away. As he turned onto the taxiway and called for the After Landing Check List, his eyes swept his panel and locked on the OFF flag.

He spun to glare daggers at me. "Did you pull that circuit breaker?"

"Yes sir. I pulled it at the Outer Marker."

MacMahan was howling and pounding his knees. "He's gotcha, Reynolds. You flew five miles and never saw that flag. Well, hell, everybody makes mistakes. If you write George his ticket, I think I can persuade Jerry to keep his mouth shut about this." Later, a happy George stood in the

Training Department office, holding his new ticket. As soon as Reynolds walked out, Jack related the story to a crowd of laughing instructors. Well, I never heard Jack promise *he* wouldn't tell. He only promised to try to get *me* to shut up. Reynolds, of course, learned he was a laughingstock and hated me thereafter, but who cares?

Flights on the CV-880 with Captain McBride were very educational for me. This old mail plane pilot had truly magic fingers and that incredible precision was awe inspiring to watch. The standard requires Captains to perform maneuvers within tolerances of five-degrees, five knots and fifty-feet. A steep turn, for example, required a full circle at a forty-five-degree bank with entry and rollout headings, speed and altitude to remain within these limits.

"Lee" McBride would first demonstrate the above by perching his coffee cup on the glare shield over his lap. He would then roll into a *sixty*-degree bank. Sitting casually with fingertips on the controls, he would continue a conversation as the airplane flew a circle in one direction and, then, rolled into another circle in the opposite direction. He would often pick up his coffee cup for a sip while the horizon rolled around. Watching his instrument panel was mesmerizing, because it appeared frozen except for the rotating compass dial!

After his demonstration, he would tell the Captain-in-training, "All right, now you do one."

His fault as an instructor was his lack of patience with the learning curve through which a trainee had to work. Explanations of how he did something were not forthcoming and his biting comments regarding sloppy' work would often humble a senior Captain. I eventually concluded that his skill level was so automatic to him that he didn't know how to explain what he did.

His landings intrigued me. The four wheels of each main gear were mounted on a "bogie." Looking like an upside down T, this bogie was free to pivot, or tip, on takeoffs and landings. This allowed all four tires to contact the pavement, even though the supporting strut was not perpendicular to the bogie. On takeoffs a leveling cylinder would return the tipped bogie to perpendicular, so it would fit into its wheel well. To prevent any attempt to retract the gear with the bogie in a tipped position, it caused a solenoid-activated bar to lock over the gear handle whenever a bogie was not level. You could hear the *clack!* of this solenoid and it also triggered a yellow caution light.

McBride's astonishing touch was consistently demonstrated on landings, which produced the *clack!* and the yellow light before you could feel any wheel contact! He rolled the rear tires of the bogies on and tipped the bogie before any weight settled on the landing gear. After watching him do this for the umpteenth time, I finally decided just to ask him how he did it.

His eyes crinkled as he drawled, "Waal, I do cheat just a bit."

"You cheat?"

"Yeah, I just get her all trimmed up on speed and aim at the runway. When I get about twenty-feet off the ground, I ease her nose up a bit and slide off some power. Then I level her off with the tires about three or four inches off and take off the rest of the power. Then I just sorta... give up."

Oh, *now* the whole thing made perfect sense! Seeing that I was not going to get a straight answer, I resolved to watch him more closely. I knew this crusty old coot liked me, because he was generous with flying time. Little by little, I unraveled his secrets. Trimming the airplane for fingertip control and a locked steady airspeed were the first requirements. Easing off some power in the flare prevented any balloon back up. Eyes on the far end of the runway to judge a slowly rising nose came next. Learning to trust one's instinct and peripheral vision to judge height was the final brick. Working my ass off one day, I finally heard a *clack!* before I felt the wheels touch.

McBride just nodded and growled, "You might be getting the hang of it."

Some pilots reading this may be thinking, *So what. I can make nice landings too.* Well, so could I. Every student pilot is taught how to flare into a nice landing. I considered myself, without undue bragging, to be a pretty good stick and rudder man, but striving to reach Lee McBride's level, with occasional success, was a whole new plateau, like a first solo all over again. The man had over forty-thousand hours in his logbook and had flown everything from open cockpit mail planes to modern jets. To this day, I have never seen a man with a better feel for his machine. The only contenders I can think of might have been Bob Hoover or Paul Mantz. I resolved to work toward this nebulous level.

I was ready to go for my DC-6 and DC-7 Captain's rating as we were working new hires out of Detroit. With Captain John Ellers, we got two Engineer check rides finished, with about forty minutes of time left. FAA Inspector Marvin Thornton was aboard. A big cheerful fellow, he was typical of most FAA types I have met. The FAA has a few bad apples, but most are decent guys trying to do a responsible job. I asked Marvin if he thought we had enough time to give me a rating ride. "Sure," he smiled. It went fast, ending with a three engine ILS and a go around, and a circle to land on two engines. After shutdown, I asked if he wanted to find an office somewhere to give me an oral exam.

"No need. You teach that stuff," he said, and handed me my first Airline Transport Rating ticket.

It was April 6, 1966 and thirty-two months after being hired by Delta. I was 27 years old. I moved into the left seat as Flight Training expanded and new Engineer Instructors were brought on board. The whole job was great fun, but exuberance needed to be tempered with caution. Without due care, even simulated failures and emergencies could become hazardous in a real airplane. Instructors can allow a trainee to crash in a simulator over and over, but you only get to do that once in the real airplane—no do-overs allowed.

Captain McBride commented that, "A superior pilot demonstrates his superiority by using his superior judgment and experience to avoid situations which might require him to demonstrate his superior skills." To avoid nasty surprises, it was his unbending rule that no FAA Inspector *ever* be allowed to lay hands on any controls or circuit breakers to set up a failure. He was to ask the instructor engineer to set up any problem. He should then whisper the setup to the Captain. It was kosher to surprise a trainee, but not the crew. Fatalities have happened and continue to happen when this rule is broken.

My first exposure to the dangers created by an uncooperative inspector occurred in Dallas. Working out of Love Field, we had an airplane from about nine at night until around three in the morning. With three trainees ready for check rides, we gathered in Operations and awaited the arrival of an unknown Inspector.

A man walked in wearing suit and tie, carrying a fancy attaché case. I introduced myself and asked if he was the Inspector for whom we were looking. With no response to my extended hand, he announced, "Yes, I'm Colonel Klink" (made-up name). A bit taken aback, I said, "I didn't know the FAA had colonels." His haughty response was, "I'm a retired Strategic Air Command Stand Board (Standardization Board) Inspector and I prefer to be addressed as *Colonel* Klink." Wow! We were off to a smashing start, aren't we? Seeing that he clearly intended to take over the entire affair, and knowing that Captain McBride would back me, I decided on an aggressive response. "Well, Colonel Klink, you can go ahead and call me by my first name... *Captain.*"

Not fully set back on his heels yet, he proceeded to explain his plan for the flight. "We'll work your first man and, then, land at Amon Carter (Ft. Worth, TX) Airport and shut down. Then, put your second man in and have him do an engine start and so on."

Shaking my head, I told him, "No, we're not going to shut down on a deserted ramp and re-start hot engines without a fire guard. It's against company policy and all good sense and I don't want to see my paycheck docked for the next twenty years to pay for a burned up airplane."

I laid out our plan for a safe operation. Explaining our "hands-off'" rule produced more argument. He finally grudgingly relented when I said we could all just go back to our hotel and cancel the whole ride. He had to be cautioned numerous times not to play with circuit breakers that night, but we finally got all three through their checks.

Captains and Instructors rotating in were warned to watch him, and all continued to have problems. Most were starting to compose letters of protest by the time I again went out with him aboard. Weather reports that night predicted a strong winter cold front to move in with snow and sleet. As it was still off to the north, I figured we could at least get some work done. We made an arrangement with Operations to give us a call on our "ramp radio" frequency as soon as they got reports of the front nearing. We departed to work northwest near Lake Grapevine.

A few hours later, we noted heavy snow flying past the windshield. A call to Approach Control revealed rapidly deteriorating conditions there. They fed us into the flow of aircraft trying to get in before the field shut down. Either we had missed the call from Operations, or they got swamped and forgot. Lining up for the ILS to thirty-one right, the tower cleared us to land and advised us of ice already collecting on the runway. Touching down as early as possible, I hauled four props into reverse, applied some throttle, and began applying the brakes. With no modern anti-skid system, the brakes were touchy and were alternately biting and sliding.

As we slowed, the props began to throw enough snow ahead to obscure vision so I eased the props out of reverse and the *inboards died*! No inboard engines meant no hydraulic pumps and no nose wheel steering. A brake accumulator was good for about four pumps on the brakes before it went flat. I pushed on moderate brakes and held them. Pulling more power on *one* and *four*, in reverse, I jockeyed the two throttles and rudder to stay on the runway and called for the trainee in the Copilot's seat to hit an aux-pump switch on his side panel to keep the brakes pumped up.

While we slid toward the end of the runway, I already understood what had happened. Goddam Colonel Klink had sneaked his fingers up and tripped the Inboard Reverse Control circuit breaker. For inboard and outboard engines, two breakers controlled the *un-reversing* sequence. With the breaker tripped, the props would remain in reverse pitch when throttles were brought out of reverse range. Engines would quickly load up and die unless fuel mixtures were quickly leaned and a bit of throttle applied. Trainees practiced this *only* on outboard engines, because there would be no hydraulics if they fumbled it on the inboards—right where Colonel Klink's stupidity had us now.

I finally stopped just short of the end and, advising the tower our position, we worked quickly to get an inboard engine started and get hydraulic pressure to taxi clear of the runway. One flight was forced to go around over us. Colonel Klink began to critique the engineer's failure to keep these two engines running as we worked.

Shaken and angry as hell, I yelled, "Get your ass out of here!!"

If memory serves, it was Instructor Fred "Flash" Gordon who grabbed the Colonel, pitched him out the cockpit door and, then, slammed and locked it. Colonel Klink followed us into Operations and a real shouting match erupted. A senior agent on duty had heard our radio calls and now realized what had gone on. He picked up a phone and dialed. After a few nods, he motioned me over and handed me the phone.

"I've got Captain Avrett on the line," he said.

I knew Captain H. Avrett was the Dallas base Chief Pilot. I introduced myself and apologized for the late hour cal, since it was almost 2 AM.

"No problem," he said. Tell me what happened." I related the events and his response was, "By God that's outrageous! I want you to call "Pre." (Captain T. P. "Pre" Ball was our Vice President of Operations, the boss of all pilots.) Write this number down. It's his home phone."

"Yes, sir," I answered. "I'll call him in the morning."

"No, call him *now*," H. said.

I dialed the number. The sweet voice of Pre's wife, Theresa, came on line. Apologizing for the hour, I explained who I was and that I was calling only on instructions from H.

"That's all right, dear," she said. "I'll get him for you."

Captain Ball came on the line, sounding alert. He was very cordial, but asked me to keep it brief. I sketched the story quickly.

"All right,' he said, "I'm glad you called, now. You hop the first flight to Atlanta and come directly to my office. I'll want letters from all of you who have dealt with this Colonel Klink. I'll take care of it. Good night."

I called another Instructor, related events, and asked him to make early calls to the others to give them a heads-up and get letters prepared. Back at the hotel, I had time for a couple of hours' sleep before catching an Early Bird out of Dallas.

This is a good point to introduce Captain Ball. Pre had come to Delta in the early 1930s and had flown as copilot for my boss, Captain Lee McBride, on the Stinson-T. He was now everybody's boss, including McBride's. A smaller man, standing around five-eight and weighing about one-hundred-sixty pounds, he still had a commanding presence. A very dapper dresser, he had a pencil-line mustache and stood ramrod straight. He had a reputation as a Master Ass Chewer as did McBride. New Hires were actually briefed about him.

They were warned that, if they ever found themselves standing at attention before his desk, they should *never try to lie to him*. His wrath was awesome to behold. It was claimed that Pre could sprint loops up the walls, across his ceiling, and down the other wall. All were warned to confess any sins, vow contrition, and take their medicine like a man. No matter what your sin, the upside of being straight with Pre was that the punishment would remain in-house. If the sinner had been truthful, Pre would stand between him and the wrath of the FAA or even God, like a battleship with all guns blazing. Our pilots adored Pre Ball. Many owed their careers to his defense. I was about to see him in action firsthand.

With little sleep and still mussed-up from travel, I approached his office around mid-morning.

"Come on in," was his booming response to my tap on his open door.

I assumed an erect pose before his desk.

"Tell me the whole story," he said.

As I did, his jaw clamped and his posture stiffened. Seeing his eyes, brought me a fleeting thought of what it must have felt like to stare at a pissed-off Wild Bill Hickok. As I finished, Pre popped out of his chair and stood, assessing me silently. Finally, he spoke.

"You should have thrown his ass off the first time he got out of line!"

"Yes, sir. I'm sorry."

"Well, that's all right. You're young, but file that for future reference."

"Yes, sir."

"All right. You gather up those letters. I want 'em on my desk before noon."

"Yes, sir," I replied and hurried off to the Flight Training Offices.

There, I found a secretary busily typing and another instructor pecking away on the only other typewriter. Finished with a letter, the secretary held her hand out to me.

"Give me yours, boy. You really kicked a hornet's nest, didn't you?"

A booming voice came from McBride's office. "That you, Jerry? Come in here."

Once again, I assumed good posture and again recounted the adventure. "Waal, I wish you'd told me before about this Colonel fellow, but you weren't the only one who didn't. You did a good job not wrecking the airplane. I'm glad you called Pre, 'cause I don't like gettin' up in the middle of the night anymore. Go ahead and get those letters up to Pre."

With a stack of letters in hand, I hurried back upstairs. Pre saw me coming and waved me in. Stuffing the stack in his briefcase, Pre waved toward another man standing.

"This is Frank Rox. He's Corporate Counsel. We're going to Dallas."

They marched out. I went home for some sleep. I later learned from Captain McBride what transpired in Dallas. Captain Ball and Rox marched into the FAA District Building and straight to the Director's office. Slapping a stack of letters on the startled man's desk, Pre introduced himself.

"I'm Captain Ball, Delta Vice President of Operations, and this is our Corporate Counsel, Frank Rox. We flew to Dallas today to deliver these letters and my message directly to you. You have an inspector who calls himself Colonel Klink. I am personally advising you that he is welcome on any Delta flight for which he has purchased a ticket, but by my orders, he will *never* be allowed to set foot in one of our cockpits again. Good day, sir."

The man sat speechless as Pre and Rox turned and marched out. We never saw Klink again. Whew! I joined the Captain Ball Adoration Society.

Flight Training continued to be a great adventure. It was easy to 'bum time' on any of our airplanes and I did so as often as I could. Captain Dick Gillette was one of our "certified characters" and a terrific pilot. Built like a fireplug, with no neck and a strawberry nose, he had a raucous sense of humor. Dick had been a "mud Marine." Using his G. I. benefits for flying lessons, he had conned his way into a job flying Stearman (biplane) crop dusters for a man named Bud, at Dublin, Georgia. Dick had slightly misrepresented his experience and Bud somehow got the impression that Dick had one-hundred hours in the Stearman and hired him. Dick had ten hours. He almost became a "Chinese Ace" by crashing three dusters as he learned his trade. Dick's face bore the scars from some hard-earned "lessons."

I bummed some time with Dick on the C-46 freighter one day. Dick was checking out two co-pilots. The old C-46 was great fun to fly, sort of like a John Deere tractor with wings. The big tail-dragger (planes that sat on the tarmac with their tails resting on the ground on a little tail wheel) had earned a reputation during WWII. Known by the Air Corps as the Curtis Commando, the tough old bird hauled freight over the Burma hump into China. With a pair of Pratt & Whitney R-2800 engines and a forty-eight-thousand pound gross weight, it was about twice the size of the look-alike DC-3.

Few know that Curtis designed the airplane to be the first pressurized cabin airliner. Its telltale, scalloped fuselage, shaped like an eight, was intended to be pressurized. It was also to be the first airliner with "tricycle" (a plane that sat on the tarmac on its main gear and resting on its nose wheel, which provided better visibility for the pilot) landing gear. Following Pearl Harbor, the Air Corps ordered Curtis to forget pressurization and to slap a conventional gear under it and build it. By war's end, it was too outdated to be an airliner.

Dick put me in the left seat for the hop up to Chattanooga and a few landings. After my stolen time, I set the brake and we swapped seats. Dick pointed at one of the trainees and asked, "You got any conventional gear time?"

He nodded.

"Okay, you're first in the barrel. Hop in," Dick said. As they rolled onto the runway, Dick locked the tail wheel. "Okay, you've got it. We'll stay in the pattern awhile for some landings."

With power up, she began to lumber down the runway. A shallow curve began to steepen as she swerved toward the right edge of the runway. "I got it!" Dick yelled as he hauled off throttles and we rolled onto the grass. "Haw, haw, *haw!*" he laughed while his stubby finger poked the startled copilot in the ribs. "You're a little rusty, boy!" followed as he rolled back onto the taxiway.

A deep drawl came from the tower. "Say, Delta, if you're gonna do that trick again, I'll call down for the boys on coffee break so's they kin hurry up heah an' watch."

"He gets three swings at bat," a laughing Gillette answered,

"Waal, you're clear to try it again any time y'all are ready. We ain't got any traffic raht now."

Back on the runway, power up, off into the grass again. Gillette's face is now turning red with his heaving laughter. "You *really* are rusty, boy. You gotta take charge a' this old thang."

A voice from the tower: "That was a real good 'un, even fancier then the first 'un. The boys are gettin' up a bettin' pool now. We got our money down, so y'all go ahead an' try her again."

We got back on the runway again, power up, and ended back off into the grass. A howling, red-faced Gillette pawed tears from his eyes as he rolled up off the grass and set the parking brake. The shaken trainee is doing a great imitation of a deer in the headlights.

Gillette, now gasping for breath, said, "You said you had some conventional gear time, son."

The trainee stares at Dick and stammers, "Well, yes, sir, but I've never flown anything with a tail wheel."

This set Dick off into another bout of laughter. Struggling for breath, he patiently explained. "Son, this is a conventional gear airplane. It has a tail wheel."

He patiently explained how you had to fly the airplane from the very start of its takeoff roll to the end of a landing, how the tail has to be raised as soon as possible to get the rudder up into the airflow where it's effective.

"You gotta use your ailerons and rudder and be aggressive," he said.

Dick reaches over to pat the man's shoulder. "It's all right, son. Anybody who claims he's never rolled one of these things off into the weeds is either a liar or he hasn't got a hundred hours in it. Just figure you're getting your trips through the weeds out of the way early. Take a couple a' deep breaths and remember that the only reason a good pilot straps on his seatbelt is to make sure the airplane follows along wherever his ass is goin'."

As we line up for the fourth try, Dick had stopped laughing and calmly coached the man to "Take charge of this old bucket." As the wheels lifted off, Gillette slapped the man's shoulder and yelled, "All right, that's the way!"

With his confidence restored, the man followed Gillette's coaching to a decent landing, just one more example of why Dick Gillette owned a reputation as a superb instructor.

I was awakened right at dawn one morning by the roaring of a motorcycle. A peek out my bedroom window revealed Dick Gillette riding his Harley in circles around my house over my lawn. I dressed quickly and flagged him down to come in for some coffee. Over his coffee mug, he explained that we were going flying that day. He had borrowed the use of a Stearman and announced that he was going to check me out in.

Arriving at South Expressway Airport, we rolled the old biplane out of her hangar. This one had been re-converted from a crop duster and restored. Its forward cockpit had been re-installed and it still had its four-hundred-fifty horsepower Pratt & Whitney radial engine! With me in the front "hole," Dick made the first takeoff from the narrow, forty-foot-wide runway. We headed for Nunan Airport. I followed through on the controls as Dick made the first touch-and-go landing.

After yelling at me not to touch the brakes, which are notorious for putting a Stearman over on its back, he waved his hands at me and propped his elbows on the cockpit coaming (raised edge). I shot a half-dozen progressively better touch-and-go landings.

Dick yelled at me to follow the highway down to Dublin, Georgia, where I knew he had worked as a "duster" pilot. As the airport came into view, Dick waggled the stick and I turned the plane over to him. Dick aimed at a building near the parking ramp in a shallow dive and throttled back. Assuming that he was going to make a "wakeup" low pass, I relaxed.

115

About a hundred feet from the building, Dick opened up the big P&W with a roar, cocked the wings and rolled the wheels over the corrugated steel roof! As he pulled up in a climbing turn, I was able to look back at the building. People were squirting out of every door, and one guy was climbing out a window! Some fifteen people stood watching as Dick taxied in and shut down.

An old timer, wearing a faded ball cap, ambled over and looked up at Dick. "I knew it had to be you, you crazy bastard," he drawled. "I'm not gonna get any work out a' my people today after that crazy stunt, so y'all might as well climb down and we'll go get some lunch."

That was my introduction to Bud, Dick's old crop duster boss. After lunch, I got in four or five more landings. It had been a long day by the time we pushed the old girl back into her hangar. I already knew that Dick Gillette was a wild man, so that day only added another piece of evidence to the indictment. Crazy or not, I still learned a lot from this superb pilot.

Chapter 9 | "Characters"

Our cast of certified characters was not limited to pilots. There were some stewardesses who fully qualified as well. One such was a British born gal I shall call Bobby Warden. Bobby spoke in a crisp British accent and possessed a rapier-quick wit and a devilish sense of humor. She could slice and dice the unwary or the foolish before they realized they were bleeding. Bobby possessed the belief that new flight engineers should be subject to an exam to assess their poise and ability to concentrate on their jobs under pressure. The test she devised was pure wickedness.

A DC-6 Engineer sat on a small fold-down seat. Starting the R-2800 required fast fingers and both hands. The reader may gain a sense of the procedure by sitting on the forward edge of a kitchen chair. Reach high with your right hand and turn an engine selector knob. With your left hand raised, squeeze two paddle switches toward each other with your thumb and middle finger. You have engaged the starter and the prop will begin to rotate. After the watching pilot has counted and called "Six blades," reach with your right hand to turn *on* an ignition magneto switch. Now, still holding starter switches with your left thumb and middle finger, depress another paddle switch with your left index finger. This is the ignition boost switch, which engages a coil to add extra power to a row of spark plugs. Now, with your left ring finger, begin working a fourth paddle switch to shoot fuel into the engine from a primer pump. As the engine comes to life, your ring finger needs to feed it more and more fuel shots. As it comes up toward a one-thousand RPM idle speed, your right hand drops to a throttle while your left fingers release all switches except the primer, which is now held steadily *on* by your ring finger. Reach quickly between your knees with right hand and lift the mixture control to Auto Rich while simultaneously releasing the primer under your left ring finger. You have just started an R-2800. That was a snap, wasn't it?

Riding a cockpit jump seat home from Detroit one evening, I witnessed Bobby administer her "test" to one of our newly minted engineers. Slipping quietly into the cockpit, she stood silently behind him as the first prop began to rotate. He flicked the mag switch on and his ring finger began its dance on the primer. As the engine began its first belches of life, Bobby kneeled and, reaching under the seat, began gently to tickle and explore his privates. The poor fellow's fingers went spastic and the engine protested its poorly fed diet of fuel with a series of loud *bangs!*

The copilot, knowing what was coming, brought the mixture lever up and got the engine settled down. Bobby responded to a glare of indignation from the "testee" with a sweet smile. In clipped British tones, she admonished him.

"I say, young fellow, that horrid racket you just made has surely frightened my passengers."

Having failed the concentration portion of Bobby's exam, he proceeded to blow any chance of recovering a few points for poise.

"Well, if you think you could do better, you're welcome to try," he snarled.

"That would be smashing great fun," Bobby trilled. "Oh, Captain, may I really?"

Captain Jim Bain shot a glance of pity at the young man, which sailed over his head. "Hell, yeah," he said, "Let her give it a try."

Bain, a charter member of the "Certified Characters Fraternity" watched with a poker face as the young fellow bounded out of his seat, bowed and directed Bobby in. He wore a self-satisfied smirk as she sat.

"Clear four," she called and went through all the motions necessary.

His smirk looked a bit frozen as number four spun smoothly up to idle. By the time Bobby had the last two engines humming sweetly, he stared slack-jawed in a good imitation of the village idiot.

Bobby stood and clapped her hands like a happy schoolgirl. "Oh, thank you, Captain Bain, that was jolly good fun." Smiling sweetly at the poleaxed victim of her prank, she said, "You see, darling, if you do it quietly, you won't be frightening everyone half out of their wits."

Bain and his Copilot just smiled sadly at the poor guy. I actually felt sorry for him. Wicked!

Another character whose company I enjoyed in Flight Training was a Captain Beau Morgan. A Southern Boy, if the name didn't give you a clue, Beau spoke in a slow, laid back drawl. I never saw Beau move any faster than a leisurely stroll, but his mind worked at the speed of today's computers.

Beau considered himself an entrepreneur. Some called him a con man, but probably just out of jealousy. He had a lot of irons in the fire. One iron was a lease on a city owned hangar, which sat next to Delta's original hangar. Slow speaking Beau had negotiated a lease which gave him ongoing first rights to renew the lease. Delta wanted use of the hangar.

When Captain Pre Ball asked Beau about taking over the lease, Beau said, "Sure, Pre. Gimme a million cash and I'll sign it over." Pre went ballistic and threatened to fire him. "Go ahead," Beau drawled.

Nobody learned the terms of their truce, but Beau kept the hangar and kept showing up at work. Beau ran a small F. B. O. (Fixed Base Operation) out of that hangar. An example of his mind at work is the day he captured all of the refueling business for the Canadian Air Force. Working in his office one day, he heard a Canadian Air Force transport on his Tower frequency monitor radio. Knowing that they bought fuel from one of the *big* F. B. O.s on the field, his brain hatched an instant plan. After a quick call to a package store on Virginia Avenue, he jumped into his old runabout station wagon and sped over to the *big* F. B. O. He made it in time to nab the crew as they deplaned. After a quick conversation, he drove back to his office.

Soon, the big transport taxied onto Beau's ramp and shut down. He loaded the entire crew into the wagon and headed for Virginia Avenue. At the package store, Beau treated each man to a case of the adult beverages of his choice. His quick phone conversation with the manager had resulted in a hefty corporate discount, based upon the upcoming surge in business with the Canadians.

Beau once sold a Cessna aircraft to a man with the pitch that his son could learn to fly cheaper if they had their own plane. By the time the boy attained his student pilot's license, Dad was beginning to sweat a bit over the bills. He approached Beau and asked if there might be some way to defray some of the costs. Beau said he would work something out. He set the boy up flying skydivers and gave him a little briefing. All went well for a while, but the FAA eventually got wind of something smelly going on.

Detailed to watch the airplane one weekend, an inspector finally observed suspicious activity. He took notes as three men handed the boy money, donned parachutes and departed. Sometime later, the boy taxied in alone and shut down. The inspector, now sure he had nabbed a culprit, ordered the boy to show his license. The boy pulled out his ticket, held it in both hands so the Inspector could see it and, then, put it back in his pocket. An angry Inspector told the boy that he was writing up a citation because he had personally witnessed him taking money and flying for hire.

"Your Student Pilot License only allows you to fly *solo*," he added as he strode off.

When the citation arrived, the boy did as briefed and took it to Beau. He led the boy into the FAA offices and straight to the Director's desk. There, he tore the citation in half and dropped it on the man's desk.

"Your man's citation on this boy will never stick, because he didn't do what it says he did," Beau drawled.

The inspector was called in and detailed what he had personally witnessed. Beau laughed at him.

"Well, now, you didn't see what you thought you saw. See, this boy's daddy owns the airplane, and he rented the use of it to those men. The boy wasn't taking money for flying, just collecting rent for his daddy."

"Even so, he still can't fly *people* for free," came the rejoinder. "He can only fly *solo*."

"Let's get the regs out and read it," Beau smiled and said.

They produced the book, turned to regulation 61.89 and the inspector slowly read it out loud. The inspector slapped the book shut with finality

"I think it's quite clear that a student pilot may not touch the controls unless he is *solo*!"

Beau nodded. "That's absolutely correct," he said, smiling. "You see, the fellow you saw get into the right seat is a Southern Airways Captain. *He* flew the airplane. After his two friends jumped out, he jumped out, and that left the boy, here, *solo*. He didn't violate any part of that reg, because it doesn't say a word about how he *gets to be solo*. So you don't have a leg to stand on."

We didn't study regs in Flight Training for nothin', by golly Ollie!

Captain Jim Carlton had a reputation for outrageous practical jokes, among other things. A frequent target was a contemporary we shall call Elroy Hager. Referred to by some as Empty Helmet, he was a big, somber fellow who simply lacked the gene to "get" subtle humor.

One of our newly "hatched" flight engineers approached Carlton one morning. Introducing himself, as briefed, to his captain, he revealed that this was his first line trip. Greeted warmly by the always jovial Carlton, he was reassured that, "We'll have a great time, don't worry. Are any of your buddies here for their first day?" Carlton asked.

"Yes, sir, I think so."

Carlton grabbed the young man's elbow and steered him back to the sign-in desk. "Show me any of your buddies here," he said. The young fellow ran his finger down the list, pointing out a couple of names. Stabbing his finger at a name,

Carlton said, "He's already signed in. You gotta find him for me."

Looking around, the fellow spotted his buddy and led Carlton to him. Carlton greeted the fellow and whispered that he needed to confide some things to him. After leading him to a quiet corner, Carlton proceeded to brief him in confidential tones.

"I just saw on the sign-in sheet that you're going out with Captain Hager today, so I'm gonna pass on some stuff to make your day a lot easier."

"Yes, sir, thank you, sir," the young fellow said.

"Okay, look. The first thing is that he likes the cockpit as cool as you can get it. He's kinda slow, so be sure to laugh at his corny jokes. Now, this is real important. Be sure to write very legibly in the logbook and especially on the pay sheet log."

"Yes, sir, thank you very much for telling me these things."

Carlton clapped the young fellow on the shoulder and, turning to leave, he added, "Say, I almost forgot. You may find Elroy a bit strange, but if you ever get the chance for a look-see, he's famous for being hung like a horse."

"Oh, well, uh, yes, sir. Uh, thank you, sir."

A few minutes later, Carlton spotted Elroy at the sign-in desk. "Good mornin', Elroy, how ya doin'?"

"Mornin', Jim."

"Elroy, I gotta talk to ya a minute. Come over here where it's quiet."

"Well, Jim, what is it ya gotta tell me?"

"Elroy, I gotta let ya in on somethin' important."

"Yeah?"

"Well, Elroy, it's like this. I had a talk with a new young fella goin' with me today an' he let on somethin' you prob'ly oughta know."

"What's that, Jim?"

"Well, Elroy, he's got a classmate goin' out with you this mornin'."

"Yeah?"

"Well, he says this fellow is a homosexual, and..."

"Oh, my gawd, Jim! Is it true? Why did you tell *me*?"

"Listen, Elroy, I'm only tellin' ya so ya won't be tellin' any a' yer crude jokes and hurt the fella's feelin's. Ya gotta learn to be more tolerant, Elroy. Why, I met him and he's a nice young fella. His buddy told me he's real sharp an don't act funny, an you'd just never know, so I'm just suggestin' that ya might wanna loosen up a bit and give the fella a fair break, Elroy."

"Well, Jim, it was good of you to tell me about this and I'll try to be fair minded about it. I will."

A day later, the inevitable event occurred. Standing side by side at a urinal, the poor fellow's curiosity led to a quick sideways glance. Elroy remained forever convinced the kid made a "pass" at him. The young fellow's reputation as the famous "queer engineer" actually gained him points for being part of one of Carlton's classics. People laughed every time Elroy indignantly told the story. He never caught on that they laughed because he had once again swallowed one of Carlton's pranks hook, line, and sinker.

It would seem incredible that *anyone* could be sucked in by another Empty Helmet classic. Around the mid '60s, Captain's hats began to sport "scrambled eggs" on the visor. The date for wearing the new hats dawned at the beginning of a month. Elroy showed up in his new hat and proceeded to gripe about the cost.

"I already bought a new hat just a couple months ago, an' now I gotta waste another forty bucks for this one."

Elroy must have had some terrier genes, because he just *wouldn't* let go. His crew soon tired of his griping and began a project. Over the next weeks, they carefully added thin strips of paper under the inside hatband. By mid-month, Elroy had to scrunch the hat on.

"Forty bucks for this dang hat and the sumbitch is shrinkin!" he griped.

Many were, by now, in the know and would innocently ask Elroy why he had bought a hat that was too small. His freshly triggered outrage was entertaining.

Having shrunk the hat as far as they dared, Part B was put in motion. On their way to a layover hotel in the crew limo, they suggested to Elroy that they were all weary of his complaints about the shrinking hat. They reported that a dry cleaner had been discovered only a block from the hotel and, by great good fortune, this place advertised the steam blocking of hats. It was suggested to Elroy that, for a measly four bucks, his problem could be solved. Elroy brightened up and, thanking his loyal and caring crew for the great idea, vowed to carry the hat in as soon as he got settled at the hotel.

The next morning the crew gathered for their limo pick-up. A smiling Elroy lifted and re-seated his hat a couple of times to show how well it now fit. He thanked his helpful crew for the great idea. Over the next weeks that this crew flew trips together, the hat mysteriously began to stretch. You, the reader, being far sharper than Empty Helmet, have by now solved the mystery. Of course! The crew, under Part B of their plan, had been slowly removing the paper, which the cleaners had been bribed to leave in place as they steamed Elroy's hat to fit.

By the end of this crew's month together, the hat sat down on Elroy's ears. Fuming about wasting forty bucks on cheap products that shrink and then stretched, Elroy trashed the hat. He bought yet another new hat from a second uniform supply store and forever vowed that the first outfit sold shoddy products. It never dawned on him that the two hats bore the same manufacturer's label. I realize that you, the reader, will find it difficult to credit such a level of gullibility, but that is a true story.

Another certified character was Captain Jim Bain. Back then, crews turned in a pay sheet at the end of each rotation. The sheet detailed flying times, cab costs, tips, meals, etc. Bain once submitted a pay sheet which claimed the cost of a new hat. The head of Payroll, a man named Stevens, bounced the claim. Bain called to argue the point. He said that the hat had blown off as they were starting engines on a DC-7 and had been mangled in the spinning prop. It was, therefore, an "in the line of duty loss." Stevens remained adamant that Delta would not pay for it.

At the end of his next rotation a week later, Bain hand-carried the pay sheet to Stevens. Slapping the sheet on Stevens' desk, Bain challenged him to check it over. Stevens read over the sheet, punched some numbers in his adding machine and finally nodded his approval.

"Well, the hat's in there, you cheap s. o. b.," Bain snarled "You find it!" He stomped out.

Chapter 10 | Flying the DC-9

Back in Flight Training, Captain McBride having had the foresight to lie about his age back in 1929, was now into his seventies. Everybody knew he was well past normal retirement age, but nobody could prove it. It was a real experience to work for this crusty old-timer. He set our standards well above the FAA's par and stood behind us like the Rock of Gibraltar. Under Captain McBride, an Instructor bore the weight of an added role. No pilot undergoing a check ride would be left standing alone before the FAA. We were to stand before *him* as a shield, sort of a "defense council."

Most Inspectors were decent and fair-minded, but a Colonel Klink, or a Gary Reynolds, could always pop up. Strong differences of opinion could occur, even with the good guys. Captains faced a check ride every six months. No lawyer, or doctor, has ever been required to *demonstrate* competence in such a way, just pilots.

While added training and re-checks were available, "busting" a check ride placed a man in an uphill battle. Thus, every check ride was looked upon as a "bet-your-ticket" event. Disputes could quickly become an adversarial situation. It is entirely possible to force the most competent pilot to "bust a ride." Problems could simply be piled on top of one another until even a superb pilot could no longer juggle all the balls in the air. Trickery can also be employed. In a training or practice session, such "loading-up" could be a good learning tool.

There were, and are, Inspectors who think like an old-fashioned barber, or a town traffic cop. If there isn't enough hair on the floor, or speeding tickets on the pad, they haven't done the job properly. Part of an Instructor's job was to ensure that a check ride was fair. Captain McBride decreed that, any time an instructor felt that events were becoming unfair; he was to step in and call a time out. If the dispute could not be resolved to his satisfaction, an Instructor was to terminate the flight and return to base. This would force the inspector to write an "incomplete," rather than a "failure" for the check ride.

The dispute then went to McBride's office. Instructors would gather to hear the explosions from behind McBride's closed door. Inevitably, a chastened inspector would slink away, while McBride could be heard on the phone demanding that the FAA office "Send an Inspector over here who knows his goddam job!" McBride never lost those battles, because he knew what ground to stand on and always fought on the offensive.

We were gearing up to put the new DC-9 into service. Nobody had seen one yet, when a group of us went off to Ground School to learn all about it. Flight checkouts would await delivery of the first plane and be scheduled by seniority in the department. Still fairly junior, I was well down the list.

Captain Dick Gillette rotated back to Flight Training from one of his occasional R & R shuffles back to flying the line. He was scheduled to perform some instruction on the Convair 880, pending the start of DC-9 ground school. We now had gained a new position called Flight Training Assistant Chief Pilot.

Captain McBride's new assistant was rather dull-witted and ponderous. He greeted Gillette's return with his patented stolid frown and informed Dick that he thought it would be a good idea to have him fly a check ride with Harry. Dick stared at him for a few seconds and then responded.

"I don't see any need for that, I'm sure Harry flies the airplane just fine." He turned and walked away to a room full of snickers.

The new DC-9 we studied was the DASH-14 series. This short-coupled aircraft would later be known as the "Baby 9," when stretched versions were developed. The original had no leading edge devices, or slats, on its clean wing. As we studied, we learned that its "full flying" horizontal stabilizer incorporated a curious feature. Pushing the control column full forward would cause a hydraulic accumulator to release its pent-up pressure into a cylinder, which would ram the entire stabilizer into a full nose-down position. My previous studies of aerodynamic engineering caused a loud *ping* in my head upon learning that. What curious flight characteristic had brought about such an unheard-of device? Ground school provided no answer.

The first aircraft, aircraft number N3301L, was finally delivered, but a couple of weeks late. It had failed to meet the designated number of seconds for retracting its landing gear. Douglas, unable to discover a reason for the extra few seconds, rewrote the specs and the FAA signed off on the new number.

Checkouts were scheduled by seniority, and Captain Pre Ball was among the first. He was aboard on one of the first flights, doing touch and go landings at Augusta, Georgia. On retraction of the landing gear, a hydraulic reservoir burst and dumped all the fluid. The landing gear was designed to free-fall into a down and locked position, so that presented no concern as they returned to Atlanta. However, unless retracted, they would hang down further than the tires. Douglas had designed a hand crank, which would draw up the cables and return the doors to a locked and up position. Captain Ball occupied the right seat and drew the job of winding the little crank handle. It was apparently a stiff little bugger. He got the doors partially up before the knob slipped from his grip. Trying to grab the madly spinning knob, he got some good raps on his knuckles.

"Screw it! Land with the damned doors down," Pre said, holding his smarting hand. After grinding a half a foot off the hanging doors, an inspection of the burst reservoir revealed some eye-opening news. Some worker had deposited his empty lunch sack in it! The sack had floated about until it chanced to cover the vent hole. Returning fluid had then pressurized the non-vented reservoir and burst it. The mystery of the slow retracting gear was solved. Trainees going for their FAA oral exam were advised to clarify any question about gear retraction time. They should ask if the inspector wanted the time with or without the lunch sack.

Pre called Douglas and angrily told them to trash all their damned cranks and pulleys and cables. He told them that Delta would solve the hanging door problem in-house. Pilots flying later iterations of the DC-9 now know the origin of those skid shoes on their inboard doors.

The mystery of the hydraulic tipping system for the horizontal stabilizer was also revealed. As the airplane approached a stall, the design provided that a warning would be given to the errant pilot. This warning was triggered well before an actual stall and was impossible to ignore. While the control column shook madly, bright red lights flashed and a klaxon horn (copied from a German U-boat) drowned out all thought or ability to communicate verbally. No shut off button was provided. This triggered comments that a relay system should be invented to set off a klaxon under the desk of every FAA Inspector coast to coast. What demon was this airplane hiding that could justify such a system?

The arrival of the Douglas test pilot Jerry Heimerdinger revealed the answer. Flying the airplane into an actual deep stall was impossible, unless you ignored all the racket and did it *on purpose*! On the theory that it could happen in a training scenario, instructors were scheduled for a little demo ride with Heimerdinger. Taken in groups of three or four, they took turns handling a deep stall. All returned with shaking knees and very pale faces. With the warning system circuit breaker pulled, they each listened as Heimerdinger coached them into a stall. "Whatever you do, don't touch the rudders, just push all the way forward and level the wings. Don't touch the rudders, *please*, whatever you do, *don't touch the rudders!*" he chanted. Asked how many times he had done this, Heimerdinger responded, "Dozens of times, and it still scares the shit out of me."

The dirty little secret had to do with the shortness of the airplane and its high T tail. Any stable aircraft carries its center of gravity forward of the center of lift of its wing. Its horizontal stabilizer therefore pushes *downward* to hold the nose up. As the nose of this aircraft was held higher and higher into a stall, its fuselage and wing would suddenly blank airflow over the tail. Thus blanked, the tail would lose any grip on the air and the plane would tumble end over end! Whoop-dee-do! Its wing, reaching stall at about the same time — and across its entire span — would drop to left, or right.

A training flight under the command of our new Flight Training Assistant Chief Pilot managed to tumble from around twenty-four-thousand feet down to about four-thousand feet before they got control of the little beast. As the milk-white group filed back into Flight Training, Dick Gillett looked up from paperwork and inquired, "Which student was in the seat when it dumped?"

Our shaken leader, the Flight Training Assistant Chief Pilot, snarled, "What do you want to know that for?"

Dick stared at him a few seconds before answering, "I was just curious who saved the airplane." Ouch! *Ouch!*

I was eventually slotted into the DC-9 checkout program and flew my four training rides. A great old Captain, Roy Layton, conducted my rating ride with Inspector 'Pappy' Estep in May 1967. Roy had flown B-24s over Germany so no training fiascos ever caused him to break a sweat. I flew with him on many different aircraft and it was always a treat.

With three years and four months now spent in Flight Training, I was beginning to feel itchy for a change. My seniority would now allow a line copilot's slot on the new DC-9. Simulators were coming, which would mean more time in a box in the basement and less real flying. Not appealing. The kicker was that I was going to have to work under the new Assistant Chief. The more I thought about that, the gloomier I felt. No leadership, no fun.

Our new Assistant Chief called me at home the day after my rating ride and insisted that I report to his office forthwith. Upon my arrival there, he informed me that he had a complaint from Inspector Estep that I had behaved in an arrogant fashion. I asked him to explain what that meant. He answered that I had flown my check ride in a suit and tie and he obviously figured that this was an arrogant thing to do. I was astonished by his pompous ignorance. I explained that most of us wore a suit and tie on days we were scheduled to fly home from Jackson, Mississippi. I informed him that the DC-9 used for training also made up the first available flight out to Atlanta. There was very little time to change clothes and the next available flight was hours later. I said that it was obvious that Inspector Estep was not aware of the situation and added that he wore a suit and tie as well.

I expected that my explanation would satisfy the misunderstanding, but the Assistant Chief clod still acted as if I had misbehaved. His attitude solidified my decision whether to go back to the line. I stood up.

"I don't think I want to work for you," I said. "I quit."

Instructor Captain Ben Truesdale had listened to my "interview" with our new Assistant Chief. He stood and said, "I don't think I want to work for you either. I quit."

Instructing teaches a lot about technique, but it's still a sort of artificial world. I needed to get out into the real world of flying the line. I spoke with Captain McBride and he was very supportive of my decision. His agreement eased my mind about the move. I would miss him very much.

Chapter 11 | Back To the Line

In August, 1967, with a Captain's rating in my pocket, I went to work in the copilot's seat of the DC-9. The "Nine" served routes from Dallas to New York and Chicago to Miami. Line flying is about *learning* the airports and the tracks between them. Jeppeson Approach Charts tell all about an instrument approach to an airport, but there remains a vast store of needed knowledge that can't be put on a page.

For one thing, the "Jepps" don't teach you how to cheat. An example was Chattanooga. Landing to the south, you have a precision ILS to follow. Landings to the North offered only Non-Precision guidance from an ADF needle and a much higher MDA (Minimum Descent Altitude). To cheat, you first looked for the glow of light from a large shopping mall to shine through whatever weather "glop" you were in. With the mall located, you could sneak a couple hundred feet down. Now you looked for the large, bright red, Buster

Brown Shoes sign. Roaring over the shoe store at two-hundred to three-hundred feet, locked on a runway heading, you counted off for ten seconds, and *et voilà*! there was the runway. There were many more like this and they were definitely *not* on the Jepp charts. One just had to *know* the airport.

A large part of this lore was learning when *not* to cheat. One cannot expect to learn this lore by paying tuition at some airline-training academy for the simple reason that they don't *know* it. It can *only* be learned by flying with an experienced captain, who knows why rabbits drop little pellets, horses drop apples, and cows drop patties.

We learn habit patterns to stay out of trouble. A night flight through bad weather from Detroit to Columbus to Cincinnati to Knoxville to Chattanooga to Atlanta, might take only two hours and 45 minutes of flying time. On a nasty night, with five instrument approaches, that's not a flight plan… it's a yo-yo. If you dropped your pencil, you might never catch up. So, develop *habits*! You may complete the checklist, but you still *recheck* the landing gear at five-hundred feet. You choose one of the taxi light switches to use as a worry-bead and turn it *on* every time you hear the tower say, "Cleared to land." You turn a little orange heading-bug on your compass dial to the takeoff runway heading before you leave the gate.

That little habit would have prevented a recent crash at Lexington, Kentucky. LEX has two runways which overlap at their north ends like the capital letter A. One is for light planes and is too short for an airliner. A little orange heading-bug would have alerted the crew that they were on the *wrong* runway. A lot of people died because two guys never learned a little habit from an old pro.

It would take too many pages to list all the accidents caused by a lack of habits, which can only be learned by an apprenticeship to an old pro. Due to seniority, there was a time when no pilot could ever reach the left seat without serving this apprenticeship. FAA experience requirements for obtaining a Captain's rating assume this situation, and remain basically unchanged since the 1930s. The regs allow that a pilot who has a Commercial Multi-Engine Instrument Rating and fifteen-hundred hrs in his logbook is eligible for a Captain's Type Rating on a Boeing 747! Back when the regs were written, such a situation was never foreseen, but with new airlines popping up every month, this has actually happened!

The regs badly need a re-write, but it will apparently take many more mangled bodies before that happens. Note to the public: Shopping for cheap deals on shoes or furniture is economics. Shopping for cheap deals on air travel can be more like Russian roulette.

My flying apprenticeship exposed me to great Captains such as Jim "Cheyenne" Bode, Dan Butler, Arch Fairbairn, Andy Croft, Billy Bishop and many others. Each was an individual who offered new nuggets to drop into my growing bag of lore.

Andy Croft was a great character with whom to fly. It took me a day to decode why Andy often gave me two legs in a row. I finally realized that Andy knew which legs included food service. I flew those legs, while Andy got to eat. Andy had a fair sized paunch and, if he was kidded about it, he would describe his belly as his "anti-stall device," because it prevented the yoke from being pulled far enough back to stall the airplane.

When Andy wasn't eating, he had a cigar clamped in his teeth. Thankfully, they were good quality cigars. We finished flying in a layover city one day. I was very hungry, having watched Andy eat three meals. I had obtained a quarter-inch bolt from a mechanic at our previous stop. As we taxied in, I fumbled my pen as an excuse to bend over and dropped the bolt into a hole on Andy's seat track. As I walked out of the cockpit, Andy was trying to force his seat to slide back. His belly would not allow him to get out of the seat past the yoke.

In Operations, I could hear Andy calling on the radio for a mechanic to come out and fix his seat latch and get him out. A few minutes later, he came in holding up the little bolt. "I think you lost this," he said and then started laughing. Andy had a great sense of humor, and got laughs telling about the great joke I had played on him.

A great nugget was offered by Billy Bishop one nasty night as we neared Columbus, Ohio (CMH). Minimums for a Class I ILS are generally a two-hundred foot ceiling and a half-mile of visibility. RVR (Runway Visual Range in feet) meters were coming into use, and the CMH main east-west instrument runway (9 Right) had one. The distance you can see through whatever glop is measured by shining a bright beam of light at a distant photocell. The photocell converts whatever light it can see into a value in feet and *et voilà!* we now have a number which says whether we may, or may not, conduct an approach. If a runway *has* an RVR, then its reading becomes primary law. This night, the RVR said, "You may not come in!"

Billy Bishop *knew* his airport. He called the tower and asked, "Well, what would you guys call the prevailing ceiling and visibility?"

Now, the Navajo Code Talkers are not the only people who speak in code. A sharp tower controller decoded Billy's question.

"I'd call it two-hundred feet and a half-mile," he responded.

"Well... do you s'pose you could light up the old runway and flip on the ILS?" a smiling Billy said,

"I'll feed some quarters into the meter right now," drawled the old hand, "and you are cleared for the ILS to 9 left," he added.

We had to "look close," but our flight ran on time to Columbus once again. "Look close" is also code. Eastern, United, or American were competitors in the market. When instrument approaches dropped to minimums, they were brothers who spoke the truth, often in code.

An Eastern flight, which just landed ahead, might be asked, "How was the visibility?" He would never admit to cheating a bit below minimums. His response of, "We've made it okay, but you'll have to look close," decoded to mean that we were going to have to be locked-on the beam and expect to cheat a few feet.

One old-timer I flew with was known for putting a few hundred extra gallons of fuel aboard. I learned that he looked very closely at weather reports and made his own estimate of fuel he might need. We had a very competent group of dispatchers in our Flight Control Department. They would build our flight plans and fuel load, based upon weather and whatever alternate destination might be required. On the line, it requires the captain and dispatcher to agree on any *go, no go* decision. I learned to think like this old-timer about the "ultimate Captain's authority" by watching him and from a story he related.

He was flying a DC-7 from the New York area through Charlotte to Atlanta one night. A look at weather reports showed a strong winter cold front moving south along the route. He called Flight Control and ordered an extra three-hundred gallons of gas. His extra fuel meant unloading some freight and mail, but it was done on his insistence. Along the route, a cold front had moved faster than expected and any approach to Charlotte was impossible.

A DC-7 had no modern Flight Director system, and its autopilot could not be coupled to fly an ILS approach. All approaches were hand flown on raw-data ILS indicators. Upon reaching Atlanta, an approach in heavy rain, gusting winds, and lightning resulted in a missed approach and go-around. It was getting worse by the minute, and even jets, with more modern equipment, were unable to get in. It was one of those frantic nights in Flight Control with flights diverting in all directions.

This captain was now headed for his "on-paper" alternate of Birmingham, Alabama (BHM). The cold front beat him to it. By the time he was overhead, BHM had also gone under. He called Flight Control and told them he was sick of all this sorry weather and was now heading for Memphis to get on the backside of the front. Flight Control acknowledged his call. A few minutes later they called him back.

A panicky sounding voice said, "Captain, we've run some numbers, and it looks like you won't have enough gas to reach Memphis!"

Our old-timer drawled, "Waal, don't you boys fret none. Ah run outta *your* gas about five minutes back. I'm burnin' *my* gas now."

Message received—loud and clear!

Chapter 12 | Flying the DC-8

By December of 1967, I was able to move onto the DC-8 and another cast of characters. Captains with names such as "Noisy" Wood, "Birddog" Mills, Dewitt Clinton, "Cracker" Morris, P. R. Smith, Al Bonner, and Warren Segars owned the left seat on these big "Cadillacs" of aircraft at the time.

Longer flights to great layovers in Los Angeles or San Francisco beckoned. The DC-8 was the Douglas answer to the Boeing 707, and it was an impressive answer. Having flown both, I would give the nod to the "8" for solid stability and comfort. Both the original 8 and its stretched 60-Series brother were very stable and honest airplanes. By honest, I mean that the plane always behaved the way you expected it to, with no surprises. Its good manners allowed sweet landings to become business as usual.

The DC-8-61 was stretched to seat one-hundred-ninety-five passengers very comfortably and weighed over three-hundred-thousand pounds. It did not have quite the speed of the Convair 880 but it carried over twice the passenger load and had much longer range and passengers rode in the quiet comfort of a limousine.

Flights from Atlanta to Los Angeles or San Francisco might average four hours, forty minutes there and about four hours to return. Thus, eight round trips plus a couple of short legs would fill a pay sheet for the month. Westbound flights are always longer because of prevailing winds - and could be much longer if the Jet Stream was encountered. The Jet Stream is a constant flow, usually at high latitudes, which carries core winds of one-hundred, to one-hundred-fifty knots. It occasionally dips down over the central or southern U. S. Our Flight Control and Meteorology people tried to plan westbound flights clear of it and eastbound *in* it.

The casual observer and even some pilots might think that flight times through strong west winds for a round trip, or two opposite direction flights, would average out. Not so. Any wind, encountered in two directions, will cost time and money. Simple math will illustrate. With no wind, two-thousand miles at fife-hundred knots will require four hours. With another four hours to return, it will be an eight hour round trip. Throw in a one-hundred-knot wind from the west and re-figure. Our five-hundred-knot airplane is now making four-hundred knots over the ground into this wind. It will now take *five* hours to cover two-thousand miles. That's okay. We'll make it up on the return flight, right? Let's see.

We head east and are now making a whopping six-hundred knots over the ground, so two-thousand miles at six-hundred knots will take three hours and twenty minutes! Wait a minute! Where did that extra twenty minutes come from? We made a ground speed of four-hundred one way and six-hundred the other. Doesn't that average five-hundred? Yep, it does. So, where'd the twenty minutes come from? Well, it snuck in there when you made the mistake of averaging speeds instead of averaging flight times. Still puzzled? You'll have to dig out your calculator and a scratch pad and do some doodling. You'll get it. Winds cost money.

Since Meteorology is not an exact science (Earth climate-warming gurus take note), we occasionally caught edges of the Jet Stream where it was not supposed to be. Route offsets to get out of it were not always successful. Changes in route and altitude might produce some relief, but such surprises usually meant a late arrival on westbound flights.

Bound for San Francisco one night, we ran into one-hundred-knot headwinds. Some changes in route and altitudes produced no gains. A route can only be changed so far before added distance eats up any gains in groundspeed. Altitude changes are also limited to the upper levels above twenty-nine thousand feet. Jets are only efficient at high altitudes. Down in the twenty-thousand range, they gobble fuel so fast that gains in time are wiped out by fuel costs.

On this night, we just had to swallow a late arrival, so we made an announcement to inform passengers. As we proceeded west, the winds got worse. A couple of more announcements followed as our ETA grew to about forty-five minutes late. Our irrepressible Brit, Bobby Warden, was our lead flight attendant and she reminded us of the delay when she entered the cockpit and let out an exasperated sigh.

"What's up, Bobby?"

"Oh, bloody hell, some man back there is driving me bonkers. Every time you make an announcement, he starts pestering me about being late to San Fran."

"Well, Bobby, all you can do is humor him."

"Well, I think I've finally shut him up, now."

"What did you tell him, Bobby?"

"This last time, he wanted to know just exactly how long it took to reach San Francisco. So, I told him it used to take about eight to ten weeks by horse and wagon and probably still does."

I guess that did the trick. At least, we heard no more about it. Bobby took superb care of "her" passengers and her quick wit made it great fun to have her on the crew. On another night, in similar circumstances, she answered the same question with another great shutter-upper.

"How long does it take to reach San Francisco?" an impatient man asked.

Bobby reacted like the great comedienne she was. With such a great straight-man line like that lobbed at her, she batted it back. Smiling sweetly, she answered in her clipped Brit accent.

"Actually, sir, I don't really know. You see, we've never made it."

Serving as Copilot with the men who held the left seat on the DC-8 was an experience you couldn't buy. These men were invariably WWII veterans who had learned their skills flying bombers or fighters in combat. There were no shy wallflowers among them. Our VP of Operations, Captain Pre Ball, left the Air Corps as a Major at the end of WWII. He was known to make pithy comments.

"We have a lot of people who fly from the left seat... and we also have some Captains."

To Pre, a man who had mastered his machine and also knew how to manage his crew firmly and fairly — while remaining a gentleman at all times — deserved the title "Captain." The men I flew with on the DC-8 were Captains. That's why I've capitalized the title.

There are only five true professions: doctor, lawyer, professor, soldier and the professional ship or airline captain. Only these are subject to peer review and competence testing. All other endeavors are *occupations* or *trades*, no matter how well one performs them. There are no professional plumbers. I'm sorry but that's a trade. One more small difference should be pointed out. While no Doctor has ever died on his own operating table, a captain will not survive a fatal mistake. A captain is not allowed do-overs. He must make the right decision the first time, and every time, if he hopes to reach retirement. There are no parachutes or ejection seats on an airliner.

Westbound for Los Angeles one night, I picked up another nugget from Captain "Cracker" Morris. While still a bit east of Dallas, we began to run into the south edge of a cold front, which had moved down faster than forecasted. Because large areas of New Mexico contain military test areas, there are two basic routes westbound from Dallas to Los Angeles. We were flight-planned over the northern route to pass over Albuquerque. The southern route is down over El Paso and along the Mexican border.

Bouncing through the fringe of the front, it was clear that our ride would only get worse on our present route. Cracker picked up his mike and requested that Ft. Worth Center clear us for a left turn direct to El Paso and the southern route.

It was my leg to fly, so I listened as Ft. Worth responded with, "Unable, Delta, we've got too much traffic over that route."

I was weaving around the worst of the build-ups as Cracker answered, "Well, we can climb or descend or speed up or slow down to fit in, but this weather is beatin' up my passengers and I just spilled my coffee."

Still, the answer came back, "Unable."

Cracker lapsed into his slowest Georgia drawl (he didn't get the name Cracker for his Boston accent). He keyed his mike. "Son, I gotta get somethin' straight in my own head. Am I up here in this sorry weather 'cause you're down there, settin' in your chair, or are you down there 'cause I'm up here?"

Moments of silence ensued, followed by a new voice on the radio. "Delta 895, you're cleared direct El Paso, descend to Flight Level three one zero, I'll have your new route clearance in a minute."

I banked left as Cracker thanked the man and slapped his mike back in its holder. He gave me a satisfied smile as we sailed into clear air about five minutes later.

"That feller was just too lazy to do a bit-a-work," he drawled.

Ka-chink, ka-chink, another nugget tumbled into the till.

I have since heard the following question posed various ways over the radio, but remain fairly confident that it was patented by Cracker Morris back in 1967.

Bomb threats were becoming a new source of entertainment for some of the mentally deranged among us. We were victimized one morning in San Francisco. Hours were lost as passengers, cargo, and luggage were unloaded and searched. Mechanics had to open dozens of inspection panels as they went over the plane from nose to tail. FBI Agents informed us that they knew who the caller was, but could not prove it.

Back then, anybody could go to the boarding lounges. A rude, unshaven, peddler made a regular pest of himself at the San Francisco (SFO) airport. He would accost passengers and try to sell them cheap knock-offs of brand name watches. When gate agents would throw him out of a boarding area, he would go to a pay phone and call in a bomb threat. He was clever enough to name a flight other than the one departing the area from which he'd been ejected. The FBI Agents said he always retaliated on whichever airline had last "abused his freedom of commerce." Agents reported that the only way to prove he was making the calls was to get the phone away from him and identify the party on the other end. They had tried, but he was always too quick to hang up. There were too many banks of pay phones to bug them all, so he continued to cause chaos. To add insult to injury, back in 1967, his crime was only a misdemeanor!

A couple of weeks after our episode, he put another of our crews through the same drill. This time, the FBI dragged him down to Operations to meet the crew. Their stated purpose was to allow the crew to "dialogue" with him in hopes they might persuade him of the error of his ways. As the conversation was proceeding amicably, the Agents left the room to refill coffee mugs. They were completely surprised when a crewmember came out to the coffee urn and reported that the poor man had fainted upon standing up and had taken such a horrible fall that it required an ambulance to get him to medical care quickly. The bomb calls ceased. There may be a lesson hidden somewhere in this story, applicable to dealing with rabid Muslims. Unfortunately, it would not be politically correct today.

Those long cross-country routes added some new experiences with thunderstorms. Of course, they are found everywhere and flying up and down the Mississippi will bring pretty good exposure to them, but some of the granddaddies of storms that build over Texas can easily top fifty-thousand feet. Nobody flies *into* one of these, at least not more than once.

When a flight comes upon a wall of them across a route, the crew must make some decisions. For this work, you need to learn to read a weather radar screen like Madame Sophie reads her crystal ball. If flights always turned back for thunderstorms, no one would get anywhere. Sometimes this is the only option left, but first, is there a way around the wall? If not, there are almost always holes through it. The trick is *finding* them. This cannot be done unless you have learned to tune and operate the radar and how to read what it is trying to tell you.

To the uninitiated, this scope looks like a Rorschach Ink Blot test. Radar can only "see" and "paint" water. It can only penetrate so far through water. What looks like a hole, containing only rain, may hide a monster behind the rain, which the radar cannot penetrate. Sometimes it's necessary to fly parallel to the wall and make short swerves toward it to aim the radar for a quick "look-see." When you find a hole, a decision to go for it has to be a quick one. There is no time to hang a picture on the wall and call for consultation. The hole will only be open for a couple of minutes.

The scene became common. Two heads bend over the scope. A finger points at the screen. Eyeballs turn to each other with raised eyebrows. A nod. A returned nod. A quick turn to aim for it. Once into the tunnel, there's no room to turn back. If it's a sucker hole, they're going to get the crap kicked out of them. Minutes go by as they bob and weave. Some rain or hail blasts the windshield. Suddenly, we squirt into clear sky. Whew! Did it again!

Was that safe? Well, no, not really, but then, flying is not an inherently safe thing to do in the first place. It only achieves a level of safety by the application of proper *risk management*, where people will buy tickets to do it. Most passengers, some of management, and a few green pilots, think a Captain is paid to fly from A to B. Not so. He's paid to make very quick judgments about a very simple question that comes in a variety of forms "Can I perform such and such an act with reasonable safety, right now? Yes or no?" He will learn to memorize the dictum, "When in doubt... *don't.*" Those who ignore it provide a source of scrap aluminum for the manufacture of beer cans.

While I enjoyed the DC-8, a new contract came into play. Some major changes in our scheduling formula slid me back onto the DC-9 for about five months. It provided good seasoning, bouncing around on short hops and moving fast.

During this period, our Atlanta Station employees were conducting their annual drive to raise money for a children's home they supported. Raffle tickets were sold for some great prizes. First prize was a bright yellow Volkswagen Beetle. The cute little 'Bug' had been brought through some double doors directly into the crew lounge and parked opposite the Crew Scheduling sign-in counter. As Captain Jim Carlton signed in, he got the pitch to buy tickets. Jim promised to buy some tickets, but asked if he could sit in the Bug to see if it fit him. He said that if it felt good, he'd buy a couple hundred bucks worth so he'd have a real chance to win it.

No one realized that he had already hatched another caper, so he was handed the keys. Jim recruited his Engineer to watch for Elroy Hager (Empty Helmet) crossing the ramp to Operations. He then unlocked the Bug and tossed in his suitcase, overcoat and hat. On receiving the high sign from his spy, Jim hopped in and started the engine. As Elroy appeared in his side mirror, Jim shut off the engine and climbed out.

"Mornin,' Elroy. How do you like my new car?"

"Mornin,' Jim. Is that yours?"

"Yep, just bought her. Ain't she pretty?"

Jim gathered his suitcase, coat, and hat and locked the door as Elroy stood with a puzzled frown.

"Jim, you cain't park in here, you know," Elroy predictably said.

"Elroy, I ain't leavin' this little beauty in that ole dusty, muddy parking lot. She's gonna set right here 'till I get back."

Jim walked off to sign in and Elroy buttonholed the next person to pass. "Carlton thinks he can park right here in Operations. That ain't right."

He couldn't find anybody interested in making an issue of it and finally walked off muttering and shaking his head. Of course, nobody told him it was a raffle prize, because it was too much fun watching Carlton feed him hook, line, and sinker... yet again.

I got back on the DC-8 and got to enjoy and learn from more great characters. I flew with Captain "Birddog" Mills on his last flight from LAX (Los Angeles, CA) to ATL (Atlanta, GA). Birddog's seniority had allowed him to nail down that trip.

He had become so well known by controllers that he never used the flight number when calling them. He'd just call, "Howdy, LA, this is the ole Birddog here." He knew many controllers by name and could recognize their voices. The Los Angeles employees had provided champagne for all passengers and a huge cake with a Bird-dog atop it. Birddog's family were aboard for his last flight and it was to be a big party. While they loaded baggage on the plane, he strolled down the aisles, greeting everyone. Departure time came and he took his seat.

I started to call for our departure and route clearance, but he held up his hand. "Lemme call for this last one." He picked up his mike and called, "Evenin,' LA, this is the old Birddog callin' for my last clearance tonight and I'm gonna miss all you boys."

"We are going to miss you too, Birddog. Everybody wants me to wish you a happy retirement."

"Thank you, sir. I'm gonna take my motor home and drive all over visitin' you fellas, so you'll see me again."

"That's great. Are you ready to copy your clearance?"

I poised my pen to write this stream of altitudes, headings, airways, and frequencies that would come, but the voice came on again. "Birddog, you are cleared to Atlanta. Have a great flight."

Wow! He had just been given *carte blanche*. Everybody else would be cleared out of his way. In my entire career, I have only heard a clearance like that *once*.

Some claimed that Captain Pre Ball had a copy of a recording made one evening between Birddog and Margaret, an Atlanta, controller. She had a thick, Georgia twang and a razor tongue. Flying the Convair 880 long before the two-hundred-fifty-knot speed rule, Birddog would approach Atlanta like an incoming missile. It went like this:

"Birddog, hold y'all's east headin,' descend to eight-thousand, and slow to three-hundred."

"All right, Margaret."

"Birddog, turn right to one-eight-zero, descend to six, an' slow to two-fifty."

"All right, Margaret."

"Birddog, turn right to two-seven-zero, descend to four, an' slow that thang down to two-twenty."

"Margaret, if I slow down any more I'm gonna fall outta the sky."

"Ah don't care, Birddog. Just do it, an' call me every thousand feet as you're fallin'."

I already had a habit of giving passengers a nice smooth ride, but Captain Boyd Hughes added a bit of polish to it. The original DC-8 had an autopilot with a strange pitch control system. In a climb or descent, pitch inputs were made through a rocker switch. Tapping it for up or down commands produced a little bump, which could be felt by passengers. Boyd believed his passengers should not feel even this gentle bump, so he hand-flew climbs or descents and he was silky smooth.

Boyd dealt with a small inconvenience—he was practically deaf! Years spent flying B-25 bombers had done a job on his ears. Added to the physical affliction was a psychological one. Boyd's wife was one of those sweet ladies who like to chatter constantly, so Boyd simply tuned her voice out—and every other female voice as well.

Boyd could read lips and simple hand signals covered all needed cockpit communications. Because he was such a gentleman to be with and such a fine pilot, all the copilots covered for him. Everything ran smoothly until one night going into New York.

Boyd was hand flying as I worked the radio and gave hand signals on our descent. With her galley secured, a flight attendant came up and perched on the jump seat behind Boyd. While she talked with the Engineer, she produced a cigarette and lighter.

She learned forward and asked, "Captain Hughes, do you mind if I have a cigarette?"

A glance at Boyd proved he had heard nothing. She asked again, a bit louder. No reaction. The Engineer started to laugh.

"What's so funny?" she asked.

"I'm just laughing," he said, "because Boyd can't hear you. He's deaf."

Now she looked suspicious. "What's the gag?" she asked.

"There's no gag. He's deaf."

"Really, it's not a joke," I joined in. "He'll hear you if you yell in his ear."

Now deeply suspicious, she said, "Well, I know this is some silly gag, but I'll bite."

Where she got this suspicious attitude toward pilots, I do not understand. Taking a deep breath, she leaned forward and screamed into Boyd's ear, "Captain, do you mind if I *smoke*?"

Boyd's eyelids bounced about four times. His head spun around toward the Engineer. "Smoke? *Smoke*? Where? *Where*?"

The Engineer and I both broke up, howling. The poor girl looked at us like we were maniacs. She pitched the cigarette in the trash and stomped out. All it took to start laughing again over the coming days was to repeat, "Smoke?"

Chapter 13 | Flying the Convair 440

Toward the end of 1969, a bid sheet was posted to fill Captain slots on the Convair 440. I pondered for all of about eight seconds before signing my name. I had flown the DC-6 and DC-7 as an Instructor Captain, but they were now gone. The twin-engine CV-440 would be my last chance to fly pistons as a captain on the line.

At home a few days later, I got a call from my now close friend, Captain Dick Gillette.

"I need to talk to you about a serious matter," he said. "Can you come over now?"

He would elaborate no further, so I drove to his house.

"What's going on?" I asked as sat down.

He got up and walked to his kitchen and came back with two beers and handed me one. "Congratulations! You got your slot on the 440, "he said. "You are now going to be a Captain."

"Well, thanks, Dick," I answered. "I didn't know the bids were out yet. It's no big deal. I've flown bigger stuff as Captain."

He gave me his patented iceberg stare. "This is different, because now you're gonna do it on the line."

I tried to downplay the thing some more and Dick finally said, "All right. I'll make you a bet."

"On what?" I asked.

"Twenty bucks says I'm right, that it *is* different."

"How would we settle a bet like that?" I asked.

"Simple," he retorted. "When you discover I'm right, you pay me twenty bucks. If I don't hear from you in a year, I'll pay *you* twenty bucks."

"Okay. It's a bet," I said, mostly to keep him happy.

"Okay. Now I'm gonna give you a lecture and you're gonna listen," he said, pacified.

"All right, Dick. I'll listen," I said, noting he was clearly in his dead serious mode.

"I know you're a good pilot. I know you think you're hot stuff because some of your DC-8 Captains have been letting you fly from the left seat. Now, don't interrupt me. You were still flying on *their* license, and it *is* illegal. Those guys were paying you a pretty big complement, but I want to make sure it doesn't go to your head." I went to speak. "Shut up. I'm not done yet. You've been learning from some real pros, but you're not done yet. There's always more to learn, so listen to your copilots. You're gonna be the boss now, but your copilots have stuff they learned from other pros. You gotta learn from *them*, now.

"Nobody knows everything, not even *me* and I'm the best there is. I want you to remember a true fact: Even a cat or a chimpanzee will learn from his mistakes, but only a smart man learns from the mistakes of others. I don't wanna hear about you makin' mistakes, 'cause from now on they *count*. You got all that??"

"Yes, Dick, and thank you."

"You'll do okay, but I still expect my twenty bucks."

I, and a few classmates who were also moving up, took a lot of ribbing. "Why do you want to fly a puddle jumper around the South when you could fly a DC-8 to San Francisco?" I finally came up with an answer that would shut them up. "Because it will be *mine* and I won't be losing any more arguments."

Ground School and a checkout-rating ride went quickly and were followed by a brief meeting with Captain Pre Ball. He later turned this congratulatory meeting into a seminar for new Captains called "In Command." I got a quick handshake.

"Congratulations," he said. "You're going to be signing the clearance papers, now. That means the airplane is *yours*. Your only job is to keep your passengers safe. I don't care what else you do with it, or where you park it, the only thing you cannot do with it is sell it, because I want it back when you're finished with it."

The CV-440 is a forty-eight-thousand-pound aircraft carrying 44 passengers, powered by two Pratt & Whitney R-

2800 reciprocating engines. Flown by two pilots with one stewardess (the term flight attendant had not been coined yet), it was a really fun airplane. The routes it served had now been reduced to Atlanta, Macon, Savannah, Jacksonville, and Brunswick, Georgia. I didn't care, it was still a ball.

Pilots are familiar with routes to be flown IFR (Instrument Flight Rules) and VFR (Visual Flight Rules). We had a third route called ICW (Intra Coastal Waterway). This route, flown VFR, followed the ICW from Jacksonville to Brunswick to Savannah. Flying the ICW at a thousand feet or lower, we could waggle the wings and get waves back from people on boats.

While the practice has been tamed down over the years, it was still traditional that newbies be subjected to initiation pranks. Done properly, they are harmless and only serve to create humor and a bonding of the crew as good sports.

The 440 offered the chance for a great gag and a newbie stewardess, out on her own for the first time, was too tempting a target. Most aircraft have a "P-dome" (pressure dome) at the aft end of the fuselage. This leaves the pointed cone section of the tail an unpressurized area outside of cabin pressure. The CV-440 was unique as it used this area, loaded via an exterior hatch, for an aft baggage bin and, thus, pressurized the entire aft cone. In addition, an interior hatch, about two by three feet, which required a cockpit door key to open, gave access to this area from the single aft toilet, or "Blue Room."

162

Upon parking and shutting down engines, the copilot would open his side window and slide down the escape rope. This was the start of the gag. He could walk aft on the ramp and go up the baggage belt loader to the exterior hatch to that aft compartment. After a quick step through the hatch and into the lavatory, he would wait for the last passenger to leave and then follow up the aisle. He could then greet the newbie stewardess as she bid goodbye to the last passenger.

Now, he would whisper instructions to her about checking the Blue Room before landing, and explain that he was supposed to be up with the Captain for landings. She would dutifully survey the Blue Room before taking her seat for the next landing and, again, he would follow the last passenger. Puzzled young ladies often poked their heads into the cockpit to count two bodies, and then scurried aft to check the Blue Room before the next landing.

Some people are quicker than others, so one young lady decoded the gag right away. At the next stop, she dashed down the steps and poured a pitcher of ice water over the copilot's head as she caught him slinking aft beneath the wing. Everybody got a good laugh, including the sopping wet copilot. She passed her initiation with flying colors and was now part of the "gang."

Another gag once backfired on a crew. At low altitude, it was not uncommon to fly the recips unpressurized. It actually provided a high volume of airflow through the cabin. With no cabin pressure, a pilot could open his side window and fly with an elbow hanging out.

163

The gag which this offered was said to have been created by Captain Jim Bain. Calling a new stewardess on the intercom, the Captain would excitedly tell her, "Quick! Bring a pitcher of water up here!" When she appeared with the pitcher, he would open the side window and throw the water out. Handing her the empty pitcher, he would order, "Quick! Get another one!" She would dash off and return breathless with another full pitcher. After sloshing the second pitcher out the window, he would sigh and say, "Okay, I think that got it."

A bewildered young lady could be counted upon to ask, "What's wrong, Captain?"

"Oh, nothin' serious. That engine just seems to run hot and smoke a bit, but the water seems to cool it off okay."

This is a great gag and can be milked several times on a flight. One day it backfired. The crew had run the girl up and down the aisle several times. She was finally stopped by a passenger who wanted to know what was going on with all the water. Not wishing to alarm a passenger, she told him everything was okay. He persisted, informing her that he was an Air Force pilot traveling on leave and that he would not panic if she spilled the beans. When she finally confided about the hot, smoking engine he doubled over laughing. After catching his breath, he explained that she was the victim of a prank and asked if she would like to get even. For some reason, she said yes, so he coached her.

She waited ten minutes and then burst into the cockpit and 'fumbled' another full pitcher into the Captain's lap as she yelled, "Here, Captain, throw some more water. It's smoking again!"

"*What!*" he said as he spun to look first at the engine and then back at his soaking lap a couple of times. The copilot was in stitches and reported later that the captain looked like someone following a fast tennis match for a few seconds. Well, a good gag is funny, even when it backfires.

Lest the reader think that everything is fun-and-games and silly clowning, I would like to make a point. Flying is serious business and can create enormous stresses on a professional. Working in this environment day in and day out requires a high level of attention and alertness, but once in cruise flight, things tend to settle down a bit. Watching a professional at work is not terribly revealing to the uninitiated. We do our business in a relaxed atmosphere which, unfortunately, tends to make the whole process look *too* easy. It isn't. The average light plane pilot at the controls of an airliner would put it into a smoking hole. Any sane psychiatrist (is that an oxymoron?) will tell you that the best antidote for stress is *humor* and, by God, we have that and the more outrageous and un-PC the better!

One of the reasons the CV-440 was still flying was the problem of finding a way to continue service to Brunswick, Georgia. The only airport was Malcolm MacKinnon on St. Simons Island. Its runway was far too short for jets and marginal for the CV-440. Tall trees served as windbreaks for golf courses and bordered both ends of the runway. There was no margin for error. The runway ended at a fence, then a two-lane road with trees directly across the road. At night, a string of red lights on a cable could be seen blinking, because you saw them through the trees. As soon as they appeared to quit blinking, you passed the trees and you could dump the plane down on the runway and find out if props would reverse quickly enough and if the brakes were optimal. I promise you, Virginia, you can hold your breath longer than you think.

This little airport offered some interesting challenges. The only instrument approach called for a timed leg off the VOR on Jekyll Island, some seven miles south. The lowest altitude offered by this approach was five-hundred feet. Even if you spotted the runway, you needed to execute a quick, thirty-degree right turn to line up with it. Therefore, pilots devised a "bootleg" approach. Many pilots are unaware that they can tune their VOR DME receivers to receive a Military TACAN station, which has a two or three digit channel number. Add 53 to TACAN three-digit channels, or 63 to a two-digit channel. Put a one in front of the sum and dial that on your VOR. It will now read *distance only*, no radial.

The CV-440 had one VOR DME on the left side, so you tuned it to the Brunswick Navy TACAN. The Copilot tuned Jekyll VOR and flew a leg northwest until the DME on the left side read so many miles. We were then over water and could descend to two hundred feet. A few more miles and then you made a right turn to 030 degrees. Now aimed at the runway, you looked for the Marina full of boats. Over the Marina, you now looked for the dog-bone shaped lake on a golf course. Split the middle of the dog-bone, and *et voilà*, you saw the runway! There was no tower here, but there was a Flight Service Station. I'm sure people there knew of our bootleg approach, but it could only be radar tracked by the Navy and they didn't care.

I came up the ICW from JAX one day to find the Flight Service Station reporting zero-zero, in heavy fog. They asked what we intended to do and I told him we would land. After shutting down in front of our terminal, I could barely see the building about eighty feet away. I was met at the bottom of the steps by an irate FAA man from the station.

"I know you people have got a bootleg approach in here," he stormed, "but this is too much! You landed in zero-zero weather and I'm going to file a violation on you."

I told him that I intended to file a PIREP (Pilot Report) that the weather was clear, with twenty miles visibility.

He shook his head. "That'll never fly. There are three of us here who *know* that it's zero-zero."

"Well," I said, "before you file a violation, you need to walk out across that grass and have a look at the runway."

"What?"

"Just go look at the runway, will you?" He huffed off through the fog toward the runway. A few seconds later we heard a distant, "Well, I'll be goddammed."

He wore an amazed look as he came back and I got in one last gentle dig. "It would be more helpful if you guys reported the weather at the runway, instead of what you see out your window."

That phenomenon was one I had never seen before. With almost *no* wind, a wall of sea fog had crept in and stood perfectly vertical between the buildings and runway. It was so perfect that it looked like a four-thousand-foot-tall, plastered wall painted bright white! The entire runway stood in beaming sunlight. We had seen it from 10 miles south, and could not resist the opportunity to pull one on the FSS (Flight Service Station) guys.

I was feeling quite comfortable in my new position when an event occurred in February of that year. We had flown from Jacksonville, through St. Simons to Atlanta and arrived in pouring rain. The front had reached just north of St. Simons when we left, but would be waiting for us on our afternoon return flight. The afternoon schedule was from Atlanta to Macon, St. Simons and a return to Atlanta. Our agents were passing out big umbrellas to passengers, who were dashing in groups across the wet ramp to board.

A boy and girl, about twelve and eleven, scampered up the steps. Their very pretty mom followed with Dad holding an umbrella for her. I greeted them with a "Welcome aboard."

The man looked at me and said, "Thank you, but I'm not going. I have a Cessna 310 (a four-seat twin) parked here. We have reservations at the King and Prince Hotel on St. Simons. This weather is too much for me, so I'm sending my wife and kids with you, and I'll fly my plane down as soon as the weather clears. This weather looks pretty bad, so I hope you know what you're doing."

He had made his comments in a kindly voice, but was looking me straight in the eye. *Gulp!* I was 27 years old. This older man, a private pilot, had just calmly put the most precious people in his life in my hands. I took a breath and looked him in the eye. "I promise you, sir, to deliver them safely."

We beat our way down and back through rain and turbulence, dodging thunderstorm cells. I was well wrung-out by the time I reached my car in the wet parking lot in Atlanta. I drove directly to Dick Gillette's home and rang his doorbell. When he opened the door, I handed him a twenty and, then, turned back to my car. The man had been absolutely right. The "Line" was *different*. I left because I didn't feel up to talking about it yet.

I will pass on another piece of advice, given to me, to any young pilots reading this book. Learn to trust your unconscious instincts. A perfect example of this occurred one night on the CV-440. On take-off from Savannah, bound for St. Simons and then Jacksonville, the left engine BMEP (Brake Mean Effective Pressure torque meter) read somewhat low. I pulled the throttles back and turned off the runway. Another careful run-up and mag check seemed normal. A BMEP up around two-hundred-thirty-five indicated a tired, but normal, engine. Our left one had shown around two-*twenty*-five. Logic said it was just age working toward overhaul time, but that nagging little voice insisted there was some other cause.

169

We had a good mechanic by the name of Sam Pruitt at Savannah. He came aboard for yet another run-up and listened carefully to the engine. He could detect nothing amiss, but offered no argument when I said that I just didn't trust it. We went to a hotel while Sam dug out his toolbox.

He met us early the next morning and reported that the only thing he could find were dirty ADI (Anti-Detonation Injection) screens, which he cleaned. That system pumps a water-alcohol mix into the engine at high power to prevent detonating of the fuel air mixture.

We took off for St. Simons to pick up our schedule, which should have begun in Jacksonville. Power seemed somewhat better on takeoff from Savannah. Starting our takeoff run from St. Simons, the power dropped again below two-hundred-thirty. I taxied back in and shut down. I apologized to the deplaning passengers for the unexpected cancellation. We huddled with the Station Manager and made calls to Sam and Flight Control. I was beginning to feel like a fool. The voice said, "Something is wrong," Yet, neither Sam nor I could say what it might be.

Flight Control offered no argument and made no attempt to pressure me. They only wanted to know if we were willing to ferry empty to Atlanta and they would finish the afternoon round with a substitute pilot and aircraft. We agreed. We used only modest power on the left engine for takeoff and a low cruise setting.

At the end of our day, the shuttle bus to the parking lot made its second stop behind one of our hangars. I spotted our airplane in the hangar with the left engine cowling off. Curiosity caused me to hop off and walk into the hangar. A work stand surrounded the engine and parts lay on a canvas on the floor. I called up to a mechanic and asked what they had found.

"You bring this one in?" he climbed down and asked, wiping his hands on a rag,

"Yes, I did. Did you find something wrong with it?"

"I'll show you."

He bent over the canvas and picked up a finned cylinder. He pointed the base at me and, holding it by the top, pulled his hands apart. I could see his face through the gaping crack from its mounting flange all the way across its top to the other side of the flange! Wow!

"I was about to lose a cylinder, wasn't I?"

"Not *a* cylinder, the *Master* Cylinder!" he answered smiling grimly.

He let that sink in as I stood, stunned. The master cylinder on a radial engine has a connecting rod shaped like a banjo, which is exactly what it's called. All the other eight connecting rods are connected to the rim of the Banjo by wrist pins. The old mechanic stood watching me as the implications all came together. If that cylinder (or "jug") had let go and allowed the Banjo to free spin, the front row of cylinders would have become mangled scrap metal and the prop would likely have spun off as well.

"Why'd you down the aircraft?" he asked.

171

"The only clue I had was a slightly low BMEP reading and a suspicious hunch.

I thought he might laugh or criticize my hunch, but he just nodded. "Gotta trust your hunches, son. Gotta listen when the little voice whispers."

I left feeling better for his approval. *Beat you again,* Fate is the Hunter! I thought and vowed to listen whenever that little voice whispered again.

A classmate, Captain Herb Kerr, also had a rather exciting event one night in his CV-440. Herb was reaching up for an overhead switch, and leaning slightly to his right, when the copilot's side window blew out. Herb ducked as the sudden depressurization ripped the cockpit door off its hinges and slammed it into the back of his right shoulder. From his ducked position, his right hand instinctively grabbed the tail of his copilot's coat. Copilot, "Reb" Jones, was out the window to his waist.

The cockpit lights had gone out as Herb struggled to pull Reb back in. A stunned Reb finally began to help himself and Herb, now having a grip on his belt, was able to get him back in his seat. All electrical power was now out, with no radios, but Herb spotted the Macon airport beacon and made an unexpected arrival there.

Maintenance discovered that the upper edge of the blown-in cockpit door had sheared off all the overhead switches, turning off the generator switches and shearing them off so they couldn't be turned back on. Somehow it had not engaged the prop feathering buttons as they sheared *them* off. The blast lifted Reb's headset off and its wire must have lifted the edge of his seat belt buckle and released it.

Reb explained his initial failure to help Herb get him back in. He said his first response to the sight of a huge propeller spinning a few feet from his face was, *This is a horrible nightmare and I've gotta wake up quick!"* The blast of cold air quickly woke him and convinced him the nightmare was *real*!

Ironically, the cabin heating was not working well and both were wearing their coats. Thus, the only injury was a tear and some missing buttons from Reb's coat as it scraped over the ragged edge of the broken window.

Fate is the Hunter missed again!

The last month of CV-440 service rolled around. April 26th, 1970, would mark the last piston powered flights at Delta. I had my DC-9 Captain's slot for May, and had finished with a recurrent check ride and a line check. I really wanted that last flight, but it was on my classmate Wiley Algood's line of time. I called Wiley and offered to swap, suggesting that my trip, two days earlier, would give him a whole week off. I suspect that Wiley was not conned by my pitch, but agreed because he is just a nice guy.

The day came and we departed from our layover in Jacksonville for Atlanta. The afternoon round from Atlanta through St Simon's, then back through Savannah to Atlanta, would be the final flight. Our stewardess was in her first few months of service and we knew her from previous flights.

173

Wanda Cornet was a pretty young lady from Tennessee. She had one of those bubbly, cheerful, can-do, personalities which brightened the day for everyone around her. Wanda was very excited about this 'last flight.' Arriving in Atlanta, we had about an hour-and-a-half lunch break before the afternoon final round.

As I walked back into Ops after a quick lunch, I spotted Wanda sitting in a chair in tears.

"What's wrong?" I asked.

She sobbed, "Some senior girl bumped me off the flight." I felt so sorry for her, but could do nothing except offer sympathy. I pointed out that she could always *claim* to have worked the 440 on its last day, but I knew it was small consolation.

Walking out to the plane with my flight plan and weather sheets in hand, I climbed the steps to greet a tall, redheaded stewardess boarding passengers. As I started to introduce myself, she lifted the papers from my hand and began to study the weather sheets. Satisfied, she nodded.

"Does the weather look okay for us today?" I asked and my facetious question seemed to zoom over her head.

"Oh, yes, it'll be okay, no problem," she answered.

Thanking her, I retrieved the papers and went forward to my seat.

As we leveled off at six-thousand feet on our first leg to Macon, I flipped the seatbelt light off. A few seconds later, the *ding-ding* of the intercom sounded.

I picked up the handset. "Hello?" I answered.

"I want the seatbelt light back on," an authoritative female voice announced. "It's bumpy back here."

"It will remain off," I explained, "because there's no weather and the constant light bumps are standard low-altitude springtime weather over Georgia.

"I'm coming up there," she answered. A few seconds later, the door banged open. "I'm not going to work under these conditions," the angry redhead announced. "I want that seatbelt light back *on*."

I tried once more to explain that it would be like that all day and pointed out that my coffee cup, perched on the glare shield, was not spilling. My copilot, Chaz Winstead, caught my attention with a raised eyebrow and made a 'U-turn' hand gesture. I nodded. He picked up his mike and told Departure Control that we needed to return to the airport. They okayed a one-eighty and asked whether we had an emergency.

"No, just a little personnel problem," Chaz answered.

As he rolled out of the turn, the Atlanta airport was clearly visible about twenty miles out. Our redhead looked a bit puzzled during the turn, but now spotted the airport ahead.

"What are you doing?" she asked.

"We're going back to get Wanda," I answered. "She *wanted* to do this trip."

"You can't do that," she screeched. "I could get fired if you do that!! *Turn around!*"

We droned on and the airport began to grow larger. Chaz looked at her.

"Turn around, *please*, might work."

"All right, *please*," she huffed as the airport grew even bigger.

"You might try, please, captain, sir," Chaz offered.

Now, thoroughly convinced that I was going back for Wanda (I was) she finally adopted a new tone. "*Please*, Captain, I'm sorry. I'll work the flight. Please turn back around."

The flight went smoothly after that. In St. Simons, the local paper sent a reporter to take a photo of the three of us beside our 440. Champagne and special postal covers (envelopes stamped, designating the last piston service for the whole airline) were put aboard at St. Simons and Savannah.

By about four, we had arrived back in Atlanta. An era was over. There would be no more rumbling radial engine sounds, only the whine of jets. As one wag crudely put it, "Piston engines, swinging propellers, screw their way across country. Jets only suck and blow." I was very happy to have played some part in that era and sad to see it end. Airplanes do have personalities. I had patted ship number 423 on her nose and thanked the little workhorse for her good manners and a job well done. I turned for one last look on my way across the ramp. She appeared forlorn, and I admit I was a bit choked up, too.

Some years later and out of sequence in my story, I re-met this tall redhead in a Florida boatyard. She recognized my face, but didn't make the 440 connection. She informed me that she had married, Captain Tommy Tutton, who had come to Delta from Northeast. They were living on a boat at this marina. I invited her to bring him to my nearby house.

He turned out to be a big jovial stereotype of the Boston Irishman. We hit it off immediately as we sat sipping beers and swapping stories. "Big Red," as Tommy called her, got up to browse some airline photos on the wall of my office. Tommy and I were interrupted by a loud gasp.

"Oh-mi-gawd, oh-mi-gawd, *you*!" came from my office. "Tommy, Tommy, come here!"

We all walked in to find her pointing at the photo from St. Simons.

"Oh, that's the silliest looking pillbox hat you're wearing," Tommy observed.

"You won't believe what he did to me," she said, aiming an accusing finger at me.

"Well, let's go sit down and you can tell me," Tommy offered.

He sat calmly, sipping his beer as she poured out the whole, horrid story.

"Don't you think that's just awful, Tommy?" she asked, finally winding down

Tommy took another sip as he considered her question. He looked at her.

"Red, you're just lucky he was a nice guy and didn't throw your ass off the airplane," he said slowly. "I think I just might have."

"But, but… Tommy," she spluttered.

He just shook his head at her and gently told her, "Red, you were just way out of line. You can't take over a Captain's airplane. You were wrong and you got off easy - okay?"

She thought a minute before admitting, "You're right, Tommy. I do get bossy sometimes."

They are both still dear friends, almost fifty years later.

Chapter 14 | Flying the DC-9 as Captain

In May, 1970, I went back on the DC-9, but as Captain that time. It was an easy transition, since I knew the airplane and the airports very well by now. We now had thirteen of the baby DC-9s and were buying the stretched DC-9-32 as fast as Douglas could stamp them out. We eventually would have fifty-seven of them. The rapid expansion of this fleet promoted fast growth in "lines of time," and seniority within the fleet, so I enjoyed good schedules with layovers in many interesting cities.

I should explain that airline seniority is a relative thing. You could be quite senior as a DC-8 engineer, but very junior on the next upward move to DC-9 copilot as an example. Quality of trips, or "rotations," depended on relative seniority. If a pilot chose to move up early, he could expect to be on reserve with no fixed schedule for some time. I have always chosen to move up as soon as a slot came open and have served my reserve penance for doing so. I have little respect for the few who pass up promotion because it might intrude on their days spent running a side business or competing in a golf tourney. They are placing a higher priority on outside activities than on their career as a pilot. I have known a few who sat 'sidesaddle' so long that they forgot how to fly. They made my days hell, when they finally showed up in a right seat with me, years later.

I have always tried to manage a relaxed cockpit. A sharp copilot, who could be relied on to manage his leg smoothly and exercise good judgment, was worth his weight in gold. I could continue to learn things from such a man, because it was easy to respect his abilities. A captain cannot abdicate authority on final decisions, but a sharp copilot must be brought into the loop for his valuable insights. It's nice to drive home relaxed after a three-day rotation with such a fellow.

Three days keeping tabs on a klutz would produce grinding molars and an aching jaw. A Klutz, who was trying his best, could generate some sympathy and some patience to teach him, but there was occasionally an example of total oblivion. A pilot with any experience knows to jot radio frequencies on a scratchpad, because the next frequency to which he is handed-off can be the wrong one. The controller may give a frequency in error, or it may be misheard. The error is easily corrected by a call on the last frequency. That only works if the pilot has jotted down each frequency in use.

I became very un-PC and very tactless after one klutz lost the proper frequency for the *third* time. I had asked him twice before to jot them down.

"I don't need to, I can remember them," he said

His third memory lapse found us in the busy Chicago area. Calling an Approach Control frequency listed on the Jepp chart finally got us relayed to the correct frequency. It was frustrating, embarrassing, dangerous, and entirely needless. I was pissed and became totally tactless. I ordered him to put a scratch pad on his side-window clipboard. I told him that I would now do *all* the flying for the next two days and that I was going to keep a frequency list. He was going to "learn radio." If his frequency list matched mine at the end of our rotation, I would consider letting him fly the next time we were paired together.

I was surprised on the evening I got home by a phone call. It appeared that I had hurt the sensitive feelings of this klutz by not letting him fly. He had complained to our Professional Standards rep. This captain was now obligated to call me for the rest of the story, so I told him. He laughed.

"I'll pass it on to the other captains he's scheduled with, that he needs to 'learn radio.'"

He wasn't allowed to fly for weeks, but he did "learn radio."

I thoroughly enjoyed the DC-9, a relatively fast, very responsive, and very reliable jet. The original DC-9-14 was a little hotrod and its bad manners in a deep stall were really of no concern. I have never seen a professional pilot even come close to an actual stall. This airplane's bad manners could only be induced by doing so on purpose.

A flight on one of the "Baby-9s" produced another episode of the "whispering voices." On an approach to Montgomery, my copilot commented that he felt a buzz in the rudder pedals. I put my feet on my pedals and also briefly felt it. The buzz went away as we slowed for the landing. On our next approach to New Orleans, I could feel it at a certain speed range. A look at the rudder produced no answers. Our third approach was in St. Louis. The buzz was back. Was it really getting worse or were we just becoming sensitive to it? The ground crew could see nothing amiss.

I insisted that our mechanics bring a "cherry picker" truck and put someone in the bucket for a close look. The man came down and reported that half of a skin patch, which had folded over the trailing edge of the rudder, had torn off one side. Moveable surfaces *must* be balanced on their hinge points to avoid flutter. Even repainting is cause to rebalance. Any flutter usually starts within some speed range. It can be destructive. We cancelled and went to a hotel. Mechanics and parts were flown down from Chicago to do repairs.

We reported in early the next morning to ferry an empty aircraft and the mechanics to Chicago. There we would pick up on our "busted" schedule. As I stepped aboard, a tired mechanic handed me an aluminum casting.

"Take a look," he said. I could see a large crack almost through the casting. I had a feeling I really did *not* want to know the answer, but I asked anyway. "What is this piece?"

"It's your upper rudder hinge bracket," he answered.

"So if it goes, the rudder rips off?" I asked.

He nodded slowly and purposefully. "Yep, it would have been gone."

Fate is the Hunter — beat you again! Once more, I thanked the whispering voices and renewed my vow always to listen when they spoke.

Because Douglas couldn't produce DC-9s fast enough to meet our expanding needs, Delta bought two Baby 9s from Eastern. They were truly dogs when we got them. Before our mechanics had brought them up to snuff, I drew one for a night flight through Augusta to Savannah. There was pre-frontal weather moving in as we approached Augusta. When power was pulled to idle for our descent to Augusta, the left engine oil pressure light winked on. The gauge showed about five psi, but the oil quantity was holding steady.

I called Flight Control and informed them that the airplane would require an engine change wherever we parked it. I asked if they would prefer the ship in Augusta or Savannah. They wanted it back in Atlanta. I said no and stated that I had no intention of flying single-engine back through the weather behind us, and certainly not with passengers aboard. Once more, I asked that they choose between Augusta and Savannah. Again, they ordered the flight back to Atlanta.

I just told them we were going to Savannah. Flight Control is a helpful asset with good people working there, but their priorities were not necessarily *my* priorities. They wanted passengers back because it would be easier to re-route them and an engine change in Atlanta would not require an engine and crew to be trucked to Savannah. I took Pre's advice seriously. Passenger safety came *first*.

My Copilot wanted to shut down the left engine. The Book said to do so. That JT-8 engine was fitted to many aircraft. Versions of it powered the C-135, B-707, DC-8, B-727, and many others. I knew that Pratt & Whitney had run one in a test cell for over an hour with *no* oil pressure. We had *some* oil pressure. The approach into Savannah was going to be through weather and would also be a black hole approach with no lights under the approach path. This all meant that the possibility of a go-around existed, so I opted to idle the engine and leave it running. Its temperatures were normal with no vibration. I would use it in case of a go-around.

As we parked, my old friend, mechanic Sam Pruitt stepped aboard. I told him that I had let the engine continue to run at idle. Sam only shrugged.

"Prob'ly didn't hurt it any and they got a new one on the way anyhow," he said, "so screw it."

On a DC-9 flight through Indianapolis (IND) one day, I had occasion to give thanks that I had the office and home numbers for Pat "Mother" Malone. Many of us had put her numbers in our Jeppeson manuals during her classes on FAA regs and Ops Specs. Pat was our guru on these subjects and could quote chapter and verse verbatim. On this day, IND had a cloud cover ceiling down around three-hundred feet with light rain. We flew an arrival ILS to land north with a light ten-knot tailwind. The primary NE-SW runway was shut down for repainting its markings. The remaining runway offered no ILS for landing toward the south into the wind.

We taxied out to takeoff north. Arriving at the south end of the runway, we observed the tall grass bending over from a strong south wind.

"What's the wind?" we asked the tower.

"It's one-hundred-eighty degrees at *mpf*-five knots," the answer came.

"Say again?"

"It's one-eighty at two-five knots." Well, that was way beyond any legal tailwind limits. We requested to taxi to the north end for a south departure. After arriving there, we announced "Ready to go." This was met with instructions to hold as they had a long string of arrivals landing to the north. After holding for some fifteen minutes, I requested an estimate of when we could expect takeoff clearance.

"It'll be a while," the reply came.

"So, you're allowing landings with an illegally high tailwind while denying me a legal departure?" I asked.

"You'll just have to wait," came the reply.

Fuming, I requested to taxi back to the gate. At the gate, I walked rapidly to a phone and called "Mother" Malone. Pat listened.

"All right, Darling," she said sweetly. I'm glad you called. You go ahead and taxi back out. I promise they will let you depart to the south."

Well, they *did*—with no delay! I never learned what "Mother" had said to them on the phone – but I'm sure she had their undivided attention.

I recently learned that Pat died of complications from a traffic accident with a student driver who pulled in front of her. What a tragic loss of a truly great woman. Pat was admired and loved by every pilot on the line. Delta offered Priority Emergency passes to all who wished to attend her funeral. Now, *that's* an appropriate tribute! I couldn't go, but I shedding some tears for her.

Love you, Pat.

Chapter 15 | Dealing With the FAA

A little dust-up had me talking to our leaders again. Here's how it went. On a night flight from Columbus, Ohio, we picked up an FAA Inspector, there to observe our line operation. We got him settled on the center fold-down jump seat and I gave him a little briefing. I told him that he could observe, but not to touch any controls or equipment. It was also made clear that there would be no simulated failures, as this was a passenger flight. I pointed out that we were using the overhead cockpit speakers instead of headsets, and asked that he be aware of calls for Delta 335 and stop talking.

Our stops for the night would be in Cincinnati, Lexington, Louisville, and Atlanta. He got off to a great start by talking through the delivery of our clearance. I shushed him politely and requested a repeat from Clearance Delivery. They read the clearance again, with an exasperated tone.

Short hop flights require the crew to dance-in-step

with each other in order to keep up. Some legs may take only twenty minutes for takeoff, then climb, a burst of speed, slow, descend and land. There would be at least five radio handoffs. Imagine two people square-dancing to their own caller. Now somebody starts talking through that caller's chant of steps. Soon, there are tangled feet.

Our observer proceeded to quiz us about the airplane's specs. More radio calls had to be repeated as I explained that we were both current and qualified and that we were not going to take a check ride oral exam while en route with passengers. It was becoming clear that this fellow had no idea of what observer meant. We managed to stumble through our square dance into Cincinnati.

On departure, our observer "helped" us by dialing a radio frequency... the wrong one. After backtracking to get the right numbers and once more reminding him not to touch, we got a late handoff for Lexington. We worked to get down, but could not get slowed enough for a straight in approach and were forced to do a lap outside the marker to get stabilized on speed.

Parked at the gate in Lexington, he proceeded to critique our performance. He observed that we seemed to be late in planning our last approach and that we were not coordinated in our radio procedures, often requiring messages to be repeated.

I blew up. "We don't have any trouble communicating when we don't have a dumb sonofabitch on the jump seat, who can't remember our flight number and learn to shut the hell up! Also, that circle we just had to do was because that same dumb sonofabitch got his fingers on our radio and set the *wrong* numbers on it." I was irate at this point, but his next comment blew off the pressure relief valve.

"You can't talk to me that way. I'm an FAA Inspector and I will conduct this ride as I see fit."

We had a very tall and big agent in LEX. He was standing behind the inspector in the doorway through this exchange. I did a very fast count to ten and took a deep breath.

"You are *not* conducting this flight, *I* am. You now have two options. You may ride to Atlanta in a First Class Passenger seat or you may get off here. You are no longer welcome in *my* cockpit."

The Inspector puffed up to full height and stormed, "You *cannot* keep me out of the cockpit."

I could not believe this jerk. I stared at him for a minute. "You just lost option one," I told him. "You *are* getting off here."

Our smiling agent tapped him on the shoulder. "Follow me, sir and don't forget any carry-on bags."

The Inspector puffed even more. "I'm not going anywhere with you," he told the agent "Do you know who I am?"

Our agent smiled at him. "No, sir, I don't know who you are," he answered, "but then, I don't really care, either. You can follow me or I can go fetch our Deputy Sheriff and have him take you off in handcuffs. The Captain wants you off, so you're getting off. Follow me."

We left on time, the last flight for the night. Lights were going off in the lounge as we taxied away. I had been in bed at home about five hours when the phone rang around 0930. Joyce answered and, then, woke me to take the call.

"Hello?"

"Morning, Jerry. This is Herb Farnsworth."

Oops, Captain Farnsworth, the Atlanta Chief Pilot! "Yes, sir?"

"I just had a call from the FAA about an inspector you threw off in Lexington last night."

"Yes, sir?"

"Well, they're just a bit upset. Seems this fellow got the last cab at the airport, went to the bus terminal and, then, waited for a bus to Cincinnati and more hours for a flight to Detroit. His boss just called and threatened you with all sorts of bad things. Care to tell me what happened?"

"Yes, sir." Wide-awake now, I told the story.

When I finished, Herb said, "So... you could say you threw him off for safety of flight concerns?"

"Yes, sir, that's about it."

"Works for me. Go back to bed."

I never heard another word about it. Herb Farnsworth didn't get his reputation for leadership by picking his nose.

I would like to make a point here in an attempt to explain this sort of incident. I hasten to say that most inspectors are decent guys trying to do a fair job. However, those who cannot sit back and observe, who persist in any sort of hands-on interaction with a crew, can be very dangerous. Any outside party in a cockpit, no matter how well behaved, becomes a catalyst. That is, while they may stand outside of events, they are going to influence what happens. Like a TV film crew, putting cameras on a protest gathering, what they see is *not* what would have occurred in their absence.

An Inspector who cannot keep his hands off controls is every bit as dangerous as a drunken chimpanzee running through a crowd with a straight razor. Such behavior has caused accidents and continues to do so today. The next two examples will make my point.

The first example involved one of our DC-8s in New Orleans. Captain Bill Tuero was conducting a night recurrent check for another Captain. An FAA Inspector was aboard. One of the required maneuvers to be demonstrated for competence was a circling approach to a landing with two engines out on *one side*. This is an inherently dangerous maneuver and requires that adherence to the performance envelope of the aircraft is carefully observed. As even a non-pilot will realize, the power of two operating engines on one side only will require a lot of rudder to keep the aircraft under control and in a straight line. The DC-8 has hydraulic boost to power the rudder against airflow forces. Without this boost, the rudder is deflected only by the power of direct cables and the amount of pressure a man can exert on a rudder pedal.

Thus, the DC-8 has *two* V_{MCA} (Velocity Minimum Control in the Air) numbers. Below these numbers, there is simply not enough rudder authority to counter the power of thrust on one side only. The V_{MCA} *without* hydraulic boost is considerably higher than the V_{MCA} with that hydraulic assist. The loss of two engines *and* the hydraulic system would be a highly unlikely *compound* failure. It's something which could be planned for and dealt with only if known in advance of a landing attempt.

That night, a circling approach was conducted at the required five-hundred foot altitude and *with* rudder boost. As the pilot rolled into a turn, the inspector decided to see how he handled the aircraft *without* the rudder boost. Without a word to anyone, he reached past Engineer George Piatza and threw the rudder boost lever to off.

On the voice tape transcript, you can hear George yelling. "Don't do that. Don't do that. Oh, no! *Oh, no!*"

Superimposed is the Pilot's voice. "I can't hold it. I can't *hold it!*"

There are other yelling voices and background noise and, then, silence.

It is a very *short* recording. The airplane was *already* well below its V_{MCA} without hydraulics when this curious Inspector shut off the rudder boost. The two pilots died without ever knowing *why* the plane suddenly rolled onto its back and dove into the parking lot of a motel. Even had they known the rudder boost had been shut off, there was simply no time to do anything about it. All aboard died in seconds as well as most of a high school band, practicing in the motel parking lot. An active and curious chimpanzee in the cockpit would have been far less dangerous than this Inspector. At least the crew would have known to keep an eye on the chimp.

In a more recent case, only a few years ago, a Grumman amphibian crashed in Ft. Lauderdale. The pilot had spent many months restoring the old Chalks Airline Grumman. A professional, well known by other pilots and respected by all, he planned to begin service to the Bahamas.

This very experienced pilot was getting his check ride when he lost both engines at low altitude. Without enough altitude to sort out the cause, he glided over rooftops and tried to land in a canal. He made the canal, but it was a crash landing. You have to hope that he was unconscious as he drowned, never realizing that the inspector sitting beside him had stupidly turned *off* the fuel tank valves at low altitude.

The Inspector lived, pulled out of the half-submerged cockpit by bystanders. The incredible dumbness behind this tragedy is impossible to exaggerate. Fuel valves have *never* been known to turn themselves off. Any pilot who accidentally selected that option would be rewarded by burping engines and *immediately* put the selector back where it had been!

Note to young pilots: never, *ever* allow an inspector to have free hands in your cockpit! You may have a knock down fight on the ground, but at least you'll be alive!

Chapter 16 | Flying the L-100 "Herkybird"

In 1971, Delta purchased four L-100 freighters from Lockheed. The primary reason was to allow delivery of spare engines to our fleet of jumbo jets in the event an off-line engine change was needed. These engines were over 8 feet in diameter, and the L-100 allows loading them easily via an articulated tailgate ramp. L-100 is the commercial designation for the great high-wing, low-belly freighter known to the military as the C-130.

Powered by four Allison turbine engines, spinning huge four-bladed props, it could haul an impressive load. The original version had so much power that an outboard engine failure on takeoff required some power reduction on the opposite engine to maintain directional control. The later version delivered to Delta had its fuselage stretched some ninety-six inches. Length added forward and aft of the wing allowed one more cargo pallet. It also moved the rudder far enough aft to eliminate need for any power reduction upon failure of an outboard engine.

The airplane was easy to fly and very responsive, with hydraulically boosted controls. Lockheed pioneered hydraulic "power steering" and the L-100 had dual boosters on its controls. There remained a minimum controllability speed of one-hundred-thirty-five knots with two engines out on one side.

Lockheed had supplied operating procedures essentially copied from military operations. This created a few conflicts. While an Air Force crew could lighten the load by dumping it out the tailgate, we could not. Two engine approaches, conducted in training, revealed that high power settings were required, even on an empty aircraft. This caused high rudder loads. The problem was created by the procedure of conducting such an approach with partial flaps extended.

Out of curiosity, I looked up the approach speed for a no-flap approach. The 1.3Vs (thirty percent above stall) speed was one-hundred-thirty-seven knots. Since one-hundred-thirty-five knots was an absolute control speed minimum, I reasoned that a no-flap approach at one-hundred-thirty-seven knots made more sense. Less power, and therefore less rudder angle, would be needed. It would also provide a wider performance margin for any unforeseen go-around.

I went out for my rating-ride with FAA Inspector Paul Newman. When the check ride got to the two-engine approach, I flew it no-flaps. After landing, Newman noted that I had never called for any flaps, as the procedure called for. He was debating whether to call for a repeat approach.

"What procedure?" I innocently asked.

"Well, the procedure calls for partial flaps," he answered.

He knew I was playing with him and wore an amused look as I pointed out that any two-engine approach would be cause for a declared emergency and, in such a circumstance, any procedure the captain chose would apply. Paul nodded thoughtfully and asked me to explain why I chose no flaps. When I finished, he nodded again.

"That makes sense and I think we should look at changing the book at least to reflect that option."

Newman was one of the Good Guys who really did understand flying.

The airplane flew routes between Chicago and Detroit, to Memphis, and on to Atlanta. Los Angeles was another destination. I flew these routes on an alternating "dual-pool" qualification on the DC-9. Detroit, as an example, provided full loads of containerized auto-parts. These loads, ordered that day, would be in dealer inventories when their doors opened on the morning of our arrival. We marveled at the statement by our CEO Ron Allen, that "There was no money in flying cargo." I guess he just neglected to share his wisdom with UPS and FedEx.

A night flight to Atlanta brought another small quirk into focus. We lost the Boost Hydraulic System. The Utility System still functioned. Both provided hydraulic power to flight controls and the remaining Utility System was adequate for normal flight. The question in our minds now was "How is the Utility system holding up?"

The only information provided in the cockpit were two pressure gauges forward of the copilot's left knee and the only indication of reservoir quantity was a pair of coffee-urn style sight tubes back at the wheel well area. The right (boost) was not accessible with cargo in place. Our main worry was that a loss of the Utility System would require the landing gear to be hand-cranked down.

The landing gear on an L-100 is unique. It cannot free-fall down, because it lowers on a spinning screw jack. It was possible to get at the left crank, but cargo would have to be moved to access the right side crank. The military flies the C-130 with at least two pilots, a navigator, an engineer, and a loadmaster, lots of bodies to hump cargo. Loss of the Utility System for us would mean a belly landing.

The system held up and we landed on rubber tires that night. The event set me into motion looking for a fix. The largest hydraulic reservoir on the aircraft was a three and a half gallon tank for an electric pump, which raised and lowered the cargo ramp tailgate. That's all it did. Our cockpit still had the button to activate this pump for airdropping parachuted cargo, something we never used. I contacted a Lockheed Tech-Rep from Marietta and made an appointment to meet at an aircraft.

With the Tech-Rep aboard, I pointed out how some few feet of tubing and a simple manual open-close valve would allow use of the tailgate pump to lower the landing gear. He agreed that it was easily doable and promised to look into it.

I got a call from him weeks later. He reported that, while the fix was easy, getting bureaucracy at the FAA to approve it was *not*. They were insisting upon lengthy and expensive re-certification tests prior to approval. They expressed concern that a failure in a gear-down line could cause loss of the tailgate reservoir fluid. It didn't matter to them that the tailgate system was only used on the ground!

To my knowledge, the L-100 (and C-130 military fleet) still flies with no backup hydraulic means to extend its gear. "We're from the government and we are here to help you. If a crank was good enough for your father, it's good enough for you."

How in the world could you have fun flying freight? Well, we arrived in Chicago at about three a. m. on one trip. The route came in over Chicago Heights VOR, via Victor-7 airway, to NILES intersection, then direct to O'Hare.

An obviously sleepy Approach Controller cleared us over this route at ten-thousand feet on a crystal-clear night. As we approached the Outer Marker for runway thirty-one Left, still at ten-thousand feet, we knew the controller had dozed off. This was going to be fun! Waiting until about two miles from the marker, I called and asked innocently if he planned on giving us an approach clearance. The poor guy spluttered awake.

"Oh, uh… yeah, sorry, I got sidetracked. Ah, well, if you have the runway in sight you can, ah, circle left or right, ah, your choice to, ah, get down!"

"Would straight-in be okay?" I asked innocently.

"Ah, well, whatever you, ah, want, that's okay," he stammered.

Just as the marker needle swung, we had her 'dirtied-up' with gear and flaps down. I pulled four engines to idle. Those huge, wide, four-bladed props shifted to flat pitch and made four giant speed brakes. With the nose aimed for the dirt, we easily dropped like an elevator with its cables cut. Losing ten-thousand feet in five miles is an easy maneuver. The Air Force called it an "assault landing" and it was a regular approach to limit exposure to ground fire. It sure woke up the guys in Approach Control and the tower!

Chapter 17 | Near Midair No. 2

With the exception of stupid fingers turning things off, almost all accidents are caused by a chain of events or circumstances. The links of this chain must remain connected to progress to an accident. Breaking a link anywhere along the chain will prevent an unhappy outcome.

Such a chain began one day in Evansville, Indiana. We taxied out for takeoff, bound for Chicago. Evansville has two runways which connect at their south end in the form of a V. The left leg is short and narrow and used only by light planes. The long right-hand leg is the main runway for airliners and other big aircraft.

A very light breeze from the south favored takeoffs and landings toward the south. As this whisper of air was well within our downwind limits and the south end of the V meant a far shorter taxi route, we elected to take off toward the northeast. A call of "Ready to go," produced the following response from the tower, the first "link" in the chain.

"You're cleared for takeoff. There is light plane traffic on a *right downwind* (emphasis mine) for eighteen."

For non-pilots, this meant that a light plane was *west* of the field, heading *north*, and flying a clockwise pattern. We would be departing toward the northeast, and tracking away from him. We both looked left as we lined up on the runway and also scanned ahead. No light plane in sight. Concluding that he must still be behind our field of vision, we rolled, the second "link" in the chain.

My copilot was flying. This was the third "link" in our chain. We lifted off and, since the copilot was flying, it was my duty to reach over and return the landing gear handle from the UP to NEUTRAL position. As I leaned over to reach the handle, my view angle dropped below the upper edge of the windshield. I was looking at the side of a Cessna, crossing from our right to our left and slightly above us. Its pilot wore an orange ball cap and a horrified expression, with his mouth wide open.

I had time only to slam my left elbow against the yoke and push it forward. We flashed under him and he cleared our high T-tail. My copilot recovered from the quick dip down and shot me a perplexed look. Eyes down on his instruments, he had never seen the Cessna.

We had broken the "chain" of links toward an unhappy incident.

Now recovered and climbing, I grabbed the mike. "Who's running traffic around this goddam airport?" I yelled.

"I resent your language," the tower responded, "I told you that traffic was on a *left* downwind."

"No, you said he was in *right* traffic," I angrily retorted, "and even if you knew he was on *left*, you cleared us off directly into his base turn, so you screwed up no matter *how* you cut it!"

We exchanged a few more "pleasantries" and shifted over to Departure Control.

My copilot and I discussed the event and were both certain that he had said *right* traffic for the Cessna. I pulled the circuit breaker for the cockpit voice recorder, since the tape re-records over itself every thirty minutes. I wanted to preserve the tape because I knew there would be a Near Miss Report filed. I was certain the tower would "accidentally" allow their tape to record over the evidence and, then, they would then attempt to file a safety violation against me.

This chain of events had a link broken only because it was the *copilot's* turn to fly. Had I been flying, it would have been his turn to cycle the gear handle and he would have been looking LEFT to do so. Neither of us would have seen the Cessna.

Fate is the Hunter, sometimes rode on the toss of a coin. Lucky once more.

In Chicago, I had mechanics swap out the tape and I put the evidence in my bag. Back in Atlanta, I called Captain Gillette, who was our local Safety Rep, and got the tape into his hands. Sure enough, he called the next day to inform me that Evansville had filed a Safety Violation against me. He asked if I was certain about the RIGHT traffic call from the Tower. I said yes.

"Get your butt over to Pre's office to listen to the tape," he said.

We sat in silence as Dick loaded the tape and pushed *play*. When it was over, Pre looked at me silently for a minute.

"Except for some of your language, for which I don't blame you, you were absolutely correct," he said. "They screwed up and, with this tape, we can prove it. How did you become cynical enough, at your age, to pull the recorder circuit breaker?"

I looked toward Dick Gillette. "Good teachers, sir."

Pre showed a hint of a smile. "Well, they seem to have 'lost' their tape somehow, but with this one I can stuff it down their throats."

Dick swatted me on the back as we walked out of Pre's office. "Looks like I taught you pretty good, didn't I?"

"Yeah, Dick, you did."

Lesson for young Captains: When "they" screw up, there will be *no* Tape—unless you happen to have one in your mitts. (Hint, hint.)

Chapter 18 | "'Pre" Retires

The retirement of Captain Thomas Prioleau "Pre" Ball was the major event of 1971. Pre came to Delta in 1934, serving as a Station Manager, a pilot, and finally as Vice President of Operations. He took time out to serve in the Air Corps through WWII and left as a Major. He was one of the original personalities who built the airline.

Pre was an exacting boss but always fair. Pilots knew that he valued *truth* and would protect a man who gave it to him cold. I had seen him do so first hand. Pre was not just respected and admired by our pilots. They truly loved this small "tiger."

As the date for his retirement drew near, we made plans for a gala sendoff. The pilot group contributed to a fund to finance a "going away trifle." The secrecy level was high. If the Manhattan Project had been held to this level of secrecy, it would have taken the Russians another dozen years to develop their A-bomb.

The ballroom at the old Air Host Hotel was chosen for the party site because of its size and one other feature—a loading dock and double doors to the ballroom. On the night of the party, every pilot who was not flying was at the Air Host. Attendance from bases outside of Atlanta was heavy. Rumors of large bribes paid to persuade some pilots to cover trips so others could attend abounded. Bid sheets for that month were a puzzle for sure. Senior pilots bid poor quality lines of time, if they indicated *that* night off, while junior pilots got the "gravy" runs.

The night arrived, greeted by a massive crowd of boisterous pilots. Cocktail hour was followed by dinner. Captain John McDonald served as a masterful M. C. As dinner wound down, John stepped to the podium on the bandstand and began to introduce speakers. Each speaker raised the crowd to high levels of raucous laughter and clapping, as they "roasted" Pre with hilarious tales of past events, some true and others laced with embellishment. Pre laughed as loud as anyone as wave after wave of outrageous stories assaulted his integrity, his sanity, his ego, and every other vulnerability. Everything, except the legitimacy of his birth, was fair game.

As the last speaker wrapped up his verbal assault, John stepped back to the microphone and invited Pre to come up and answer all the scurrilous charges against him. The room was in pandemonium as Pre rose from his chair.

Pre standing was the signal for action. In choreographed moves, one group took only seconds to clear tables and chairs and form a lane from a set of double doors to the center of the floor. A second group surrounded the double doors and stood six or eight men deep, to block any view as the doors to the loading dock swung open. This knot of people migrated quickly to the center of the ballroom. Pre had reached the podium and stood beside John wearing a puzzled look. The entire room was on its feet, with the dense knot standing in the center.

Dead silence prevailed as John invited Pre to answer all the lies laid against him by this 'sorry looking mob.' Pre stepped up to the mike. That was the signal for the knot standing in the center to melt aside. The mass split to reveal a spanking new, top of the line, BMW auto, sitting silently on the dance floor. Pre turned slowly toward John, wearing a questioning look, to discover John dangling a set of keys in front of him. John reached over, lifted Pre's arm and dropped the keys in his palm.

"Okay, Pre, you can speak now," John said as he backed away.

The crowd stood hushed as Pre silently surveyed the faces focused on him. His jaw was clenched as he tried to maintain a straight face. As he struggled, tears began to creep down his cheeks. There was not a dry eye in the house. Someone finally broke the spell and rescued Pre's dignity by starting to clap. The clapping released an avalanche of pent up emotions and bedlam prevailed for long minutes.

Pre had gained a tenuous grip on himself and managed to gulp and stutter his way through some "rebuttal" remarks. Again, cheering and whooping pilots rescued him. The secret had been kept without a leak. The loading dock, outside the ballroom doors, had provided the perfect means to roll the car from a rental truck directly into the ballroom.

Captain Pre Ball passed away at the ripe old age of ninety-nine. When I heard the news, I sat down and cried quietly. Admitting this causes me no embarrassment, for I'm quite certain I was not alone.

Chapter 19 | Moving to Florida

During the early summer of 1971, Joyce and I had taken some vacation time in California. I ran into some old high school pals in Newport Beach and got invited to enjoy some sailing. I also got in a bit of surfing.

Back in Georgia for another hot summer, I began to feel some pangs of homesickness. Not for California, but for some salt water. Joyce and I had built a home on an acre of woods and had been in it about three years. Toward the end of the summer, I was out in the heat on a garden tractor mowing grass one day when a friend, Captain Tom Richter, drove up. I shut down and we went inside for a cool drink. Tom proposed that I gather up my chain saw and follow him in my pickup to cut some firewood. He reported that oaks were being felled in Hapeville and that we could get some good wood.

Something snapped. I was spending summers mowing grass and cutting firewood and winters inside burning it. I told Tom that I was going to Florida and got up.

"What, *when*?" he said.

"Now," I said and went upstairs to pack a bag.

I told Joyce I would be back in a couple of days and left for the airport to hop a flight. In Florida, I grabbed some maps and contacted a pilot doing sideline real estate. It took a day to locate a nice house on the water, north of Ft. Lauderdale and called Joyce to report in.

"Buy it!" she said and I did.

The only thing I checked on first was did I have enough seniority to hold a DC-9 Captain's slot in Miami. Back in Atlanta, I signed my name to a bid sheet for Miami before driving home. When I told Tom what I had done, he went down and bought a home nearby. A few months later, we were both notified that we should be in place to fly out of Miami as of January 1, 1972. We were both ready to close on our new homes, but the sellers were not, so we would need someplace to live for a few months. We went back, seeking a rental. That's when we learned about Florida "seasonal rent" prices. We bought a little FHA 3-2 in a nice working class neighborhood.

The day after Christmas, we set off in our two pickups with trailers for Florida. Carrying a bit of bare furnishings, we set up in the little house. We both now owned two and a half houses. Our wives took turns, coming down weekly to be sure we ate more than canned chili. Our Atlanta homes eventually sold and the Florida homes closed to complete the transition.

Our Miami Chief Pilot was relieved to discover that his two newbies were already qualified, line-checked and ready to go to work. The Miami base was very senior, meaning that a pilot needed more seniority there to hold a position comparable to what he could hold elsewhere. A collection of pilots there really were characters. The lifestyles they enjoyed truly puzzled our staid corporate leaders in Atlanta. Consequently, Miami had an outlaw reputation, some of it actually earned!

Our Chief Pilot was a bit of a character himself. He made his home in the island compound once owned by Al Capone. The house and various events in it were noted in some publications. As this gentleman is a friend and a great guy, I shall skip over such tales. He ran a very laid-back operation, which puzzled some corporate types. Those who decoded his attitude realized that all he cared about, besides his various boats, was that his pilots show up on time, do their jobs, and stay out of mischief, certainly fine by me.

We had not been long in the base when Tom called me one evening to discuss a problem. He had just finished a long conversation with the copilot they paired me with for the month. I was astonished at what he told me. He said that this fellow had purposely put in his bid sheet for the month to fly with me. I asked why. Tom related that I, unknown to me, had a reputation on the DC-9 and this fellow wanted to learn to handle the airplane like I did.

I was completely taken aback. I have always worked hard to handle a plane smoothly and to set it down like it was carrying uncrated eggs. I felt some pride in doing things well, but had no yardstick to assess what my contemporaries were doing. You never get the chance to fly with people of similar seniority.

Tom then went on to explain that this fellow was so upset over his performance on our last trip that he was considering trading off his trips with me. Tom asked what had happened. By this time I had worked out what the problem was and I felt pretty low about it.

This fellow had made the last landing of our usual three-day rotation and it had been a "thumper." I had laughed and told him that I would stand in the door and take the rap for it. I was only intending to rib him a bit, but when I looked at him he had tears in his eyes. I ignored this, trying not to embarrass him. Tom related that the poor guy was completely unraveled because he thought that *I* thought he was incompetent. I felt low enough to crawl under the rug. I had no idea the guy was trying to copy me, nor that it meant so much to him. I asked Tom if he was going to speak with him again. He said he had promised to call him back.

I explained to Tom that I thought the man was competent and a very safe pilot. Tom agreed, as he had flown with him. I said his landings were all perfectly safe, but that he seemed to work too hard at the end and often created his own "pilot induced turbulence." I asked Tom if he thought I should call the man. He said no, that he would do it, so I asked that he relay my request that the fellow stay with me.

I was fully aware now that I had been guilty of doing a "Captain McBride" on the guy. I had failed to explain and teach how I did something. This poor guy was left trying to copy my landings with no explanation, or information, coming from me. The bottom line was that the problem was entirely my fault. I wanted the chance to make it right and asked Tom to convince the fellow to stay with me.

Tom managed to convince him because he was there when I signed in for the next rotation. I had to start off by apologizing to him. Then I told him that I thought he was a very competent pilot. His approaches were stable, well planned, and landings were perfectly safe. I promised to work with him on the touchdown technique. By the end of our three days—and I had given him most of the landings—he was doing some slick touchdowns.

The whole episode brought the fact home to me that part of my job should be sharing techniques and "secrets" with those with whom I flew. For any pilots reading this, I should share some information. The DC-9 shares a characteristic with all aircraft that have aft mounted engines. On the Boeing 727, this quirk is more pronounced, but it's common to all of them. The weight of aft mounted engines requires that wings be mounted further aft on the fuselage for balance. The center of lift on a straight wing is about one third of the way back from its leading edge. With swept wings, this center of lift is going to be rearward of the wing root, where it meets the fuselage. The center of gravity on a stable aircraft must always be forward of the center of lift. All these requirements mean that the main landing gear is going to be well aft of the center of lift. This is true of all aircraft, but more pronounced when engine weight is mounted aft.

What does all this gobbledygook mean in terms of flying characteristics? An abrupt pitch change, nose up or down, will cause any aircraft to rotate about its center of lift. With the gear well aft of this point, an abrupt pitch correction on landing will cause the landing gear to rotate downward. Even a small one that close to the runway will "spike" the gear down. Thus, a perfectly set up landing will turn into a sharp thump. The secret is in a nice flare and, then, looking at the far end, keep the nose coming up gently. You may be a foot or so high and still get a gentle touchdown, but a last-second nose up "snatch" will spike the gear every time, causing a hard landing.

I got this fellow to do this by coaching him to fly the landings with only his fingertips on the yoke and to keep flying until he purposely flew the nose gear down onto the pavement. You cannot snatch the yoke back with fingertips. It only happens when you have a "choke-the-chicken" full-fist grip on the yoke. Try it—you'll like it.

By the way, if you can't fly with your fingertips, you're not trimming the airplane and everything you do will be forced and ham-handed.

Chapter 20 | Flying the Boeing 727

The B-727 In Seattle:

In 1972, Delta took over Northeast Airlines and a somewhat acrimonious merger process began. Putting the pilots' seniority lists together became a problematic exercise. Delta had the Lockheed L-1011, and the DC-8. Our third down-the-pay-scale aircraft, the Convair 880, was equivalent in our pay scale to the largest Northeast aircraft, the Boeing 727. Our two larger aircraft and their pay scales made equivalency of the two seniority lists badly lopsided. A formula was finally reached, producing some degree of unhappiness on both sides.

Many Delta pilots referred to the B-727 as the Edsel, but some finally admitted than an airplane that could carry almost the number of passengers as a DC-8, fly almost at the speed of a CV-880, and get off runways as short as the DC-9 did, couldn't be all bad. Delta absorbed the Northeast B-727-

95 and B-727-295 fleet and put orders in for new B-727-232s with more powerful Dash-15 engines. Bids were let out for expanded crew positions. In keeping with my "move up early" philosophy, I signed up.

Delta had, as yet, no B-727 simulators or training program. A fairly large group filed bids to checkout on the airplane. The group was split, with half going to Ft. Worth for contracted training by American. My half went to Seattle for training at the Boeing plant. I was there for five weeks, starting in February of 1973. I looked out the window every morning at overcast skies and never even took my sunglasses out of my hotel room. Amazing!

Ground School ran about three weeks with no surprises. An FAA oral exam followed. Ditto. Then we got into the simulators for flight training. The old simulators did not fly like an airplane and I didn't care what the engineers who designed them said. They flew like what they were... a sim, so we learned to fly them.

There were interesting differences of opinion about flying techniques. Boeing's instructors were mostly retired military with no airline experience. Most had less than half the flying time and weather experience of the people they were training. One of the early disputes was over the improper rotation technique some use on takeoff, including me.

For the layman, I need to explain some numbers involved in a takeoff. V_1 is a decision speed, a *go-no-go* point. V_R is a rotation speed, where the nose gear comes off the ground. V_2

is a flying speed which is twenty-percent above stall speed. There are some other parameters involved with calculating these speeds, but they're not important for this example. One of the takeoff calculations is always, "How much weight can be lifted off a runway x-feet long and clear an imaginary fifty-foot-high obstacle (such as trees) at its end?" Many small town runways are too short to allow takeoffs at the max gross weight of an aircraft, so it becomes a selling point to get as much weight as possible out of West Hernia Airport.

Boeing convinced the FAA to allow an interesting technique to maximize the weight versus runway length equation. At V_R, you initiated a "smart," four-second rotation to bring the nose up to eighteen-degrees of pitch. The airplane would leap off the runway and attain the desired V_2 speed *after* it was fifty feet off the runway!

Back to the Boeing Instructors' critique of our rotation performance, or lack of performance in his estimation. Instructors were expecting us to perform this described maneuver. The technique and experiences of airline people is to lift the nose gear at V_R and "feel" the airplane off, looking for V_2 as the plane broke ground. My refusal (and I was not the only one) to adopt the prescribed technique generated a heated discussion.

I defended my reasoning with a couple of arguments. First, errors of weight calculations can be in orders of one-thousand or ten-thousand pound increments. Second, low level wind shears, caused by buildings or tree lines, are common. Third, while it's nice to know what the certification maneuver is, and that the plane *might* perform at that level if you ran out of concrete, it was a stupid technique to apply in daily operations. Hanging, nose-up, fifty feet off the runway is a lousy place to discover a wind shear, or that you're twenty-thousand pounds heavier than your 'Weight and Balance Sheet claimed. I cited an accident in Denver, which proved my point.

An unnamed airline had a B-727 lift off from Denver using the prescribed technique. A few dozen feet in the air, the plane ran into a tailwind shear. It came back down to the ground like a bag of cement. I could not recall injuries from the event, but damage was extensive.

The instructor was unmoved and I was getting hotter. The man had no line experience and didn't know what the hell he was talking about. He was teaching as though airplanes always operated in clear skies, with a nice ten-knot breeze down the runway, right on the nose! I finally asked him to imagine a situation.

"You're standing on the corner of a busy city street. Four lanes of traffic are zipping past. You have repeatedly pushed that button on the pole to get traffic stopped and give you the *Walk* light. It's apparently busted. Finally, in exasperation, you tuck your thumbs into your armpits and start flapping your elbows madly to fly across the street. How well do you think that's gonna work?" I asked him.

"That's ridiculous. That's not gonna work," he replied. "What's your point?"

"My point is that the airplane can fly better than you can," I retorted, "and it will when it's damned well ready and not before.

One of our funnier conflicts involved what you were supposed to call those levers which make the engines whine louder. On the old recips, they are *throttles*. Technically a throttle controls a baffle plate in a carburetor to allow more or less airflow, but the throttle on a steam locomotive controls a steam valve.

Since the jet engine was created, people have attempted to re-name this lever. The current name in favor seems to depend on who is writing the manuals. I have seen wholesale revisions issued to change from *Power Lever* to *Thrust Lever* and back again when somebody else took over the job.

I've always referred to it as a *throttle*, so I was repeatedly corrected during the sim training to call it the *Power Lever*, or maybe it was *Thrust Lever*. It was forty-six years ago, I'm not sure. After one more correction, I decided enough was enough. I was all prepared and suckered the guy in.

"Okay, I called it a *throttle*," I said. Don't you know what that is? Don't you speak English?"

"Yes, I know what you mean," The instructor patiently explained, "but it's referred to as a *Power Lever*."

He had swallowed the bait. Now, to set the hook.

"Well, if it's not a *throttle*, why did Boeing mold the words THROTTLE into the number one and three *throttle* knobs?"

He stared at the *throttle knobs* as if he had never looked at them before. He just closed his eyes and slowly shook his head, muttering, "Okay, okay."

The rigidity these guys expected was just too good a game to pass up. Commands such as, "Wheels down," would elicit a correction.

"Captain, the correct command is, 'Landing gear down.'"

"That's what I said," I responded. "Don't you speak English? Throw out the rubber!"

Phone conversations with our group in Ft. Worth revealed the same sort of byplay going on there. We were discovering that the Delta pilots had a bit of a maverick approach to terminology and a built-in resistance to ultra-rigid procedures. That's what happens when people are individuals, exercising command judgment, rather than programmed robots.

An incident at the American Airlines training center was cause for some heated discussion between the two companies. A Captain I'll refer to as Gary was flying his sim check ride with an FAA Inspector present. He flew an ILS approach. When he called, "Minimums, no runway," he began the go-around. Shoving the throttles up and rotating to climb, he called, "Takeoff power, flaps fifteen, positive rate, gear up." At this point, he expected the copilot to even up the throttles at takeoff power. Instead the instructor Engineer reached up and pulled the throttles to *Idle*. Of course, the sim crashed! Lots of vibration, flashing red lights, bells and horns, programmed to convey the idea that you're now dead!

Gary looked at this fellow. "What the *hell* did you do that for?" he asked

"Captain, at American, when you say takeoff power, we take off the power," came the arrogant answer. "The correct command is 'Max power.'"

Gary fumed as the sim is re-set to do the approach over again. The call "Minimums, no runway," came back again on the re-do approach. Again, Gary shoved up the throttles and called, "Takeoff power, flaps fifteen, positive rate, gear up." As he removed his right hand from the throttles, so they can be evened up, the instructor again reached forward. This time, Gary's huge fist slams down and pounds the instructor's wrist down onto the center console. Gary flies a perfect go-around.

The instructor turned pale, holding his wrist (which an examination later revealed had several broken bones). "What the hell did you do that for?" he bleated.

Gary calmly looked over at him. "That's to teach you what happens at Delta when you f--k with the Captain's throttles." he answered.

Uh-oh. Much hoo-hah and many phone calls ensued. A lot raucous laughter came from us, when we heard the tale. No, sir, you do *not* "f--k with the Captain's throttles!"

Another small point of dispute was over the landing technique taught by the Boeing instructors. After flaring to kill the sink rate, they wanted to see the plane pushed onto the runway. Our group universally rejected the idea of

pushing an airplane onto the runway and favored a more conventional practice of holding it off into a hose high, semi-stalled touchdown. I, frankly, could not overcome the mental hurdle necessary to push an airplane forward onto a runway on purpose.

Arguments flared until someone got the idea to invite some of these instructors to talk it out at afternoon happy hour. A fair sized group gathered at the hotel lounge. With a pitcher of beer on our table, we batted the points back and forth.

One instructor insisted that the B-727 was different and had to be pushed on. I told the man that I had flown the C-135, DC-8, DC-9, and CV-880. I pointed out that they were all swept-wing jets, like the B-727, and invited him to explain exactly why the B-727 had to be landed differently than these other four planes. He frowned and sat silently, thinking.

One of his colleagues chuckled in his direction. "Go ahead. Explain," he said.

Finally he sighed and answered. "Okay, I'm gonna deny I said this if you repeat it." (I've cleaned this up to a certain level of PC.) "We sell airplanes all over the world. We have to train people from disadvantaged countries to fly them. Some of these people have barely mastered the "high-tech" principles of things like bicycle chains and sprockets. They are very hard to convince that our calculated approach speeds are correct, so they fly faster. The 727 is a very clean airplane. We teach pushing onto the runway to keep these guys from floating the entire length of the runway into the trees off the far end. If you're experienced enough to fly on-speed and get it on with runway left for stopping, you can land without pushing it on."

Everybody started laughing. "All right, that's all we wanted to hear, the truth," I said.

We established an unwritten truce and said no more about pushing.

The B-727 after Seattle:

The B-727 program in Seattle was the first checkout I had experienced where they split the check ride between simulator and aircraft. The oral exam and sim check ride were done in Seattle. That left approaches and landings in the aircraft to be completed later. With the Seattle portion completed, I returned to Miami for another month on the DC-9. The second part of the checkout was finally set up at the airport in Jackson, Mississippi (JAN).

JAN is a good place to work, with light traffic. The work-up training day went well and the FAA was set up for a check the following day. One of the maneuvers would be an autopilot 'coupled' approach to one-hundred feet. There, the autopilot would actually fly the ILS beam. The pilot was expected to set up the autopilot, monitor the approach progress and make appropriate decisions. The problem this day was that JAN had only one ILS system, an approach to runway Fifteen Left, which is a southeasterly heading. Our wind that day was from the west at eighteen to twenty-five knots. This created a quartering tailwind well outside the parameters of the autopilot's ability to cope.

Looking at our weather as we prepared to begin the ride, I was mentally betting that the autopilot could not make a successful approach. The pilot flying wore a hood to block outside references. The Instructor in the right seat, the "safety," had full visual cues. A successful approach would align the aircraft with the runway and put it in a position to land at the one-hundred-foot height. I remember thinking that I had never "busted" a check-ride and did not intend to let it happen that day. I snuck in a moment in the men's room with the Pilot's Handbook to refresh my memory on the crosswind and tailwind parameters for which the autopilot had been certified. Satisfied that the numbers in my memory were correct, I walked out and the check-ride began.

I performed visual approaches, a no-flaps approach, a two-engines-out approach and a circling pattern at five-hundred feet to runway Thirty-three Right, into the wind. The "coupled" ILS followed. All the way down the beam, the autopilot hung off the downwind side, making inadequate corrections to get centered on the "Localizer.", "This is a bad approach," I said at five-hundred feet, "and I would go-around at this point."

"Okay, but keep coming. I have a good view," the safety pilot instructor said.

At the one-hundred-foot point, he reached over and raised my hood. We were a good fifty yards left of the runway with no way safely to land. I went around.

"Well, that's a busted approach. We'll have to do it over," the FAA Inspector said as we climbed out.

I told the Instructor that he had the airplane and turned to the inspector.

"For the purposes of this ride, that was a successful approach and I have no intention of doing it again," I said. "The next scheduled maneuver is to hand-fly the same approach using the Flight Director. I'll put the airplane on the runway with this hand-flown approach, but I *will* not repeat an autopilot coupled approach."

His response was to the effect that he wanted a repeat. As in all things in life, it helps to know where you stand legally.

"I conducted the approach correctly and made the proper decision to go-around at the five-hundred-foot point," I replied. "The autopilot had actually failed to align with the runway because it was operating outside of its certified performance envelope. If you want to 'recertify' the autopilot, that's between you and Boeing. All my actions were correct. Either I continue with a hand-flown approach or we terminate the flight now."

At that point, the instructor chimed in to back up my position. After a short hesitation, the inspector relented. I hand-flew the second approach to a landing and the check-ride was over.

The point of this story is primarily for the young pilot. Any check-ride puts your "ticket" in jeopardy, so it pays to have a solid knowledge of exactly what you are supposed to demonstrate and what the limits of your equipment are.

When you're being pushed out on a limb, you're always better off to call a halt before the limb gets so skinny you slide off, or it breaks.

A good instructor, if one is aboard, should stand up for what's fair, but you may have only an inspector aboard. So, know what's properly required of you and what the required parameters are.

On the Line in the B-727:

Flying the Line on the B-727 was a real joy. For one thing, it uses a three-man crew. Having an Engineer aboard really makes the workload much easier to manage, especially in weather. The extra man can handle walk-arounds, deal with mechanics, and do other airplane business. This leaves the two pilots free to coordinate on weather, clearances, etc. We were now flying some of the Northeast routes, up to Bangor and Portland, Maine and into Boston, etc.

Some of the Northeast aircraft were up for sale and were still in the "Yellowbird" colors of Northeast Airlines. There were still some hard feelings from some of the Northeast people. The seniority lists had been merged to maintain "relative seniority," that is, a man who held middle seniority as a B-727 copilot would remain in that position. Northeast had copilots with more total years than some of our captains and they expected to jump ahead. The Delta list had advanced, through expansion, much faster.

I had been a Captain for over three years at the time of the merger and would have been set back to DC-9 Copilot by their formula. The formula they finally settled upon put a Northeast pilot into the list on a five-to-one ratio. Nobody changed seats or lost "relative seniority."

This still did not satisfy everyone. There was probably no way to be totally fair to all personnel, but nobody lost pay or got downgraded. Those of us on the line had no part of the negotiations and expected everyone to suck it up and perform like pros. Some feathers did fly and I had one such incident.

Stepping into the cockpit one morning, I greeted a copilot I didn't know.

"Good morning, I'm Jerry," I said and stuck my paw out.

A stony-faced silent scowl and no handshake met me. This was to be a three-day rotation and with the first leg into winter weather in Boston. I just didn't feel like putting up with "attitude" for three days of hard work in nasty weather. I picked up a mike and dialed our ramp control frequency.

"Kindly call Crew Scheduling for me and find out how much delay it would cause to get a reserve copilot out here for the flight."

"Will do," he said. "I'll call you right back."

My unnamed copilot now sat up straight, with wide eyes. "What the hell are you doing?" he asked.

"I'm getting a copilot who has the courtesy to shake my hand and tell me his name," I answered. "I don't feel like spending three days with somebody who's pissed off at me for something I did not do," I added.

He stared at me for a few seconds and, then, shook his head. "I'm sorry," he said.

226

I stepped out to the galley and got a cup of coffee. When I came back, I started over with, "Good morning, I'm Jerry" and stuck out my hand.

That time I got a handshake and a name. Things worked out okay and we became friends over time.

My attitude has always been that if I'm gonna pack a bag and leave home to fly, I intend to have a good time doing it. If it's not fun, it's not worth doing. Part of my briefing to new copilots is to tell them to relax and enjoy the job. I always told them, and engineers, to feel free to question anything I might do with which they were not comfortable. I would explain that we all make mistakes, but there are three of us to catch them before they become serious. If somebody calls a mistake and it turns out *not* to be a mistake, there is no damage—no harm, no foul—and nobody's feelings should be hurt.

In other words, we should back each other up and operate as a *team*. I always made sure that our engineer was in this loop as well. On a low minimums approach, he can see *both* instrument panels. If he should note a discrepancy, he should call it out. If there isn't time to sort it out, he should be free to call for a go-around. It's always better to blow some fuel and time than to continue an approach when something does not look right to any crewmember. Even if his suspicion turns out to be unfounded, there is no harm done and he's learned something.

By the time my tenth date of hire anniversary rolled around, I had been flying the B-727 for six months. I was having a ball!

Sitting at the gate in Ft. Lauderdale one morning, we had a strange surprise. We were doing our cockpit preflight as passengers were boarding for the flight to Boston, when a booming voice with a heavy Boston accent came from behind us.

"I hope you bastards know what you're doin.'"

Certain that it was my new friend, Tommy Tutton, pulling our chain, I did not immediately turn around, desperately trying to think of a good comeback for Tommy. Coming up blank, I turned around to greet him. Instead of Tommy standing in the doorway with his toothy grin, I saw a scowling red-faced Ted Kennedy. His upper lip lifted in a sneer as he turned and walked unsteadily to his first class seat in the first row behind the galley. Well, how's that for a morning greeting? The s. o. b. was serious!

I have always enjoyed layovers in Boston — great people, super restaurants, and many historic sites, but some of the laws still puzzle me. Why is the penalty for drunken vehicular manslaughter continuous re-election to the Senate?

More Fun on the B-727:
Most non-pilots would look at my old logbooks and conclude that flying the line must be a boring business. Months will show rotations flying through the same cities over and over. Actually, the layovers in great cities like Boston, New Orleans, Montreal, and dozens of others, offer terrific opportunities for sightseeing and learning. Pilots always

228

search out the best eating spots and many become unofficial clubs.

As an example, Orono, near Bangor, Maine, offered a family-owned restaurant that would treat crews to a true five-star feast. The table would be loaded with steamer clams, fresh corn, cornbread muffins, vegetables, salads, homemade jams, etc. Newcomers were encouraged to order the prime rib. It was hilarious to watch their faces as a fourteen-inch platter was set before them, covered by a huge slab of inch-and-a-quarter thick prime beef. The restaurant would always carefully package up the three quarters of it that a hungry man could not finish. Flight Attendants would often make snacks and sandwiches for us from the leftover slab for the next two days.

The flying was never boring, either. The same route never offered the same weather or the same sunrise or sunset, or the same people. We always managed to create fun. An example is a three-day rotation flown with a great Copilot, Jerry Fulleton. Jerry was a super pilot and a very funny guy around whom to be. He always wore a smile and his sense of humor was infectious, always looking for a target. This rotation was a three on, four off schedule, so we always flew the same legs on the same weekday. The third day had a leg from Cincinnati to Chicago. That's just a short half hour sprint. At the time, the routes were "canned" and published in our Jeppeson approach chart pages. The route was direct to Chicago Heights VOR, then to Victor 7 airway to Niles intersection. Altitude was listed as FL-240 (Flight Level twenty-four-thousand feet). We had direct competition on this route from American Airlines. Their CVG (Cincinnati) departure was a couple of minutes ahead of ours, so they were usually backing out of the gate as we were closing the door.

Taxiing out behind them on our first rotation for the month, Fulleton picked up his mike.

"Hey, Americano gringo?" he whispered

A few seconds later, we heard, "Si?"

"I hope joo got a fast horse, gringo," Fulleton whispered. "We geeve joo a head start."

"Well, we'll have to see about that," came the whispered reply.

The race was on. It was a sucker-bet, because we had a new B-727-232 with Dash-15 engines. With American in sight ahead, climbing to twenty-four-thousand feet, we requested twenty-two-thousand from Departure Control. As we blew past him, we made a little announcement and did some S-turns so our passengers could wave from both sides to "any friends or family who may be riding with American today."

Meanwhile, Fulleton made whispered comments on the radio. "Joo horse look like she tired today, gringo."

Great fun!

The next week Fulleton asked, "Hey, Americano gringo, ees dat joo again?"

"Si."

"I hope dat joo feed joo horse some oats, gringo."

"Si."

This time, we came over to Departure Control in time to hear American get his requested twenty-two-thousand feet, so he's out in front and blocking the altitude we used the previous week. Okay, we go on up to twenty-four-thousand feet. He thinks he's got us, because we will need to be about five miles ahead before Chicago Approach Control will allow us to descend through his altitude ahead of him and he's pushing it today.

Fulleton teases as we blow past. "Joo need to feed dat horse more oats, gringo."

The third week comes. "Hey, gringo, joo got a faster horse today?"

"Si." This time he goes to twenty-two-thousand feet and we steam past at twenty-thousand! Taxiing in at O'Hare, Fulleton asks a flight attendant to fix up a fancy Shirley Temple drink with ginger ale and cherries on a stick. She builds a great one, with cherries and limes and a parasol. As soon as we gate, we're off up the hall to the American gate. Fulleton tells the agent we have a gift for his Captain, so we follow him down to the jetway. As the 'gringo with the tired horse' taxis into the gate, we stand on the edge holding a salute. He's so startled he taxis over his nose wheel chock. The three of us stand in a line against the jetway wall, thanking deplaning passengers for "flying Delta." It sails over the heads of most, but produces startled double-takes from others. With passengers gone, we knock on the cockpit door.

Fulleton presents the fancy Shirley Temple to a stunned Captain. "Hey, gringo, joo deed the bess joo can do weeth old tired horse today. Joo lose tree inna row, so we geeve joo consolation prize of thees nice dreenk."

The American crew were very good sports about the gag. They asked how we were able simply to blow past them. When told we had a new plane with Dash-15 engines, they just groaned.

"You guys really suckered us in. There's no way we could keep up with you in this old bucket."

We parted with handshakes and a laugh. Great guys!

Navigation

One of the fascinating things about flying is learning and applying the art of navigation. The beginning navigator learns techniques which make the practice appear to be a science. Experience teaches that it's more art than a science. With the input of many pieces of information, the art is to judge how much weight, or confidence, to put on sometimes-conflicting information. A good navigator makes those judgments almost subconsciously.

Modern gee-whiz stuff like INS (Inertial Navigation System) and GPS (Global Positioning System) lull many into thinking that the art of navigation is passé. Just follow the dotted line on the screen. I admit to my old-fashioned bias. It causes me to ask, "How do you know when your gee-whiz gadget is lying to you?" I can think of one case where a crew, who were not navigating in their heads (lack of situational awareness), allowed their gee-whiz system to turn the wrong way and fly them into a mountain. They forgot, or never knew that any computer yet built is perfectly willing to kill itself!

The GPS system can locate one on the earth to an accuracy of a few feet. It has made a Bahamian friend, who owns Overseas Salvage Company, a wealthy man. He drags boats off reefs or re-floats them after they have sunk. The advent of GPS has been a major boost to his business. Why? Because people who will not learn the art of navigation go out with total trust in their little electronic gadget – and *hit* things! How can that be? Simple.

First, some three-fifths of the earth has not yet been accurately charted. Hazards are not always in the *right place* on your chart. Second, fast fingers can punch one wrong button and make your GPS lie to you! Trusting a gee-whiz gadget without also applying the old-fashioned art of navigation can lead to disaster.

Most people have never thought about *why* the art of navigation was developed in the first place. Many who have only navigated streets and highways have never questioned how one finds his way across a trackless sea or sky.

If our planet had no winds and no ocean currents, there would be no need for navigators. It would be necessary only to publish a large volume in which one could look up courses and distances from one place to another. The direction and number of paces from your front door to your curbside mailbox never changes, but the winds and currents between earthly locations change constantly, thus the need for navigation.

In the air, there is a third dimension—the *vertical*. Many pilots virtually ignore this dimension. Beyond looking at wind speeds at various altitudes in order to plan their cruising altitude, they make no changes in their vertical navigation.

Every aircraft manual publishes its most efficient climb speed. This ideal climb speed is the best choice *only* on a no-wind day! Very few (or should I say the lazy?) make any adjustment to it for the winds they encounter. Now for the technical stuff....

It would appear obvious that climbing into an increasing tailwind will provide a boost. Climbing into a headwind results in a penalty, but what can you do about it?

Here's an example: The B-727 has a climb speed of three-hundred-twenty KIAS (Knots Indicated Air Speed) until reaching a crossover point of point-eighty mach (eighty-percent of the speed of sound). Again, this is the best speed, but *only with no wind*. How should you adjust that speed? Keep in mind that it is miles covered over the *ground* which determines how efficient you are. Obviously, you should be in no great hurry to climb up into a sixty-knot headwind, so apply a rule of thumb. Add one third of that sixty-knot penalty to your climb speed. Your three-hundred-twenty KIAS climb speed now becomes three-hundred-forty KIAS. Clearly, there are *limits* as to how far one should take it. That's the art. My limit is about three-hundred-fifty KIAS.

"But that means you will take longer and burn more fuel to reach cruise altitude," I can hear you say. That's true, but you can't compare my climb with the fellow who stayed at three-hundred-twenty KIAS until you add in the fuel he burned to reach the geographic point down the track where I reach Top of Climb. Then you must add the fact that I'm miles ahead of him and will have a shorter flight.

How about a tailwind? Reverse the correction. Steepen up the climb to get up into the boost earlier.

Descending offers more opportunities to fine-tune your vertical navigation. The airlines teach a three-for-one rule. This means that you would take three times a cruise altitude of thirty-five thousand feet and begin descending one-hundred-five miles out from an airport. That works, but it's far from the most efficient way to slice the pie. Put me wingtip to wingtip with a guy who's going to use that three-for-one formula. I will beat him to the airport by three to four minutes every time and burn less fuel doing it too. How? It's called *energy management*.

The lazy fellow won't use it because it requires constant mental math. First, I must explain that I hate the use of speed brakes. Those panels on top of the wing are raised to kill off speed and allow a steeper descent. They also cause the cabin to shake, rattle, and roll and they are not efficient. Their use is like drag racing from stoplight to stoplight only to slam on the brakes at each red light.

How does my descent work? I build imaginary *gates* in the sky, starting at the airport (or the outer marker for an ILS approach) and working outward. I want to be over the marker at two-hundred KIAS, clean and at idle power. It will take five NM (nautical miles) to coast from two-hundred-fifty KIAS down to two-hundred KIAS. From ten-thousand feet, the plane will coast down at fifteen-hundred feet-per-minute at two-hundred-fifty KIAS. I need to coast down eighty-five hundred feet to the fifteen-hundred-foot crossing altitude over the marker. That's going to take a bit under four minutes. Two-hundred-fifty KIAS is a bit over four miles-per-minute. Call it five miles per minute, times four minutes, which gives twenty NM. It will take ten NM at ten-thousand feet to slow from Barber Pole (max speed) down to two-hundred-fifty KIAS. Add it all up (5 + 20 + 10) and Gate #4 is thirty-five NM out from the marker at ten-thousand feet and max speed at idle power. Gate #3 is at twenty-two thousand feet. The plane will drop at max speed at three-thousand feet per minute at idle power, so, from twenty-two-thousand feet to ten-thousand feet feet at three-thousand feet per minute will take four minutes. At eight-plus miles per minute that's another thirty-five NM, so Gate #3 is now seventy miles out. Gate #2 is at thirty-thousand feet. From Gate #2 down to Gate #3 is a drop of eight-thousand feet at two-thousand feet-per-minute. That's four minutes and about thirty-five NM, so Gate #2 is now one-hundred-five NM out. Gate #1 is at cruise altitude, say thirty-five-thousand feet. Descent will be at one-thousand feet-per-minute at eight-plus NM per minute for five minutes. That's forty to forty-five NM. Add it all up (35 + 35 + 35 + 45) and I'm going to leave thirty-five feet at one-hundred-fifty to one-hundred-fifty-five NM out. I'm going to be on the Barber Pole all the way down to ten-thousand feet and reducing power all the way. At about twenty-two-thousand feet, I'll be at idle power. If you draw this profile, it looks like a series of ratchets in descent rate (one-thousand FPM, two-thousand FPM, three-thousand FPM, and fifteen-hundred FPM). In practice, it's an ever-steepening curve down to ten-thousand feet as you do the mental math and fine-tune this energy management curve along the way.

You can't always fly this efficient profile. A traffic controller may lay on a crossing altitude which busts your profile, but you can always salvage part of your ideal profile. In addition, this profile will often allow you to make a surprise crossing point *without* the use of speed brakes, simply by going to idle power early.

If repeated arrivals to some airport reveal a recurring crossing point which affects the profile, you can re-build your profile to accommodate it. I firmly believe that speed brakes should only be used to correct for poor planning on the part of a traffic controller. They should not have to be used to correct for poor planning on *my* part.

Why bother with all of this? I believe that, if I'm going to do the job at all, I should do it as efficiently as I can. Out of curiosity, I once accumulated ten months' worth of my old flight plans. They showed that my profiles beat flight plan times by an average of almost four minutes. They also beat the predicted fuel burn by an average of almost nineteen-hundred pounds. It doesn't sound like much, but it's about two-hundred-eighty gallons. You do the math! I would have been tickled to get a monthly bonus check for the fuel saved!

I should mention that *all* jet aircraft will fit these profiles with very little tweaking. Why a little DC-9 and a huge L-1011 will *both* coast down at fifteen-hundred feet per minute at two-hundred-fifty KIAS at *idle* power requires a deeper look at aerodynamics than we need right now.

Our old Piper Aztec climbed at one-hundred-forty KIAS and descended on a six-to-one formula. Like *all* light aircraft, its profiles can be tweaked for more efficient flying. That's the challenge of being a real navigator. If you're too lazy to navigate, just stay with the published speeds and profiles.

And I'll beat you every time!

Chapter 21 | Flying Dignitaries

I have carried dozens of well-known people over the years and it's usually interesting to meet them. A few stick in my mind as outstanding for one reason or another. I have mentioned Teddy Kennedy. Well, 'nuff said about that.

Patricia Neal was pre-boarded in Atlanta for a flight to JFK (Kennedy International Airport in New York). She had a traveling companion and they both stepped into the cockpit to greet us. She was, of course, suffering from the stroke which ended her great career. She spoke and walked with some difficulty, but still had great poise and a warm charm. The whole crew gathered to greet her and tell her how much we enjoyed her work. Her response was genuine, open, and very charming. I had always admired her work, but now fell in love with this very courageous lady.

We seated her at a window with her companion on the aisle. She read a magazine as the other passengers boarded and nobody tagged her for an autograph. I doubt that most even recognized her. We worked hard to give his lady an extra smooth ride to New York. She remained seated until other passengers had deplaned, then came forward. I got a hug and a kiss as she handed me a note of thanks. The note, with her shaky signature is still stapled into my logbook.

Another note which is also stapled into my log is from Evel Kneivel. Boarding in Ft. Lauderdale one day, our agent informed me we would be a few minutes late. He said we were waiting for a passenger who had arrived on time, but was being held up at the security-screening checkpoint. Standing at the door, I chose to make the P. A. (Public Announcement) to our seated passengers. I promised a short delay and an on time arrival in Atlanta.

After some five or six minutes, one of our agents escorted an out of breath Evel to the door. He was very apologetic for the delay and begged me to let him make a P. A. to the passengers to tell them it was his fault and not Delta's. I handed him the mike. He was hilarious. He made his apology and took all the blame for not allowing enough time to get past the screening. He said, "I'm carrying so many pounds of steel rods, nuts, bolts, and screws (in his body) that I always set off the metal detectors. Your agent told these people who I am, but they were still trying to decide whether to strip search me. I told them it was not gonna be a pretty sight, 'cause, naked, I look like Dr. Frankenstein's monster." He walked the whole aisle, shaking hands and apologizing to people for the few minutes of delay. Kids got autographs and

240

he handed out picture cards. He was a master showman, and also a helluva nice guy.

I'm not a fan of Jimmy Carter but his mother, Miss Lillian, is a real piece of work. This old Southern lady was tough as nails and spoke her mind. While the Ayatollah Khomeini held our diplomats prisoner in Tehran, Jimmy hid in the Rose Garden and sucked his thumb. Reporters got a hold of Miss Lillian and asked what she thought should be done. She didn't mince words or hem and haw.

"I think I'd put a couple million dollars on his head, an' see what happens," she fired back.

Whoa! Jimmy's minders whisked her away and reporters never got another chance to ask her opinions about anything. I carried this grand lady and her Secret Service chaperones from Bangor to Boston. She was spry, charming, feisty, and quick as a whip.

A humorous meeting happened one night in Charleston. We landed one Friday night around eight p. m. Because it was to be a fairly short layover, we stayed at a hotel on the airport grounds. Upon checking in, we noticed the place was packed. It turned out to be an Air National Guard weekend. We needed a bite before sleeping and the lounge bar served great burgers, so the crew did a quick change and met in the lobby. Our Flight Attendants all elected to do a 'slam-click' and order from room service.

As the three of us entered the lounge, it was clearly packed and very dark. After our eyes adjusted, we spotted a table big enough for about six people. There were only two guys seated there, so we went over and asked if we might join them. One of the men waved at the empty chairs.

"Sure, have a seat," he said,

A waitress soon appeared to take our orders. When she turned on her little flashlight to write on her pad, we could see the faces of the two guys we had joined. We were about to enjoy our burgers with Paul Newman and Tom Cruise! I hastily asked if they would prefer their privacy. Both assured us we were welcome and they asked if we were Air Guard pilots. We told them we were an airline crew and asked them what brought them there. Turned out they were to be racing (a Porsche, if I recall correctly) in a local event.

They were both very friendly as we chatted, so I decided to ask if they would mind if we invited our flight attendants to meet them if they promised not to ask for autographs. Both readily agreed. I went out to the lobby and grabbed a house phone. One of them answered.

"Hello?"

"Hi, this is Jerry. I'm in the lobby and we're down in the lounge having dinner with Paul Newman and Tom Cruise. We were wondering if you might like to come down and meet them."

"Yeah, right, nice try." CLICK.

Other calls followed a similar script, so I walked back in and sat down.

"So, are they coming down?" one of my crew asked.

"Well, no," I answered.

"Either these two guys are not interesting enough for them to get dressed again, or they just don't believe me."

Newman and Cruise both laughed and one of them said, "You look like an honest guy. I wonder why they don't believe you!"

The next morning my crew met in the coffee shop for breakfast. Again, we sat at a table with Newman and Cruise. As we finished, our flight attendants all walked in to get cups of coffee to go. They all did a great imitation of deer in the headlights as we got up and said goodbye to Paul and Tom, wishing them good luck in their race.

In the hotel shuttle bus, our flight attendants rode silently most of the way to the terminal. Finally, one spoke. In exasperated tones, she asked why we had not introduced them to Newman and Cruise.

"I called all of you last night and none of you seemed interested." I answered,

More silence. I've never understood why flight attendants are so suspicious of pilots.

Another interesting gentleman was Prime Minister Fukuda of Japan. He came aboard in Atlanta for a flight to New York La Guardia. He separated from his retinue to step into the cockpit and greet us. He impressed me as a very dignified man, yet was also quite open, relaxed and friendly. He noticed that I had been making an entry in my logbook and asked if he might sign it. I promptly handed it over. I can read his bold signature, but not the Japanese characters which follow it.

On a Sunday evening flight from La Guardia to Portland, Maine, I once noticed we had only one passenger in First Class. In Portland, I was surprised to say goodnight to James Cagney. He was cheerfully cordial and thanked me for a nice flight.

A very young flight attendant asked if I knew that "very nice old man."

"No but that's Jimmy Cagney," I answered.

I got a blank look.

Oh well….

The next week in La Guardia, I mentioned Cagney to our gate agent.

"Oh, he's aboard every Sunday evening," he answered. "He's doing a one-man matinee show every Saturday and Sunday and then he flies home to his farm near Portland. He'll be aboard tonight."

As he deplaned in Portland, I stopped him to ask a question. "Mr. Cagney, whatever happened to the *Swift*?"

"The *Swift*, the *Swift*. What's that?"

"The old sailing pirate ship you had moored in front of your home in Newport Beach."

"Oh, *that* old thing – I gave it to the Sea Scouts. How do you know about the *Swift*?"

"Well, sir, I grew up in Newport Beach, and remember that boat in front of your house."

244

"Well it's a small world. You made my night recalling that old boat. Thanks for the nice flight."

He shook my hand and, then, walked off with a jaunty step, chuckling and shaking his head.

Chapter 22 | Crew Relations

Dealing with "Events"

Within a few years after the Northeast merger, things were pretty well settled. Pilots from both companies had formed friendships and worked well together in crews, but there were exceptions.

One Captain, whom I shall call Gene, was a leftover from the days of engineer-mechanics. When the airline decreed that all crew should be pilots, he had been forced to undergo pilot training. The results were not spectacular.

Copilots were encouraged to watch him and a few were known to have taken the airplane away from him. One very talented copilot, with whom I always enjoyed flying, told me about such an event. Gene hadn't the good sense to thank this man for keeping him out of trouble, but complained to our Chief Pilot instead. The copilot got an evening phone call from the Chief Pilot. He was asked if it was true that he had usurped the Captain's authority by taking over Gene's airplane. He admitted that he had done so.

"Good boy! Good night," the Chief Pilot said and hung up.

Another copilot got even for Gene's bad temper in a hilarious way. Many of our rotations would start in Miami and end, days later, in Ft. Lauderdale, sometimes the other way around. To avoid the hour shuttle ride one way or the other, many pilots made arrangements to have their cars delivered by a later crew to their arrival airport. They could then drive straight home after their flight arrival.

Arriving in Ft. Lauderdale at around one thirty in the morning, this copilot had his plan in gear. The Flight Attendants had scurried off and had picked up the shuttle voucher ticket for the ride to Miami.

He gathered his bag and turned to Gene with a parting comment.

"Gene, you're the biggest horse's ass I've ever been stuck with for three whole days. Good night!"

As he marched off, Gene followed on his heels, proclaiming that he should not be spoken to with such disrespect. He was still chewing on the copilot as they piled into the shuttle bus. Just before the driver began to pull out, the copilot spoke to him.

"Gene, shut up a minute, 'cause I've got to tell you something."

"What?" Gene shouted.

"You left your bags on the airplane."

247

"Oh, goddam it!" Gene yelled. "Gimme that damn voucher."

With the shuttle voucher in hand, so he would not be left, he dashed back into the terminal. Minutes later, he dashed back out with bags in hand and piled in. All the way down I-95 to Miami he ranted at his disrespectful copilot.

Reaching the crew parking lot in Miami, everybody scrambled to get out and away from Gene. The copilot made a time-out hand signal and told the spluttering Gene to give the driver his five-dollar tip. Gene dug out his wallet and handed over the tip while resuming his tirade. Again, the time-out gesture.

"Gene, I've got one more thing to tell you."

"What?" Gene fumed.

"Your car is in Ft. Lauderdale. Good night."

Whoops of laughter echoed around the parking lot. Gene had to bribe the driver to take him back to his car up in Ft. Lauderdale.

The copilot, who engineered that spectacular coup, getting Gene so mad that he forgot where his car was parked, was a great guy with whom to fly. I shouldn't reveal who he was, but I can give a hint. His initials are Bill Arnold.

Some Thoughts on Pilots of Other Ethnic, Religious, or Gender Persuasions

In general, most pilots don't care about these so-called issues. We live in a world where performance and ability are what matter. Flying ability cannot be identified with any of the above categories.

From my high school days, I recall Paul Mantz expressing his opinion about Amelia Earhart. She hired him to teach her how to fly her Lockheed Electra. He said she was flighty, unstable and would not listen to the advice he gave. She collapsed the gear on her airplane in Hawaii because he could not convince her to stop jockeying throttles to deal with crosswinds. Mantz was not knocking women pilots, per se, because he went on to say that women pilots such as Jackie Cochran or Pancho Barnes would have been able to complete a successful round-the-world flight.

In 1940, Jackie Cochran went to England to fly for the British Air Transport Auxiliary (ATA), and also was part of "Wings for Britain" crew that delivered American built aircraft to Britain. In June, 1941, General 'Hap' Arnold was placed in command of the U. S. Army Air Forces (created from the U. S. Army Air Corps) and was finally convinced by the winning performance of women pilots ferrying those military aircraft to England. Cochran's squadron was called the 319th Women's Flying Training Detachment (WFTD). Lt. General William H. Turner also began using another woman's piloting skills. Under Gen. Turner's tutelage, test pilot Nancy Harkness Love created a proposal to free up more male pilots for combat roles, leading to formation of the paramilitary Women's Auxiliary Ferrying Squadron (WAFS) in September, 1942. Jackie Cochran eventually became head of the Women's Air Service Pilots (WASPs), formed in July 1943, merging Cochran's and Love's Squadrons.

Even earlier than that, four women got together in the fall of 1929, writing to every licensed female pilot in the United States — all one-hundred-seventeen of them — to create an organization of licensed women pilots. The name eventually chosen was The Ninety-nines, because ninety-nine responded to the letter.

I'm an honorary member of the Ninety-Nines Flying Association. I knew one of them, Thelma Cronin. As a young WASP, Thelma flew every WWII aircraft we produced. The WASPs delivered new aircraft to bases around the world. Thelma told about delivering new Bell P-39 Air Cobra fighters to our Russian allies. Having flown solo a couple of thousand miles to a remote field in Alaska, she was met by a nineteen-year-old male Russian pilot. The Air Corps had decided it was too dangerous for a woman to fly another twenty miles across the Bering Strait to Siberia! I guess he didn't know that another woman, Harriet Quimby, was the first person to fly across the English Channel in 1908.

Our dear friend Ruth Jacobs is in the Guinness Book of Records. Her husband, Jim, an old Alaska bush pilot, encouraged her and she became the only person to have flown a light plane, solo, around the world, landing on every continent. Is Ruth a competent pilot? It would appear so.

My wife Dotty retired as a Captain on the Boeing 727. Now, I flew that airplane for eight-thousand, seven-hundred

250

hours and saw pilots who ranged from excellent to passable. An Academy classmate once said, "If a minimum standard wasn't acceptable, there wouldn't *be* a minimum standard." I flew with Dotty enough to observe that I never saw anyone, man or woman, handle the 727 *better* than she did. She just happens to be one of those people who are "naturals."

Dotty once came home, upset about harassment from "those men," who didn't think she deserved to occupy the left seat. I told her the men were not her problem. The real men were all for her. It was the insecure "little boys" who were the problem. Thereafter, she ignored the little boys.

Blacks are still under-represented in aviation. The situation is improving for them, but still rather slow. I happen to know a number of excellent black pilots.

One was Leon Clark, with whom I personally flew a lot. I always enjoyed working with Leon because he made my job easier. He was an excellent pilot who I did not have to "keep an eye on" and he was a gentleman to be around.

Anyone who still harbors a prejudice against the abilities of a black pilot needs to read about the Tuskegee Airmen, or see the movie. The experiment to train black pilots early in WWII was an abject failure. Why? it was, because the experiment was aimed at proving that blacks were too dumb to train to fly.

Dotty and I have met a number of the few still living Tuskegee Airmen at various air shows. These quiet, dignified gentlemen established a war record which is quite literally impossible. Their 332nd Fighter Group flew P-51 Mustangs.

Over a thirteen-month tour of duty, their job was to escort and protect our bombers over Germany against Luftwaffe fighters. How well did they do? I said that their record was impossible. No bombers escorted by these men were lost to Luftwaffe fighters, not *one*! Many of these men died to create a record that no other fighter group even came close to matching. Yet, when these men came home to America with chests covered with medals, no airline would talk to them.

I pray that Americans will continue to outgrow such foolishness. Good people and good pilots come from every ethnic and gender background. My dear friend, Captain Steve Berman, said that he once enjoyed a special and unique status. He claimed he was Delta's "token Jew pilot." Then, they went and ruined everything by hiring more Jewish pilots! Poor Steve!

Chapter 23 | Other Adventures

Flights into Montreal offered a great layover downtown, with lots of interesting places to see and fabulous restaurants. The only roach in the soup was running into the occasional Quebecois attitude about the French language. The battles to make Canada English were won almost two centuries ago. Yet Quebec still fights the battle to remain French. Imagine the people of Louisiana insisting on "French only" today. When people from Quebec visit France, they are laughed at for their provincial accent, yet they persist and can be quite arrogant at it.

In town, this attitude produces only occasional annoyance. In flying, it can be deadly. The worldwide language of aviation is English for a number of reasons. America and England produced the bulk of aircraft and did more of the pioneer flying and worldwide airline routes require a common language to function.

I'm reminded of a story told by one of my wife Dotty's old classmates. This gent is now a retired Army Brigadier General. The story takes place at a NATO reception. Officers from many countries stood about in groups, enjoying cocktails. A French general approached a group of them, carrying his glass of wine and stood listening. Finally, he spoke.

"I notice that we are always speaking English at these affairs, never French. Why is this so?"

Surprised by his arrogant question, the group fell silent. An American General finally broke the silence.

"Well, it may have something to do with the Brits and Americans and Canadians and Aussies and New Zealanders all getting together and fixing things up so you wouldn't have to learn German." Ouch!

I have a dear friend, retired Air Canada Captain Pierre Charbonneau who has worked to address this problem. He is French Canadian by birth. His family has been in Quebec for over two hundred years. His mother, whom I loved, always referred to herself as French, never as Canadian.

The problem with this stubborn attitude, when applied to aviation, is that it erases the safety feature of a common language. Air Traffic Controllers in Quebec — and particularly at the Montreal airport — mixed English and French, depending upon who they were addressing. Pierre fought to stop this dangerous practice to the point of getting death threats.

How is this practice dangerous? Humans make errors. Airplanes, zipping around a busy airport, create a traffic situation which can be compared to a roomful of people engaged in an intimate square dance. The Air Traffic Controller serves the function of the dance caller. If all the dancers are attuned to his calls, the steps run smoothly. What would the room look like if he made a call in a language only one group understood and which ran one group into another?   Here's what happened when one of them did that to me.

We were approaching Montreal during one of their winter blizzards. Traffic was backed up as they struggled to keep runways cleared. We were put into a holding pattern at around sixteen-thousand feet. Others were in this stack, but hidden in clouds. Flights would be peeled off the bottom of the stack to make instrument approaches and everyone in the stack would ratchet down a thousand feet.

Flying a holding pattern, a racetrack, is easy... and boring. Crews engage in idle chitchat. A professional pilot learns to listen to radio calls and create a mental picture of the other flights around him. It becomes almost an unconscious habit. He may be in conversation, but one ear is attuned to what the controller is saying to traffic around him.

As my crew idly conversed, our controller alternated from English to French. I speak some Spanish, but the only thing I can say in French is Coupe de Ville, probably because I once owned one. As I relaxed, the controller said something in French. I still do not know what it was that suddenly galvanized me to grab the yoke, trip off the autopilot, and quickly drop about two hundred feet off altitude, but just as I did it, an Air Canada DC-9 slid over us two hundred feet above. We only got a quick glimpse through some breaks in the cloud. Our Controller came over immediately with excited instructions to descend to the next thousand-foot level. In *English* too!

He had put the Air Canada flight into the stack at *our* level. I 'rogered' our descent to the next altitude, then asked him, "How do I say, in French, I'm very sorry that I f--ked up?"

The next voice over the radio was a different one and he apologized in English. The error made by the first Controller is not unheard of and would be easily caught with everybody speaking English. Since I don't speak French, I still cannot explain what triggered my alarm bell.

My language can be explained, because it does tend to slip into gutter words when I'm really pissed off. I know it's a character fault and I'm still working on it.

Fate is the Hunter — beat ya once more!!

Flying through a hurricane can be an interesting experience, too. Eloise had pushed up into the Gulf Coast area as we departed Palm Beach for Tampa and then on to Boston. Weather was nasty, but flyable — barely. Thunderstorms, heavy rain and gusty winds still covered Florida. My log shows two hours of moderate to heavy turbulence, which persisted until we finally got far enough north on the leg to

Boston. From Boston, we flew to Washington, D.C. and, then, on to Atlanta.

By the time we arrived in the Atlanta area, Eloise had also arrived. Another hour of moderate to heavy turbulence greeted our arrival and followed us into the inevitable holding pattern. By the time we were finally peeled off the bottom of the holding stack, approach weather was advertised as a five hundred foot overcast with east-southeast winds gusting to thirty-five knots. Well, that didn't sound so bad. We had good surface visibility below the clouds and the wind not too far off the heading for runway Nine Left. The ride wasn't much worse than running in the Baja Race down a Mexican highway at a hundred or so.

Getting a much-needed cup of coffee was out of the question as we ricocheted around on our vectors to reach the Nine Left ILS approach course. Crossing the Outer Marker and bracketing the glide slope signal, I was mildly curious as to why it was taking a heading of one-hundred-forty to one-hundred-fifty degrees to stay anywhere near the ninety-degree Localizer course. *Must be some much stronger winds up there than down at the surface*, I thought. At five hundred feet, we dropped out of the clouds and had a good clear look at the airport. I was looking down runway Nine Left through my *side window*! The tower had said nothing throughout our approach beyond "Cleared to land."

"Ask 'em for the wind," I said. My copilot, John Thomas, made the call. The Tower radioed back, "Winds one-hundred-eighty degrees at sixty, gusting to seventy knots. What are your intentions?" John and I just looked at each other. A dead crosswind at seventy knots and they didn't say anything till we *asked*?

I just shoved the throttles up and John cleaned up the flaps and gear as we went around. Clearly nobody was going to land there any time soon. Departure Control put us in another holding pattern. The radio was inundated with calls for clearances to alternate airports. Company Radio to Flight Control was also overwhelmed.

We did some laps in the holding pattern before Departure Control called to give us an Expected Clearance Time, which was about forty minutes away! At low altitude, we were guzzling about twelve-thousand pounds of fuel per hour. A quick check with Engineer, George Mason, confirmed that we no longer had enough fuel to mill about that long. We needed to go someplace.

John and I conferred. We agreed that, with these winds, we needed a north-south aligned runway. Augusta, Georgia, had what we needed. Calls for a clearance to AGS (Augusta) produced only promises that "We're working on it."

John and I agreed that we should just go, before we faced a low fuel problem. We headed out of the holding stack and dropped to Visual Flight Rules altitude of fifteen-thousand-five hundred feet, heading direct to Augusta. Our call to the Tower at Bush Field produced a surprised clearance to land.

We parked amid a large gaggle of other diverted flights. Many had arrived with very little fuel left. We still had over an hour's worth remaining. We would not have been so comfortable had we stayed in a holding pattern over Atlanta. While it was outside of our Operations Specifications to operate a jet under VFR rules, it was perfectly safe to do so. Clue to young pilots: when the system is 'broke,' do whatever it takes!

Another weather experience with a nasty crosswind occurred one night in Portland, Maine. We arrived in the area with the Tower reporting good visibility, but a heavy wind from the south at thirty-five knots gusting to forty. That meant a dead crosswind for the active runway 11 (on a one-hundred-ten degree heading). The runway was reported to be snow covered with patchy ice and they could offer no braking action report. My copilot, Fern Forrest came from Northeast Airlines. He was an experienced and solid pilot and I was glad to have him with me that night. We discussed whether to make a landing, or go on to Bangor. Most of our passengers were for Portland, so we wanted to get in if it was possible to do it safely.

I had about four-thousand hours in the Boeing by now and Fern had a lot of time in it as well. The B-727 has a lot of capabilities and we were both comfortable with is characteristics. Against a decision to go in were a couple of factors. Runway 11 sloped a bit downhill and ended in the harbor. Not good, especially with no report on braking conditions. With a south crosswind, we could come in over the harbor and land to the west on runway 29. That would offer some uphill slope and a flat run-out area off the west end. Another factor was sort of a Catch-22. The Boeing has a max-demonstrated crosswind component of nineteen knots. That's not actually a limit, nor is it the most the airplane can deal with if handed skillfully. The published number is sort of a "weasel way" for Boeing and the FAA to avoid actually committing themselves to a published limit. What it really says is that, if you operate beyond this number and slide off a runway, we will all point our fingers at *you*!

A word here for young pilots. The rest of you can skip ahead. Light plane pilots are taught to handle a crosswind by putting a wing down in the flare and using the rudder to align with the runway. This works because a light aircraft carries very little momentum and is quickly pushed sideways by a crosswind. A large and heavy aircraft should be handled differently. First, its low wing does not allow much wing down before you start curling the outboard edge of your flaps on the runway. The second and subtle factor has to do with momentum. Remember old Isaac Newton? He was a clever fellow. He told us that a body in motion tends to stay in motion until acted upon by an outside force. So what does that have to do with landing in a crosswind? Well, a one-hundred-fifty-thousand pound airplane, approaching at one-hundred-forty knots, carries a hell of a lot of momentum. It's going to take quite a bit of force and some time to change the track it's on.

A heavy airplane, tracking in alignment with a runway, carries momentum which wants to stay in alignment, right down that runway. Flying an approach with a heading crabbed off, to correct for a crosswind, has nothing to do with the track that momentum is following. The point is that if the crab-angle is carried into the landing flare and ruddered out to align with the runway just before the wheels touch, the crosswind has little time to exert side forces. The aircraft momentum remains aimed down the center of the runway, but it does require some fine timing.

Fern and I decided to make a "look-see" approach to runway 29 with a planned go-around. We wanted a look at the runway surface condition. In addition, we wanted to see if we had enough rudder to kick us into alignment and hold us from drifting for long enough to make a solid touchdown. Passengers were advised that we would not land on the first approach and that we were only going to get a look at the runway.

The flight was lumpy. At two-hundred feet, I ruddered into alignment and added enough power to sail down the runway for a good 'look-see.' Our track held well and the runway looked dry with some bare patches showing. We cleaned up on the go-around and looked at each other. We both nodded. I asked our Engineer, Russ Harlow, if he was comfortable with making a landing. He nodded.

"Go for it," he said.

Fern and I worked it out that, before I pulled power off, I would call out "Land" or "Go-around." He would reach across and deploy the speed brakes as soon as the wheels touched. That would put our weight firmly on the landing gear. It would also allow me to keep my hand on the throttles and pull them into reverse as soon as the wheels touched.

As we neared the runway, the tower began chanting out wind speeds. Over the runway, I kicked in some rudder and called "Land" just as he chanted forty-five knots. He was trying to help, but it was just a distraction. Our plan worked like a gypsy charm. It took only light braking to turn off at a mid-field taxiway.

This account is not particularly unusual. It's offered as an example of what the line pilot will deal with from time to time. If you do it right, nobody says anything. If you don't, you make headlines. It's all part of the package.

An event which is not supposed to be part of the package happened one night while leaving the Dallas Fort Worth (DFW) airport. Myself, Copilot Terry O'Donnell and Engineer Bob Fredrickson shared the cockpit on that night. We had a crystal clear sky and a bit of moon as we taxied out behind an American Airlines B-727 for a south takeoff. Our flight would be heading east to Jackson, Mississippi. Lifting off right after the American flight, we were handed off to Departure Control. They responded that we were in radar contact and asked if we had the American in sight ahead. Terry was flying. I handled the radio and answered that he was in sight.

"Keep him in sight and expect diverging headings," Departure said.

"American 123 turn left heading zero-nine-zero, Delta 1027 turn left heading zero-nine-zero," he called a minute or so later.

We both acknowledged and turned east at almost the same time, since Departure had given the two instructions in one sentence. We were now climbing parallel to each other and about two miles apart. Our initial climb clearance was to ten-thousand feet. Probably due to our lighter weight, we were climbing slightly faster than the American B-727.

Climbing through about seven-thousand feet, we appeared to be level with him. Having been told to "expect diverging headings," we were waiting for a turn to the left or to hear him given a turn to the right. He was clearly visible off our right wing.

"American 123, turn *left* to zero-four-zero degrees," the Controller called.

Both our heads snapped to the right as they acknowledged the turn.

I had just enough time to shove my left elbow against the yoke and call out, "Look out! Here he comes!!"

We had pushed over at about eighty-four-hundred feet and, seconds later, he flashed out of sight directly over us and, boy, he was *loud* going over! It was over so fast there was no time for fear, only anger.

I grabbed the mike and yelled, "What the hell were you doing giving American a *left* turn?"

I expected to hear something along the lines of, "I'm sorry, I goofed." Instead, the Controller fired back, "You were told to keep him in sight!"

Our anger boiled!

"Well, we did that!" I yelled back. "That's why we're still able to talk to you, but I never expected to have to dodge him after you aimed him at us."

Another controller, probably the supervisor, came on the radio and argued that we were "not where we were supposed to be." Still no apology. I asked for a phone number and we carried on to Jackson.

Fuming mad at the stupid mistake and then the bullshit about it afterward, I knew they were going to play c. y. a., so, once again, I pulled the voice recorder and flight recorder circuit breakers. In Jackson, I had mechanics pull both tapes and forward them to Atlanta. My phone call to Dallas produced more b. s. I couldn't speak to the controller because he had been relieved and sent home. Yet, the supervisor would not admit that he had made a blunder.

"Then, why the hell did you send him home?" I asked.

More b. s. All I wanted to hear was a simple apology. The event was over. Nobody got hurt. It was close, but that only counts in horseshoes, hand grenades, and nukes. The supervisor hinted that he thought we "may have been flying too fast." I told him to go to hell and we headed for our hotel. We filed a NASA Near Miss Report.

A day after the rotation ended I got a call from Pat "Mother" Malone. As you may remember, Pat was our resident expert on Operations Specifications and Federal Air Regs and she was a court recognized *expert witness*. "Mother" could quote those heavy books by paragraph and sentence, verbatim. She taught the classes. Most pilots kept her phone numbers inked in their Jeppeson books. She advised us that Dallas had filed a violation against me. They had decided, in their cover-your-ass mode that I *had* to have exceeded the two-hundred-fifty knot speed limit to have caught up to the American flight.

The explanation of how we caught up is quite simple. Stand behind someone and ask them to starting walking. After they have taken two paces, you step off behind them. Now, on command, both of you turn left 90 degrees and keep walking. As soon as you both turned left, you have caught up. You're now even. I asked Pat if she had yet reviewed the flight recording.

"Oh yes, Darling," she answered. "You never got over two-hundred-fifty knots. I'll call them and tell them we have the recorder and voice tapes and that will end it."

I was mad as hell all over again. I told Pat that I would like for her not to tell them we had the tapes. I asked her to let it go to a hearing, so I could stuff it down their throats. The bastards had screwed up and now wanted to blame me! All I wanted from them was a simple apology. Pat said it wasn't worth the trouble, but that she would properly "stuff them" with the recorder evidence. That was the last I heard about it.

Hint to young pilots: Don't expect everybody to be honest about mistakes. When you face an "event," keep all the notes and evidence you can. I've been accused of being a cynic. Not so. I'm a *realist*. A cynic expects everybody to be dishonest. A realist just knows that *some* are dishonest.

Chapter 24 | Anatomy of an Accident

The subject of accidents is not a pleasant topic, but I think that a book of this sort should include some discussion of it to be complete. The public is always horrified at the report of a major crash and properly so. Every person with feelings is shaken by a mass loss of life. A major airline accident is always front-page news. Unnamed sources can always be counted upon to speculate about the cause and hint darkly about some pilot blunder.

Official findings by the National Transportation Safety Board (NTSB) will not appear until months, or years, after the event. They will not be published by CNN or Fox or any of the others. By then, those findings will be old news. The media will have fresh tragedies to hold our attention and sell soap flakes or appliances. Paul Harvey tells us a tale and, then, goes to a commercial. When he comes back, he says,

"…and now, the *rest* of the story," and, then, tells the punch lines that bring the tale together.

With airline accidents, the public rarely learns the rest of the story. It's usually only working pilots who learn what really happened, so, in an effort to educate, I will share a story with you. It's painful to write this account because I knew the crew and many of the flight attendants. It's been some thirty-four years since Delta Flight 191, a Lockheed L-1011, approached Dallas Fort Worth (DFW) airport in a thunderstorm. The crew consisted of Captain Ted Connors, Copilot Rudy Price, and Engineer Nick Nassick. Ted's reputation was solid. He was known to be cautious. Rudy had flown with me on the B-727. I know, first hand, that he was a talented pilot. I also knew Nick to be well qualified. So, what happened?

First, I must set the stage. The vast majority of accidents are the end result of a chain of events, rather than some single factor. DFW airport grounds are bigger than Manhattan and Texas can brew up some monster thunderstorms. Such storms can produce what have come to be called "microbursts." This phenomenon has only been studied by meteorologists for a couple of decades. The mechanism that produces a microburst is still not completely understood, nor are they predictable. What happens is that air rises in a thunderstorm, cools, condenses, and begins to fall. This usually produces the rain we are used to. Occasionally, however, this cold, wet air mass falls in a concentrated, dense column, straight down. It can be so tightly packed that it may be only hundreds of yards in diameter. This column carries tremendous weight and travels at high speed. Since it cannot penetrate the Earth, it must spread out violently as it hits the surface. To see what happens in miniature, climb a ladder and dump a five-gallon bucket of water on your driveway. Observe carefully how the water propels to the sides. Now imagine the force of a three-hundred-yard wide column falling like your bucketful of water.

The outflow from that column is a horizontal gust of wind. An airplane approaching this column feels, first, a strong headwind and, then, a strong down draft under the column. The real killer follows, a sudden and powerful *tailwind*. The momentum of a large aircraft cannot be altered in only a few seconds, so what the airplane experiences is a sudden *increase* in airspeed quickly followed by a sudden major *loss* of airspeed. The speed that mass of airplane is traveling over the ground is meaningless. It's only the speed of airflow over the *wing* which matters.

DFW is so big that weather at one corner can be different from its opposite corner. Major differences in wind from one corner to another are a good indicator that some local phenomenon is at work and it could be dangerous.

Radar cannot see air, but it can see *raindrops* in the air. Doppler radar can sense the speed of these drops and thus report the wind speed. DFW had a Doppler radar system in operation. Four corner units compared their sensors with a central, master unit. Differences beyond a set threshold triggered an alarm, which indicated the possibility of wind shear or a microburst.

Pilots familiar with DFW are aware of this system. It's comforting to know that it would warn of major wind discrepancies. DFW also had a dedicated weather radar and observer. Traffic control radar is not capable of painting weather very well, so it's comforting to know somebody is watching a weather unit. Now, the stage is set.

Ted and crew were vectored by Approach Control toward the ILS Approach Course. They were flying through light rain, so they had no visual cues. Rudy was flying on instruments. Everything was going as expected on a rainy day. They knew they were spaced behind a Learjet. <u>Link one of the chain.</u>

The Doppler radar wind shear detection system had been popping alarms so regularly that it had become annoying, so it had been turned off and nobody thought this fact was important enough to mention to the crew. <u>Link two of the chain.</u>

The dedicated weather radar observer had taken a lunch break, so nobody was looking at the scope, again, not important enough to mention to the crew. <u>Link three of the chain.</u>

The Learjet had landed and its shaken pilot radioed the tower. "You've gotta shut down this approach. We almost lost it. We lost forty-knots in seconds out there!!"

Because Ted was still beyond the outer marker and had not been handed off from Approach Control to the tower frequency, they didn't hear the report of danger from the Lear. When he did shift over to the tower frequency, he was given a clearance to land and nobody saw any reason to pass on the warning from the Learjet. <u>Link four of the chain.</u>

The flight was at low altitude and close in when they flew into the microburst. Voice and flight recorders both proved that Ted and Rudy reacted to the first gust almost instantly, both realizing what that sudden increase in airspeed meant. Pushing the throttles to full power, they flew through the core and suddenly hit the tailwind on the other side. The Flight Recorder showed a major loss of airspeed in only three seconds. Already too low to trade off some altitude for needed speed, even with engines at full power, there were simply no more options left to recover the major loss of airspeed and momentum needed to fly out of that downburst. With turbulence bouncing the airspeed all over the dial, they still managed to hold the airplane at the edge of a stall with the "stick shaker" triggering off intermittently. This is now the recommended technique for such a recovery, so they were already doing everything that hindsight says they should have done. They were simply victims of *Fate is the Hunter.* Had they been a few hundred feet higher when they encountered the microburst, they likely would have been able to fly out of it, but they simply ran out of time and altitude.

The airplane touched down in open terrain and lifted off again, struggling to fly. An engine struck a car on a perimeter road as the plane settled onto the grass east of the runway. At this point, the accident would likely have been survivable for most of those aboard, but there remained... <u>link five of the chain.</u>

As they skidded over the grass, ahead of them sat a large, round, steel water tank. With no way to steer, the impact was head-on, and massively violent. Having done everything correctly, they were still victims of an unbroken chain of events. Had any of the first four links been broken, Ted would have abandoned the approach early enough to escape.

Immediately after the accident, I looked at the plan-view of the airport on the back of page 11-1 of the Jeppeson manual. I could find no depiction of a water tank. It's there now. I have always wondered if Ted thought he was aimed at a clear, flat strip of grass.

A preliminary report by the NTSB tried to lay most of the blame on Ted. An outraged pilots' union forced them to acknowledge "mitigating circumstances." The flight recorder preserved a clear record of speeds, altitudes, headings, g-loads, aircraft configuration and more.

The real tragedy of Flight 191 was that after everything was digested and understood and procedures put in place to recover from a microburst, they could see that Ted and Rudy had *already* followed those *exact* procedures!

They programmed a simulator to duplicate the conditions encountered so that pilots could practice a recovery. Very few succeeded in flying through that event without crashing the simulator. It took me six tries to fly a successful recovery and I *know* that was just a random fluke. What they faced was simply *not* recoverable. Yet, the FAA tried to blame Ted to cover all four of *their* procedural failures!

So... now you know "the rest of the story." Rest easy, old friends. It wasn't your fault.

Chapter 25 | The L-1011 Checkout

I had logged eighty-seven-hundred hours in the left seat of the B-727. Sixty more hours would have made it a year in the seat. It was time to move up. In 1987, I reported to Atlanta in mid-August for ground school on the Lockheed L-1011 Tri-Star. It had earned a reputation as a great airplane. Its pedigree came from the design shop of the genius Kelly Johnson and his Lockheed Skunk Works. To a pilot, that pretty much said it all.

For those who have never heard of Kelly Johnson and his Lockheed Skunk Works, I'll offer a quick sketch. Johnson was a genius of an aeronautical engineer. He was also a management genius. He set up his shop so that, as a new aircraft was built, the designers' offices were in the same building. People could walk from the assembly floor directly upstairs to an engineer's desk and say, "Come down here and show me."

His products included the fabulous WWII P-38 Lightning fighter. The Japanese called it the "Forked Tail Devil," as it had twin engines and twin booms supporting its tail. Major Dick Bong – the highest scoring ace in American history – shot down 40 Japanese planes with his P-38. Captain Thomas Lamphier shot down and killed Admiral Yamamoto (the architect of Pearl Harbor) with one. Kelly's P-80 Shooting Star was the first Air Force jet and first to down a MIG-15 in Korea. His F-104 Starfighter was the first fighter which could accelerate to supersonic speeds while climbing straight up. It was called the "missile with a man in it." His great four-engine Constellation has already been mentioned. Kelly's C-130 cargo plane with 4 turbo-props has been in production now for over sixty years simply because there's nothing else that can do what it does so well. He built the U-2 spy plane, and then its successor, the incredible SR-71 Blackbird. The SR-71, built in the 1960s, cruised at three times the speed of sound (Mach 3). Today, it still remains the fastest plane ever built.

This is the pedigree behind the L-1011 Tri-Star, in which I was about to check out. I was excited about the chance finally to get my hands on this thoroughbred. The more I learned, the more I marveled at the engineering genius that went into this airplane. She had none of the faults of her sister Jumbo, the DC-10.

Controls on a ship this size simply require that they be moved by hydraulic power. That immediately raises a question in the mind of a pilot. *What the hell am I gonna do if the hydraulics fail?* Nagging at the back of his mind, a pilot sees a horrific scenario. He sees himself pushing and pulling on controls that are no longer connected to anything! This nightmare ranks about number two, behind having a wing fall off!

Well, never fear... Lockheed is here! Lockheed pioneered hydraulic boost way back in the late 1940s on the old P-80 and T-33. They also used it on the L-1049 Connie and the C-130 (L-100) and the Electra. All of these aircraft allowed for manual control in event of hydraulic failure. Input forces were extremely heavy, but Lockheed engineers cleverly calculated what the adrenalin levels would be. They concluded that pilots, motivated by fear, would have no problem moving the almost locked controls.

I recalled a day from my past in the Training Department. A few of us experimented with flying the L-100 with all the boost packs turned off. The controls felt like they were set in concrete and the plane was barely flyable. We were obviously not motivated enough. We knew the boost could be restored with the flick of some switches. For the L-1011, Lockheed had obviously spent considerable time pondering this question.

Their solution was clear genius. They installed *four* hydraulic systems. A combination of twelve engine-driven and electrically driven pumps powered the four systems. Control surfaces (ailerons – rudder – elevator) were powered by multiple systems in such a way that loss of any THREE would still leave the aircraft flyable. As a cherry on the banana split, they also added a ram air turbine (RAT) which powered a thirteenth pump. The RAT nestled in the belly on a spring-loaded arm. If a sensor ever detected a loss of pressure in all four systems, the RAT would slam down and allow airflow to spin its turbine. Therefore, if by some incredible chance one should lose all three engines and find oneself suddenly at the controls of the world's biggest *glider*, that glider would be fully flyable! Okay, okay, I'm sold!! I'll buy one!

It's difficult to convey, especially to a non-pilot, the incredible level of sophisticated design genius which went into this airplane. It's almost unfair to use an accident to illustrate the point, but it may be the only clear way to do so.

I doubt there is anyone who was living at the time and was over five years of age who cannot recall the vivid horror of watching a United DC-10 crash land at Sioux City, Iowa. More than half of the passengers survived the crash and break-up of this DC-10. The events leading up to the landing attempt lasted long enough for film crews to be on hand to record it. The failure which caused this event suddenly and without warning rendered this DC-10 totally un-flyable. The eight-foot diameter, spinning, forward fan turbine wheel on the top-mounted center engine, suddenly disintegrated. Pieces of flying shrapnel cut into the top of the fuselage. They severed all three hydraulic lines powering the elevator and rudder. Douglas engineers had, incredibly, laid all three lines together down the top of the fuselage!

Captain Al Haynes and his crew now faced a pilot's worst nightmare... no control! With help from a deadheading instructor pilot, they somehow coaxed the crippled plane to Sioux City. Using differential power from the two outboard engines, they incredibly juggled forces to coax the plane toward a runway. As they neared safety, they were unable to keep the left wing from dropping. It touched first and the aircraft tumbled down the runway and broke up.

Any pilot will attest that Captain Haynes having gotten that airplane anywhere near a runway was a totally impossible piece of flying. That airplane in the condition that it was should have become uncontrollable and broken up long before they got to Sioux City. That crew performed as professionals. They did not give up. Their skill, impossibly, saved more than half of their passengers. They earned every bit of the praise laid on them.

The sad point of telling this story is that had they been flying an L-1011, the entire drama would never have happened. Lockheed engineers, probably thinking in terms of battle damage, spaced the four hydraulic lines to these critical controls around the fuselage. A disintegrating engine could have cut, at most, the two upper lines. The Tri-Star would have flown on to a no sweat, engine-out normal landing.

One small mistake in design philosophy made all the difference. Redundancy (belt *and* suspenders!) is how a total failure is avoided. Three hydraulic systems to power a control follows this philosophy. Then, to place all three lines together in a vulnerable place defeats the whole point. Engineers are prone to think in terms of *What are the odds of such-and-such happening?* They tend to be pleased when odds are reduced to, say, one in a hundred thousand. Pilots think more along the lines of *What do I do* when *it happens?* We know that if a thing is possible, it will happen. The proper question becomes not if, but when. As I studied the L-1011, I grew more and more pleased and excited. Lockheed engineers clearly thought like pilots.

I find no procedure in the manual to deal with a wing falling off, but then, no other builder has one either, so I guess that's too much to expect. Everything else in the 'not-good' list seems to be covered by redundancy or a well-designed procedure. I was really itching to fly that beauty!

However, first came the simulator practice and check ride. The sim has full motion and full visual presentation. Therefore, all training, including the rating ride, would be conducted while still "bolted to the floor." I was surprised that the sim flew so beautifully and wondered if the airplane really flew the same!

Some perception adjustments were needed. The nose gear on the B-727 is just about under the cockpit door. On the L-1011, it's back under about the fourth row of seats, some forty feet behind my seat. Swinging my butt out over the grass to line up on a runway seemed a bit odd at first, but after a couple of times it seemed natural enough.

Landing, with my eye-level some fifty feet above the runway when the wheels touched, was another mental hurdle. I'm amazed that it began to look normal after some half dozen repetitions. Learned from Captain McBride years ago, my habit of looking at the far end of a runway to judge small pitch changes helped there.

The sim sessions were a real workout. Emergency procedures, abnormal landings, and other drills were hammered in. As all the new stuff fell into mental slots, I found that I actually had fun. I found that flying the sim didn't actually feel any different than flying the B-727. If anything, it seemed even more responsive, with no perception that it was more than twice the weight of a B-727, over five-hundred-thousand pounds of massive gross weight. I still harbored the suspicion that the actual airplane couldn't possibly handle as smoothly and quickly as that sim and I realized that was probably guarding against being disappointed by the real thing.

Rating Ride Day came around and I was excited. I take some pride from the fact that I'd never busted a check ride and that string is now over fifty-nine-years long. I also admit that some degree of ego is at work there, at least as a motivating force, but, ego doesn't account for success. The answer is really quite simple. The way to face a check ride or *any* test in life is first, to be prepared. There's no point in facing any test if you haven't learned the material. Then, it must be accepted that there is no such thing as a check-ride without mistakes. The successful approach is to have confidence that you can do what others have done, picture some of the dummies who have already succeeded and see them doing it wearing only their underpants, stay mentally relaxed enough to deal with the unexpected and recognize your own mistakes and correct them. You're going to make 'em. Just expect them, catch them, and fix them. If you know what you're doing, you're not going to make any big killer-blunders, so don't waste mental energy worrying about it.

I have seen literally hundreds of check rides, both as instructor and as a trainee. The only people who busted were those who allowed some small, almost inevitable, error to get to them. They allowed their minds to latch onto a small failure, blow it all out of proportion, and erode all their poise to carry on. We have all watched a football team come apart, usually over some fumble or busted play. It's sad to watch. When we see it, we all know the game is over. They may as well head for the showers. The truth is that losers may still have egos, but ego has no power. Only a solid, *earned* pride has the power to push one on to success. That's from where the "I will not quit" mindset comes.

The Rating Ride was a breeze and, now, I would soon lay hands on the real airplane. Classmate, Captain Dan Baba, was the Instructor on the ride up to Huntsville, Alabama. I shot six landings and fell in love with the L-1011. It handled like a dream. Lockheed built such a "feel" into purely hydraulic controls that the plane could be handled like a sports car using only my fingertips. It almost seemed to go where I was *thinking*. I've flown dozens of different aircraft over the years. Few ever felt so completely natural.

Chapter 26 | The L-1011 "On the Line"

Flying the L-1011 on the line was great fun. Routes ran from the Orient to Europe and Alaska to Puerto Rico, lots of variety from which to choose. International flying and Domestic flying were in two different departments, each with their own chief pilot. International routes paid incrementally higher rates. However, there were some International routes under the Domestic umbrella. Flights to Canada, Mexico, Puerto Rico, Bahamas, and Bermuda fell under the Domestic Department.

I have never enjoyed long, overwater flying. My idea of fun flying is with hands on the controls. Takeoffs, approaches, and landings require flying skill. Sitting for eight or ten hours, watching a Flight Management System navigate across the ocean is not my idea of fun. *B-o-r-i-n-g*. At the end of that safari, somebody got to make a landing and, then, you were in a five-hour time zone change and possibly even in

France. Pilots flying such routes might average four or five landings a month.

On the other hand, a flight to Puerto Rico might take a shade over three hours. It offered international pay, no time zone change, a hotel on the beach, friendly people, good food, and a nice swim in warm water... and you're *not* in France. How can you beat that?

Puerto Rico flights offered another opportunity for fun. I have cruised the Bahamas since the early 1970s and have lots of Bahamian friends. Passing overhead, I could call and visit with them, using a portable VHF Marine radio. These little radios only have about three Watts output power, but I once got a good lesson on the importance of antenna height. I wanted to call a friend who was the caretaker on Musha Cay and could not recall his radio "handle," so I just called "Musha Cay (pronounced key)" about four times. I finally got a response, "This is the Miami Coast Guard – who's calling *mayday?*"

Holy Cow! They are over two hundred miles away and "Musha Cay" sounds like *"Mayday"* to them! "Negative *mayday!* Negative *mayday!*" I answered. Three Watts sure goes a long way from thirty-five-thousand feet!

Charter flights are often fun, because passengers are part of a single group and are off to some exciting location. I once picked up a double run from Atlanta to Nassau. Two loads of sales winners for Snapper Comet lawnmowers were scheduled.

The Flight Attendants for such charters usually come from the very junior reserve pool. I briefed the cabin crew and pointed out that the flight was only an hour-and-a-half, not much time to serve over three hundred people. The last meals had been served as we started down over Grand Bahama Island. Nearing Nassau, they were scrambling to secure the cabin. They needed some time and Nassau Approach Control was perfectly happy to have us do a "sightseeing lap" around the island. I know the island well, so was able to give a good narration as we circled once around counterclockwise. At the end of the lap, our cabin crew still needed a couple more minutes, so we did a clockwise lap for our right side passengers. Our deplaning passengers raved about the "tour!" Empty, we hustled back to Atlanta for our second load. As passengers boarded, I was approached by their coordinator, carrying a clipboard. He said that everyone was very excited and looking forward to the great tour around the island! I was astonished. I think my mouth fell open.

"How did you know about that?" I asked.

"Oh, our first group called to tell us about it. They loved it. So, we're all excited too!" he answered, Well, we were there to please, so, obviously, we had to do it again. Nassau Approach also loved it. "Mon, we t'ink all de airlines should give dey people a look at our be-oo-ti-ful island home."

Months later, Dino, dock master at Nassau Yacht Haven, asked me about the day he saw a huge L-1011 circle the island four times. I pulled his chain a bit. Told him I was trying to get his attention and that he should pay more attention to his radio. I had the hook in him for a couple of minutes, but I couldn't keep a straight face and finally had to tell him the truth. Flights to Bermuda were great fun.

We got the occasional layover. The islands are very beautiful and "Veddy veddy British, old chap." Navigating to Bermuda, or missing its dangerous reefs, used to be a major challenge for sailors. The Spanish were not the greatest navigators and were also very superstitious. After the Spanish Admiral Bermudez wrecked his whole fleet on the outlying reefs, the Spaniards gave the islands a wide berth. They believed the "Devil Islands" moved around in the ocean. Their fear of going anywhere near the islands resulted in British control. When the second fleet of colonists for Jamestown also wrecked on Bermuda's reefs, survivors were able to settle there simply because the Spanish avoided the place. It is possible the FAA believes some of the Spanish superstition about the islands moving around, because their rules require a line check for Captains to fly there. I flew to Bermuda for years, yet have never had a line check to the place.

My first flight out there on the B-727 actually came as a surprise. I had hurriedly filled in a bid sheet one month, looking mostly at dates and paying scant attention to destinations. I had a copilot from Northeast. Going through Boston we had time for lunch and chanced to meet the Boston chief pilot. My copilot introduced me. In idle conversation, he asked where we were going next.

"Bermuda," I answered.

"Have you had a line check?" he asked.

"No. Why?"

"Well, you're supposed to have a line-check," he answered. We were due out in about forty-five minutes and, since I worked for the Atlanta chief pilot, I just shrugged. I told the astonished Boston chief that I had flown there in the Air Force and for Capitol Airways. I added that, unless the islands had moved sometime in the past twelve years, I was fairly confident that I could find them again. Happily, they had stayed right where I thought they were.

Years later on the L-1011, a scheduled check pilot simply failed to show up as we stopped in Atlanta. With a full passenger load and looking forward to dinner in Bermuda, I just went on. Yup, the islands had again stayed put.

There are legitimate safety concerns to be considered when flying overwater to a small island, but finding the place is no longer one of them. Years ago, on an Air Force flight from Spain, we used celestial navigation to approach from the east on the right latitude. Navigation is no longer the primary concern. What must be considered, now, is that the island has only one long runway. A thunderstorm or an airplane sitting in the middle of the runway with a buckled landing gear could close the airport, so you need to carry enough fuel for some delay in the area, plus enough to reach an alternate airport and the only alternate airports are clear back on the mainland. Fuel planning has become the primary concern. Water landings with airliners are not exactly prohibited, but you can only do it once and there will be lots of awkward questions to answer later.

For pilots who fly overwater, I'll share a little known tidbit about the use of your HF (high frequency) radios. Some thirty years ago, there was an international conference to "clean up" all the Marine HF frequencies. I took the HF off my boat to the shop to be re-programmed. When I got it back, I noticed that there were no longer any frequencies with decimal numbers, for instance, no 4592.7, just whole numbers like 4593. Overwater aircraft usually have fully synthesized HFs, which can tune any whole number. Each of the new Marine bands — 2, 4, 6, 8, 12 Mega Hertz (MHz) — have two or three ship-to-ship frequencies and they each have a Coast Guard frequency. Did this mean what I think it did? Yes, Virginia, you can talk to an ocean liner from thirty-five-thousand feet, or to the Coast Guard in event you have some reason to do so.

Now, the Federal Communications Commission would frown on an airline pilot having a midnight chat with a tugboat captain on the Mississippi or a shrimper out in the Gulf. *If* I were ever to do such a thing and *if* they ever found out about it, they would really fume over a call to friends on their sailboat in the Bahamas. Of course, I never did any of those things.

If you have ever operated a Marine HF, you would have noted that a call sign such as "Sundowner Whiskey Papa Alpha six-seven-four-two," doesn't sound like it's coming from your cell phone. I only mention this as a point of interest, not as any sort of suggestion and, since you pilots are not supposed to use your HFs like that anyway, I'll refrain from listing those "secret frequencies," which are only available from any marine electronics shop anyway.

On a serious note, in an emergency, FCC rules allow that you may broadcast on *any* frequency, even on TV. So, if you wanted to tuck a page of Marine frequencies into your Jeppeson book, just for emergencies… well, why not?

One of the rewards of flying is the eagle's eye view of some of the spectacular geology of our Earth. I will always be able to pull up memories of flights to Anchorage, Alaska where approaches from the south funnel descending flights right down Turn Again Arm.

Back in the 1670s, Captain James Cook surveyed this area. With his Lieutenants Bligh and Vancouver, he searched for a Northwest Passage. As he sailed up one fjord after another, they each came to a dead end. By the time he ventured up the one leading south from Anchorage, some frustration was apparent. Reaching its end, he had to come about once more, so he named it Turn Again. Incredibly beautiful glaciers spill into this rugged looking fjord. Dozens of flights down this gap never presented the same picture. Time of day and sun angle always painted a new view.

Most of my flights to Anchorage included a hotel layover and a chance to explore the town. However, one schedule was a turnaround and presented an interesting compression of time. Riding from the hotel in Portland, Oregon, we watched the sun set over the mountains. Our takeoff was in the dark. Climbing toward the northwest, the sun rose again to the west and gave a view of the rugged coastline all the way to Alaska. A spectacular sunset followed us in the descent down Turn Again Arm. It was a night landing in Anchorage. After a snack at the airport restaurant, we took off in the dark for Salt Lake City. As we climbed to cruising altitude, we were treated to a lovely sunrise in the northeast! We were all hungry upon arrival in Salt Lake City, but, after two sunsets and two sunrises in some ten hours, there was some confusion whether to order breakfast or dinner. Oh, well, it still beats eight to five in an office cubical next to Dilbert.

An airline pilot may fly hours and hours each month and earn all his pay in a few short minutes. Arriving in Atlanta just after sunrise, those night flights from the West Coast often presented one of the most difficult instrument approaches there is. Any low visibility instrument approach requires that the crew pay attention. Weather conditions vary widely and the problems presented by those conditions determine the degree of "pucker factor."

At night, or under deep storm clouds, you can expect to get a good look at the string of lead-in lights and, then, runway lights, or at least pick up their glow through the rain or snow. The worst condition, however, is bright sunlight in fog. There are no contrasts. The world looks like the inside of a ping-pong ball in daylight. That condition happens when night cooling causes condensation fog over the airport.

In Atlanta, this fog drifts up from lower land to the east and south. It may be only one-hundred feet thick, allowing a fairly clear view of the land as you fly over and look down. Once down in it, with the low morning sun in your face, it's a different story trying to see horizontally through it to pick out lights and runway features.

The L-1011 is certified for CAT III flying. That means we're legal for approaches when the Runway Visual Range (RVR) is down to six-hundred feet. There is no decision height. The fog can be right down on the runway. At our approach speed — around one-hundred-forty-five knots — you can expect to see objects about two-and-a-half seconds ahead. The L-1011 was our only aircraft certified to do this. It required *two* three-channel autopilots. That is, elevators, ailerons, and rudder. Both autopilots have to be engaged. In addition, an auto-throttle was required to hold a pre-set speed. Working through a computer, this system would Auto-Land. It flew the approach, made the landing flare, reduced power to idle, and steered down the runway centerline. Sounds like a snap! Just latch in some switches and let her bring you home.

Well… it's not quite so simple. You see, it's supposed to do all this magic, but someone has to watch what that gee-whiz gizmo is doing. No one has yet built a computer with a sense of self-preservation. The guys operating this thing have to be mentally capable, not just keeping up with it, but staying ahead of it. There are some pilots who will never get hurt in an aircraft accident, because they're always five to eight miles behind it! Check rides do a pretty good job of weeding out those types who should never be allowed to play with gee-whiz toys... or sharp tools.

That gizmo's not a kitchen appliance. You don't just turn it on and watch it work. A thorough crew briefing is required, well before the approach begins. An experienced captain will make sure his copilot and engineer are part of a *team* operation. The captain will stay head-down to monitor instruments and autopilot performance. At the latter stages near the runway, the copilot will keep his eyes outside for visual cues and call out what he sees.

Some pilots try to perform both these functions. Bad idea! You're dealing in seconds and few people, over the age of about ten, can refocus their eyes from distance to arm's length fast enough to gather meaningful information from outside and an instrument panel at the same time. It's far more efficient and safer for two people to divide these areas.

What about the engineer? We may tease him and call him "the plumber" at times, but on the above sort of approach, his role is vital and where a three-man crew really has the edge. The instrument panels of the captain and copilot are going to display information from *two separate* ILS receivers. The displayed information should always be identical. Sitting centered behind the two pilots, the Engineer is the *only* one who can monitor both panels and, because his eyes are five or six feet from the panels, he can easily refocus from inside to outside rapidly.

A smart Captain will wrap up his briefing by making certain that both the copilot and engineer understand that they have the authority to *command* a go-around any time something doesn't look right. There may not be time to question or explain a discrepancy and a go-around only costs some time and fuel. The time spent explaining, rather than acting when something looks wrong, can cost a helluva lot more!

How does this all play out? We'll pick up the chatter at two-hundred feet above the runway. This will all take about three seconds.

Engineer: "Two-hundred feet to touchdown."

Captain: "We're centered."

Engineer: "One-hundred feet."

Copilot: (as we dive into the fog) "Threshold lights passed."

Engineer: (reading Radio Altimeter) "seventy-five feet. Fifty feet."

Copilot: "Edge lights. We're centered."

Engineer: "Forty feet, thirty, twenty, ten, touchdown."

Copilot: (as Captain pulls Ground Spoiler lever and, pulls the throttles into reverse) "On centerline, one-hundred-ten knots. On center, ninety knots."

At touchdown, the Captain is looking outside, but the Copilot continues to call cues. As the aircraft slows, both are watching for the blue turnoff lights. We're down in good form and headed for the gate.

Piece of cake! Anybody could do it.

Chapter 27 | Some Bad News

I have omitted scenes of personal life from this story as they are irrelevant to the subject. However, a life-changing event hit me in 1991. I had a long-term solid marriage to a wonderful woman. We had no children as a result of a childhood fever which resulted in her having blocked tubes. Efforts to fix the problem failed and we adjusted. We worked and played happily together.

Joyce had spent three years with thirteen different doctors trying to discover why she often suffered back pains. I'll skip a long story here. She was finally diagnosed with pancreatic cancer. An operation proved too late. The prognosis was death in four to six months. Devastating news!

I knew I had to stay with her, becasue I could not function, flying around thousands of miles away while she faced the end alone. Carrying passengers safely demands that your mind stays focused on the business of flying. I realized that I simply could not do that in the face of what was happening at home and Joyce deserved my care and constant presence, for whatever time remained. Major conflict.

I tried to get a leave of absence. No luck. A clever and compassionate Chief Pilot offered some good advice, so I took a disability leave. A psychologist agreed that I could not perform safely with the burden of my wife in terminal condition. There were a few who challenged my decision, claiming that I should be able to fly by setting other concerns aside. To these few, I responded that any man, who could put aside his wife's imminent death at will, was someone I had no desire to know, or with which to fly.

I'd discovered that the most difficult condition for me to accept is the realization of total helplessness. I have always been an action-oriented person. Every challenge in my past was surmountable by hard work and study. If I put in enough effort, I felt I could control the outcome. Wrong! I knew this was something I couldn't fix. Knowing it and *accepting* it, however, are two different things entirely.

I stayed with Joyce and cared for her. During that time, I didn't yet have the tools to help myself, while I did a good job of caring for her. For two and a half years I "medicated" with alcohol. I was always functional, but used alcohol to relieve stress. We beat the doctors' guesses. Joyce remained fairly functional for two-and-a-half years. The end came quickly and she died at home on September 10th, 1993.

I was a mess. I turned my home over to a Canadian friend, Pierre Charbonneau, whose boat was on my dock. I had to get away. After loading my boat with one hundred and fifty cases of beer, twelve cases of rum, and some food, I sailed for the Bahamas. Over a five-month period in company with a friend who lived on his boat with his wife, I proceeded to drink it all.

By March of 1994, I had decided I could find no answer in my current behavior and that I might as well go back to work. Leaving the boat in care of my friend, I flew home. After renewing my medical certificate, I informed the company that I was ready to return to work.

"Okay," they said, "but we want you to see our doctor in Houston because you've been out over a year." (Actually, almost three.)

On June 28, 1994, I flew to Houston, met the doctor, passed his physical and went to a hotel. The next morning, the phone rang. It was the doctor. He asked that I return. Back in his office, he slapped a paper on his desk.

"This is your lab report," he said. "How much have you been drinking?"

"Quite a lot after my wife died," I answered, "but I'm back to normal now."

"What do you call normal?"

"Only four to six beers a day."

"Well, I think you are an alcoholic, and I want you to go into a rehab program."

Strangely, I was not shocked. My immediate feeling was one of acceptance, possibly even relief. I was not yet ready to admit to being alcoholic, but I did know there was a problem.

I had been in control my entire career and had rigidly separated flying and drinking, but I did know that the periods prior to and after Joyce's death had not been normal. For the first time, I had doubts about my control, so I was ready to listen.

The doctor made arrangements for me to enter "post-grad drinking school" (as I called it) at South Miami Hospital two weeks later. On the flight home, a flight attendant offered me a beer. I declined in favor of a Coke. Arriving home, I opened a utility room refrigerator and pulled out a Coke. As I sat sipping my Coke, I was suddenly surprised to realize that I had actually not wanted the beer on the flight, nor one from my own refrigerator, which got me to thinking. Perhaps I should get rid of the case or so in my refrigerator, perhaps not. I was very curious about this strange and sudden lack of any desire. Two weeks rolled past as I awaited entry at South Miami. The beer remained in my refrigerator, but I felt no desire to pick one up.

I'll shorten the story of my recovery by saying that I *am* an alcoholic, but apparently a very odd one. It took a long time to accept that my decades long "control firewall" which separated flying and drinking, was alcoholic behavior. The very act of thinking that consciously planning while drinking is okay is proof of alcoholic behavior. Normal drinkers don't have to control and plan when a drink is appropriate.

I have now been sober for over twenty-five years. According to AA friends, I am an oddity. From that day in the doctor's office in Houston, I have felt no desire to drink

295

and I'm comfortable in the company of people who are drinking. The desire simply has gone. I still can't explain why that is so and claim no credit for it. I cannot point to some epiphany or event to explain it. It just happened. All I can do is accept it and thank my Higher Power for it.

Chapter 28 | Some Good News

To continue my story, I must back up a bit. Joyce and I had developed a habit of leaving our ketch-rigged sailboat, Paladin, in the Bahamas after a vacation cruise. It was cared for by my friend Graham and his wife Jeannie. Those six to eight month periods allowed us to fly back to the Exumas (as district of the Bahamas) for a few days when time allowed.

In 1988, we went out to the local island airstrip for a flight home. A fairly regular service was run by a charter company, operating a Piper Navajo, a ten-place twin-propeller, aircraft. On that day, we arrived to see a very beautiful blonde woman in uniform, doing her walk around on the Navajo. I introduced us and gave her my airline card. She gave her name as Dotty and readily agreed to my request to occupy the right seat. I had never ridden in a Navajo and was curious to learn about it. Joyce was seated back to back behind our beautiful pilot. Lively three-way chatter occupied us for the hour-and-forty-minute flight to Ft. Lauderdale.

I realized early in the flight that this lady was a very accomplished pilot. She "wore" the aircraft very comfortably and set it down in Ft. Lauderdale like a feather. I was suitably impressed.

Driving home, Joyce gave me a knowing grin and asked, "You really liked that girl, didn't you?"

"Who?" I answered, always quick on the uptake.

"The pilot, silly," she said, rolling her eyes.

"Oh, yeah," I replied. "I thought she was very nice."

Joyce gave me one of her patented "I know you" grins. "Well, I thought she was a *doll*! I'm going to invite her to our next party," she said and she did.

Months later, it was time to bring the boat home. I recruited three pals from our sailing club to make the four-day run home. Finding no flight available for the day we needed to go, I called Dotty. She agreed to a rental flight in her own Piper Seneca. Since one of my crew could not get free until that afternoon, it would be a late flight and Dotty would have to stay aboard and fly back the next day.

Joyce briefed her, explaining that she would have the forward bunk and head to herself, where to find bedding and towels, etc. On arrival, we took the boat out of the marina to an anchorage near Graham and Jeannie's boat. A party on the island was set for the night, with crews from a couple of other boats. We had time for a nice swim. Dotty is a blond Norwegian/Swede. She looked great in her flying uniform. In

298

a bathing suit, she was spectacular. The four of us fellows tried to act like gentlemen, but we could not help ogling. Dotty pretended not to notice and. I felt sure it was not the first time men drooled over her. She flew out the next morning, back to work.

Back to my timeline. I returned from my binge in the islands in March, 1994 and it was time for my Canadian friend to return home. Those dear friends, Pierre and his wife, Lise, had been lifesavers. We discussed my future and we all agreed that I should not expect ever to replace what had been lost with Joyce's death. Nobody got that lucky twice. Nevertheless, I had reached a point in my recovery where I desired some female company.

My thoughts turned to Dotty, the beautiful blond pilot from six years previously. I kept a half-inch stack of business cards near the phone, which I sorted periodically to keep the size down. Those of no use got tossed. Others were dropped in a drawer. Dotty's card was still in the stack after six years. Hmmm.

I thought, perhaps, she would like to go to dinner with me, so I began to tap in her numbers, but a little voice chimed in. *"This is silly. You haven't seen her in six years. She'll be remarried or have a boyfriend. You're just going to make a fool of yourself."* I put the phone down.

My visit to the doctor in Houston followed. I entered the rehab program, a four-week "post grad" program in AA. Sometime during that program, I realized that my thoughts often returned to Dotty. I finally resolved that I would make that phone call, just to settle things one way or another.

I was looking forward to a return to flying. The airlines now had a solid program to save the recovering alcoholic. It involved meetings, monitoring, and is very successful. My thought was that, on the remote chance of some sort of relationship with this woman, I had two things to accomplish before I could make that phone call. First, I should be back on my feet and back to the work I loved. Second, I'd need to learn enough about the disease of alcoholism, so I could explain what I was doing to recover in such a clear way that she would understand and not slam the door shut in my face. With that plan of action decided, I set the question aside and got on with the program.

On August 17, 1994, a Wednesday, representatives from the airline HIMS program, including one of my old drinking buddies, gathered for my "graduation." Two days later, Friday, August 19, was my fifty-fourth birthday. I would celebrate by attending my first BOAF (Birds of a Feather) meeting, an AA group open to pilots only. Following instructions to a meeting place across town, I arrived about twenty-minutes early. I introduced myself to some new faces as others arrived. A group of about a dozen men had arrived and stood talking outside. Just as we turned to go in and begin the meeting, a Toyota convertible zipped into a spot beside us and shut off. The door popped open and a beautiful blond hopped out. As she stepped toward our group into the porch light, my mouth dropped open.

300

"Dotty? what are you doing here?" I asked, incredulous.

She flashed a smile that would have melted a glacier. "Oh, I've been in this program for seven years. Welcome, it's nice to see you."

I was stunned. The first thought that flashed across my mind was, *That eliminates number two. I won't have to explain AA.*

The meeting was a fantastic experience with a great bunch of sober pilots offering help, experience and support. Speaking to Dotty after the meeting, I learned that she was a "free woman." I was astonished that meeting her again could have happened in that way and on my birthday, yet! Her open personality and her beauty were more stunning than my six-year-old memories of her. I realized that I was powerfully attracted to her. It surprised me that I felt hesitant to ask her for a date, but I did manage to ask if she might go to dinner with me. She immediately said yes.

Chapter 29 | Back in the Saddle

The airline offered me a choice of attending a recurrent training class, or an initial training class, as I went back to work. I had no yardstick to judge what information may have faded. Wanting to be on solid ground, I opted for the longer initial checkout.

I was gratified and somewhat surprised by how easily my rusty edges polished off. Everything seemed to fall right back into place. One of my instructors, a young woman, made me feel very happy one day in the simulator. I had just finished programming the Flight Management System (FMS) computer. She said, "That was fast. I was scheduled in here today to re-train you on the FMS because nobody thought you would remember the steps. Well, I guess I'm done. Nice job." I saw no reason to tell her that I had reviewed and studied my old three-by-five "cheat cards" prior to the checkout.

I shared simulator time with some Captains who were new to the L-1011. Some struggled a bit learning not to overcorrect on a precision approach. Some pilots just seemed to expect that, because the L-1011 is *big*, it must be horsed around, but it's actually very sensitive and quick to respond to fingertip inputs.

On my second day back in the box, my instructor had me set up to hand fly an ILS approach. I turned to look behind me when I heard him say, "Now you guys watch how this should be done." He had gathered five or six of the new trainees to watch. He leaned over and whispered, "CAT III, keep going to a landing." This approach, flown by hand, would be illegal to do in the actual aircraft, but it is fun to practice in the simulator. Using the old Captain McBride Fingertip Method. I flew to a landing. The old ego got a huge boost when the instructor told his audience, "Only the autopilot is supposed to be able to do that, so don't try it on the airplane."

My instructor was complementary in our after-session briefing. I could not resist pulling his leg. I told him that I thought it was no big deal and that my wife could probably do the same thing with a bit of coaching. That got a huge laugh. So, I told him that she was coming up to visit tonight and offered a ten-dollar bet that she could fly that approach if he would let me bring her to the next day's session.

"I'll coach her some tonight," I added.

He fell for it. "You're on for ten bucks," he said, laughing. "It could be fun to watch."

I coached her on the L-1011 that night. Next day, I introduced her to my instructor. He seemed a bit surprised, probably didn't think I could *get* a wife, especially not one who looked like Dotty. He grinned cheerfully as we got her set up in the seat. The grin slowly faded to puzzlement and, then, slack jawed amazement as she smoothly slid down the ILS to a nice landing.

I tried to milk the gag a bit more. "See, all it took was some coaching. Anybody could do it. You owe me a ten." Dotty gave it away when she started laughing.

"I think I've been had," he said, so we 'fessed up and let him off the hook, explaining that she flew the B-727.

My check ride, and then a line check, went off smoothly. I was back in the saddle again.

I guess I should back up and explain how Dotty and I got from our first AA meeting to getting married. We had quickly realized that our attraction was mutual and powerful. About six months passed between leaving rehab and the start of recurrent training. The HIMS program occupies this period with AA and the airline group meetings. This, with satisfactory performance, leads to a provisional medical certificate, which allows a return to flying. A period of two to five years of probation follows. Ongoing AA and "coached" meetings follow weekly. It is a great program and boasts a very high success rate.

One of the AA admonitions advises against starting a new relationship in the first year of sobriety. Dotty and I were seeing each other regularly. We were being very careful to keep things from becoming intimate, a concession to avoid mistakes. It was not easy. I repeatedly drew flak in aftercare meetings for seeing her. I was not about to shut her out, because I knew that our feelings were solid and right.

I finally got mad during a meeting and let fly. "That advice against a relationship is not a goddam rule, it's a suggestion, based on the assumption that a drinker has screwed up a marriage. I had a great marriage. I know what a good marriage looks like, feels like, and smells like. I did not screw up a marriage. I was not divorced. My wife *died*. I intend to keep seeing this woman, so why don't you people, especially those of you who are divorced, just shut the hell up and tend to your own business, which is staying sober!" That was the last I heard on the subject.

Dotty and I carried on cautiously. We came close to heading for the bedroom one evening. "I don't want to start us off on an affair," I told her, "because I think I might ask you to marry me at some point."

"Yes," she said.

"I'm not asking you to marry me," I responded.

"I know, but I said yes, so that's settled."

"Oh. Well then, I guess it's a good idea to show you a year sober, first."

"Okay, but I'm not concerned," she answered.

Five months later, she announced that she was tired of waiting. So was I. On the dock in my back yard, we had a nice ceremony, with family and friends flying in from all over.

Best move I ever made, even though I can't claim any credit for how it happened. It really is possible to hit a jackpot twice, through sheer dumb luck, or maybe by some Higher-up Power doing the planning.

Three months later, our schedules finally allowed four days off together. We flew to the Bahamas to be on our boat, still in Graham's care. His wife Jeannie had been very close to Joyce and also knew Dotty from her flying to the area. Jeannie had nursed me after Joyce's death. She was a big sister to me, so I asked her if Joyce had ever spoken about Dotty.

"Yes," she answered. "She told me she hoped you might meet her again one day."

Well! Some Power had to be planning that scenario and I'm certain it wasn't me!

Chapter 30 | Back to the Line

Returning to the line was a great relief and a lot of fun. Once again, I realized how much I loved being in the air. I did not even mind the necessity of commuting to work.

Dotty and I often had mismatched schedules and would pass each other coming and going. Sometimes, one or the other of us simply went back out to deadhead along. We knew that the HF radios on our aircraft could talk to each other on Marine "chatter channels" from Alaska to the Caribbean, but, of course, we never used them for that.

We were often able to schedule layovers somewhere together. This sometimes presented opportunities for mischief. Arriving in the Dallas area one day, I heard Dotty check in with the same controller. The controller was operating at a lazy pace with a light traffic load. At a break, I asked if he would mind me calling another flight. He said, "Go ahead."

I called Dotty's flight and asked if she was the Captain. She answered, "Yes, why?"

"Well, I just wondered where you're going after Dallas?"

"We're through in Dallas and have tickets to deadhead home to Miami. Why?"

"Well, you sound very nice on the radio. We're going on to a layover in Salt Lake City and I wonder if you would like to go to dinner there?"

"That's a very sweet offer. Why not?"

"Great. We leave at 1047 from Gate 29."

"All right, I'll be there."

A long silence followed. Finally, our controller came back on.

"Ahem... now that you're set up for tonight, Delta, you can descend to flight level two four zero."

Other voices began to chime in.

"I've seen fast before, but that takes the cake."

"How do you know that she's not fat and ugly?"

"You're a real operator man."

Comments like that went on until the controller finally took over.

"Okay, you guys, that's enough. I never heard a move that fast before, either, but we gotta get back to work now."

One last voice. "Hey lady, how do ya know *he's* not fat and ugly? Good luck!"

It's not that I like to play jokes, but it's just that some opportunities are too good to pass up.

Dotty and I once had a layover in Orlando on the same night. She arrived first and went to a different hotel than we normally used. I had our transport drop me at her hotel. A sweet little old lady watched as I approached her check-in desk in uniform.

"Are you checking in?" she asked sweetly.

"Well, not exactly. I was talking to a lady Captain on the radio today and she invited me to come here and spend the night with her. So, can you tell me what room Captain ------ is in?"

The poor sweet lady got all huffed up. "I can't give you a room number."

"Well, could you call her and tell her the fellow she invited on the radio today is here now and ask her if it's okay to give me the number?"

Deep sigh, but she made the call. Hanging up, she gave me a disapproving look. "Room 322," she hissed.

"Thank you, Ma'am." I said, and about three steps from her desk, I turned and asked, "Were you here when she checked in?"

"Yes, I was," she huffed.

"Was she good looking?"

She turned and marched into her back office. While changing for dinner, I told Dotty about the prank.

"Omigod, that lady is here every time I check in," she said. "What is she going to think of me? We have to tell her the truth."

We stopped at the desk on our way to dinner. Dotty flashed her left hand and pointed to her wedding ring. "This is my husband and he was only playing a little prank."

The lady stared at us a moment. "Yes, of course he was," she whispered sarcastically.

Oh well, somebody has to maintain pilots' wild reputations with the public.

I thoroughly enjoyed my return to the L-1011. My seniority number was now on the first page of our list and this allowed a lot of options. Planned crew rotation pairings changed somewhat on a seasonal basis. Most pairings were three-day schedules of flights. These rotations are published and bid for monthly. The choices are awarded by seniority. Lower seniority gets the leftovers. Flying the same schedule month after month can become boring. Seniority allows a full variety of schedules. Whenever I started to feel a desire for new scenery, I could simply choose a different pairing.

I don't know how many times I've flown over Meteor Crater in Arizona. It was always fun to invite flight attendants up to see it. Many had never heard of it. "See the huge hole that meteor made when it hit, about a mile across!"

"Wow! That's really huge!"

"Yeah, and can you see the hotel there on the north rim of the crater?"

"Yes, yes, I see it!"

"Well, when that meteor hit, it blew all the windows out of that hotel and scared the hell out of everybody."

"Oh, my God, that must have been awful!!"

An invitation to come up to watch a sunset was always good for some humor and flight attendant's comments were always predictable.

"That's just gorgeous! What a spectacular sunset!"

"Well, it was okay, maybe a five or six, but not really spectacular, pretty much a standard sunset."

Such are the ways pilots entertain themselves and combat boredom. I'm still not sure how such harmless humor promotes so much suspicion of pilots among flight attendants.

Because I was based in Atlanta, Ft. Lauderdale was often a layover city. I could go home while my crew went to a hotel. On one such occasion, Dotty mentioned that her crew was ticketed to Atlanta the next morning to begin a flight there. I suggested that she ride with me in the morning, so she did. The next morning our agent boarded her into the first row of seats. The L-1011 has a forward galley sited like an island which blocks passenger view of the cockpit door. On completion of our pre-flight checks, I decided to have some fun. Putting on my hat, I stepped around the galley to view the forward area. Spotting Dotty in her Captain's uniform, I walked over and introduced myself. She stood as I quizzed her about what she flew and where she was going that day. Passengers, mostly business travelers, began to peek over their newspapers to observe us. Finally, I asked her if I could request a small favor. She smiled and nodded.

"I don't want to sound sexist," I said, "so please don't take the wrong way, but I've always wondered what kissing a captain would be like. Would you mind just a small kiss?"

The fist class passengers had fully lowered their newspapers by then and many eyes studied us.

"Well, I suppose a small kiss would be okay," Dotty answered with a smile,

I wrapped my arms around her and gave her a long, lingering kiss. Stepping back, I put my hands on her shoulders. "That was very nice," I said. "Thank you"

I turned and walked back to the cockpit.

Dotty later told me that when she turned back to her seat there were dozens of gaping mouths and wide eyes staring at her. Dotty is a cool lady. She just smiled back and pointed to her raised left hand and ring. "That's my husband. He just can't leave me alone."

In 1996, I was aware that the Company was working on a buyout program to offer early retirement to senior pilots. I was enjoying flying so much that I paid scant attention and had no desire to quit early. Then a big manila envelope arrived in the mail. After opening and reading the many pages, I was stunned. I called my tax attorney and rushed to his office. He scanned the pages for about ten minutes.

"So, what's your question?" he said.

"Well, what should I do?"

"Well, you can keep working for about seventy cents on the dollar and retire with less money, or you can take their offer. In addition, the seven-figure lump sum is only payable to you, so if you die prior to your regular retirement date, it will not be paid to your widow. It's a now-or-never offer."

"Well, hell, that sounds like one of those "offer you can't refuse" deals."

"Yup, that's about it."

I thanked him and left. After explaining the deal to Dotty, I signed my name and sent back the papers.

My last flight was scheduled for November 24th, 1996. My copilot for the month was Bruce Olmstead. Bruce was a great guy to work with. I asked him if he would mind my flying all the takeoffs and landings for my last month.

"Not at all and I don't blame you for wanting to," he very generously replied.

Dotty rode the jump seat for my last three-day rotation. Our first night was in San Juan, where we took the crew to dinner. Dotty learned from my engineer, Steve Fry that he had pulled in some favors to fly the last three days with me. She refrained from telling me until we were back in our hotel room. I was glad she did, because it choked me up to learn that he'd gone out of his way to swap schedules to be with me.

Steve was an ex-Marine flier, and he looked the part. He wore his cap brim two fingers off his nose, wore spit shined shoes and a sharply creased and ironed shirt. He always looked ready for parade inspection. His mind was as sharp as his appearance, always "ahead of the program." Steve was always ready with what I needed before I knew I needed it.

He sat sidesaddle at his panel, waiting out his seniority servitude with a cheerful personality. He's a superior Captain by now.

Pushing back from the gate in San Juan the next morning, I was somewhat puzzled that the tug pushed us all the way out to a taxiway. Then two fire trucks sped up and starting shooting a water nozzle salute over the airplane. This I had not expected. I learned from my crew that the Station Manager had ordered up the salute. I had always made a practice of visiting Ops to chat with our people and practice my Spanish. We had a sharp group in our San Juan Ops and I guess my visits and halting Spanish led to this honor. It was a touching gesture from them and one I shall remember forever.

We flew through Atlanta and on to a layover at home in Ft. Lauderdale. The last day called for a flight to Atlanta, back to Ft. Lauderdale, and a final leg to Atlanta. Since I was based in Atlanta, but lived in Ft. Lauderdale, my Chief Pilot arranged for a relief captain to ride the leg from Atlanta to Ft. Lauderdale and fly the return last leg to Atlanta after I got off.

On my last leg into Atlanta, I carried family with video cameras. Last flights allow a relaxation of some rules, so I was able to have family in the cockpit. My stepson filmed the landing from the cockpit. Unknown to me, Dotty had arranged with one of our agents to film the landing and arrival. This man ran a studio called One Brick Short Productions and he did a superb job. He got one of the best landings I ever made. His film shows about a hundred yard trail of tire smoke where they are just touching pavement but without enough weight on them to spin the tires up to speed. He also filmed the water salute, the arrival at the gate, and the reception. He later sent the film, with all the airplanes I had flown also in it, in a very professional package.

The Chief Pilot met us at the gate, where he presented a large framed photo of the L-1011, with pilot signatures all around the border. Dotty whispered to me that Steve Fry had made a P. A. after my landing.

"Captain Farquhar has just set this four-hundred-thirty-thousand pound airplane down like a butterfly with a sore foot," he told our passengers, "and there aren't many who can do that without you feeling the wheels touch."

He then went on to call up all the aircraft I had flown and the years of work for Delta. All of which I very much appreciated.

We departed from Atlanta for my last leg to Ft. Lauderdale. I had told my stepson, now a captain himself, that the L-1011 was capable of flying at point-nine-six Mach, straight and level, which met with some skepticism on his part. I had forgotten the conversation until he brought it up during our cruise south toward Florida, and again expressed his doubts. I told him to fire up his video camera as I pushed the throttles up. With that number on tape, he no longer doubts what this Lockheed thoroughbred can do!

After landing in Ft. Lauderdale, I was again surprised to taxi between two fire trucks shooting a third water salute.

What a sendoff! We shook hands all around then quietly made our way home for a small party.

Thus, a very rewarding career ended. I served thirty-three and a half years on the line. My greatest satisfaction is that I carried some two-point-five million people and delivered every one of them without a scratch or bruise—and mostly on time.

Dotty and I still flew our trusty Piper Aztec. I still use the flight bag I bought in Frankfurt, Germany, in 1962. It's showing some patches, but looks like it might outlast me.

Chapter 31 | Some Words about Management

The product of an airline is a seat moving from A to B. It's a perishable product. If it is not sold today, it cannot be sold tomorrow. It is sold directly to the ultimate consumer, a traveler. Each customer is handled one on one, either in person or by phone, as he purchases our product. He will be physically with us as his product is being created. For the entire time he is using our product he will be in contact with an agent, then a cabin crew and, then, the flight crew. He or she will judge our product by how (s)he is treated and by how personal belongings are treated.

These facts would seem obvious to anyone who has flown, but I point them out to lay some groundwork. These facts make it clear that our product requires continuous face-to-face contact with our customers. It seems obvious that there is no way a passenger is going to come away from that experience happy and satisfied after a couple of hours in contact with unhappy employees. It's why Mister Woolman counted his employees as his most important asset. If he took care of them, they would take care of the customer. This approach is what built the Delta reputation.

Following the death of C. E. Woolman, other CEOs served briefly before Dave Garrett took the chair. All followed the Woolman formula. Dave Garrett, from 1978 to 1987 was a true leader. He took care of our people and our stockholders. We all prospered. Dave Garrett retired in 1987 and Ron Allen succeeded him to the CEO chair. Delta's real troubles started on that day.

Ron Allen was not a "people person." He had ambitious plans for the airline and he was in a hurry to enact them. His plans would require large sums of money. He inherited a cash-rich business, where almost every piece of equipment carrying the Delta logo was owned by the company.

In his scramble for money, Allen mortgaged everything in sight. Allen's ego made him impervious to advice from a vast well of experience and expertise around him. He knew more than anyone about everything. That type of personality couldn't trust and delegate authority to those below him. He must micro-manage. Such a personality couldn't admit error, so he vented his rage at any bad report upon the bearer of bad news.

I'll provide some examples:

Allen wanted to start service to the Orient. He ordered, against advice from pilots and flight control dispatchers, a fleet of new MD-11 aircraft. There was no way to get those warmed-over DC-10s to carry enough fuel for non-stop flights to Japan, but Allen argued that he could buy three for the price of two B-747s. The MD-11s were a fiasco, often having to make unscheduled fuel stops. Delta lost billions!

Employee salaries became his target for more so-called savings. Delta traditionally promoted from within its own ranks. A young fellow might start as a baggage loader and rise to become an agent, or supervisor and he would know, first hand, what it took to get a plane loaded and out on time. A baggage loader was part of Delta's family and he had a stake in its success. Allen decided these people were being paid too much. If loading service could be outsourced at minimum wage, he could save on salaries and benefit costs. Allen had spent his entire career on air-conditioned "'Mahogany Row." Since he had never spent sixty seconds humping bags in the rain, he could not foresee what was going to happen and nobody wanted to trigger his wrath by telling him.

The baggage handling area in Atlanta sits under the A-Concourse. The building above is supported by rows of two-foot diameter concrete columns. Baggage carts, called "hay wagons," steer by all four wheels, designed so that a train of two or three wagons will track behind the tug like cars on a railroad. With four to six wagons, there is slippage and end wagons will track inside on a turn.

Wagons began to chew up the concrete columns and once pristine, white tugs and wagons began to look like they had gone through WWII. City Engineers began to notice the chewed up columns. It was bad enough that they warned about a weakening in structural integrity if it continued, the engines on the tugs were failing because nobody bothered to check radiator coolant. Tugs and wagons looked and performed like junk. Why? Because part-time crews just didn't give a damn. This didn't happen when Delta's own baggage loaders were still employed.

A hidden cost was the abnormally late departures on bad weather days. Dozens of part-timers would look out their windows at pouring rain and wind and say, "Screw it," so weather days would always be worked with short-handed crews. Were salary and benefits savings large enough to offset higher upkeep costs on our beat-up equipment and to offset passenger anger over late departures and missed connections and a higher lost baggage rate? I don't know and I'll bet Allen didn't either!

Allen saw the higher salaries paid for senior, experienced mechanics and maintenance supervisors as another target for savings. He forced top ranks to take early retirement and the results became quickly obvious.

There was no inherent fault with the L-1011, but more and more delays for maintenance problems cropped up. Any aircraft flown ten to fourteen hours daily is going to require constant attention. Some of the Rolls Royce RB-211 engines on the L-1011 had been in service for eighteen years! I call that reliable! However, it was an inherently complex aircraft with hundreds of systems and subsystems. With thousands of

320

parts, there is always going to be a failure rate, which will require replacements. Such failures are normal and were not the root cause of an increase in departure delay times.

The cause was the longer time it took less experienced people to do those regular maintenance chores. Allen would not admit that those growing rates were a direct result of his decision to lop off the senior people, so he blamed it on the only cause which could not be his fault — the airplane had to be at fault.

A perfect example of his micro-management happened one morning in Ft. Lauderdale. Boarding about a half-load for Atlanta, we discovered that the two forward toilets would not flush. This function was controlled by a computer system called a multiplexer. It had a glitch. Most of our passengers would be making connecting flights in Atlanta, so I told our agent that I would make the P. A. to inform passengers to use the aft "blue rooms" and that we could placard the forward rooms as "inop" and leave on time.

"No, we cannot dispatch with the forward two 'inop,'" Ron Allen said, because he was on a recent flight with friends when that happened and he was embarrassed. Therefore, we now had a directive that we could not dispatch without fixing them. I couldn't believe that Allen's meddling fingers had bypassed Flight Control, the Maintenance Coordinator, the Minimum Equipment List, Local Maintenance, the Agent, and the Captain!

I wrote him a memo, noting that, because some moron had put out such an edict, we had departed an hour and a half late. Passengers had missed connections. The aircraft and crew were re-routed for three days. With a prior alert, Atlanta Maintenance could have solved the glitch in a few minutes. Only fourteen passengers would have had to walk a few extra paces to an aft blue room. I suggested he might want to look into the identity of the moron who had thrown a wrench into the established functions of our appropriate departments. I never got a response, but the stupid order was cancelled. He may have suspected that I already knew who the moron was.

Maybe that's why he never invited me to Thanksgiving Dinner.

The sad truth is that Ron Allen had no respect for the loyal people who made the company function and he especially despised the pilot group, the people who actually guided planes through all weather and built the best safety record in the industry. They stood at the bottom of his list. He never rode in a cockpit and had no concept of what we did. Worse, he didn't want to know. We were overpaid bus drivers to him and his disdain was returned. I never met an employee of any group who had a good word for Allen.

In 1997, his high-handed attempt to bypass a Board decision and fire an executive finally became too much and the Board fired him. Unbelievably, things got even worse. We were saddled with Leo Mullin. Coming from a banking background, Leo knew enough about the airline industry to call a travel agent when he needed a ticket somewhere. His ego was a match for Allen's and shielded him from any doubts that he might not know what the hell he was doing. Leo piloted a once successful Delta into bankruptcy court.

Of course, neither Allen, nor Mullin were in any way at fault for this sad situation. All blame lay with overpaid employees, high fuel prices and upon any doorstep but their own. Thus, they fully earned the millions with which they lined their pockets before bailing out.

It cost some two-hundred-million in lawyers' fees to convince a Federal Judge that a decades-old contract for retirements didn't really mean what it said. Through no fault of Allen or Mullin, it would now be necessary to terminate all pilot retirement benefits and, since they bore no blame, it would be okay for them to keep the millions with which they walked off.

Since I spent half-a-century earning that pay, I am not an impartial observer. A detailed and impartial accounting of the misfeasance of these two clods can be found in a book called, *Airline without a Pilot*, by management consultant Harry L. Nolan, Jr. (available at www.targetbooks.com, or www.amazon.com). This work is an eye opener. It is recommended reading for anyone who wishes to understand business in America today and should be a required text at every Business School in the country.

The above management philosophy appears to be an ongoing phenomenon. As I wrote this, a new example appeared:

The new Delta CEO, Richard Anderson, announced plans to acquire Northwest Airlines. Having emerged from bankruptcy invigorated by the shedding of various contractual obligations, such as pilot pensions, Delta had the money to swallow Northwest Airlines. The plan included sixty-million dollars to be divided annually among six apparently miracle-producing executives.

They also planned to pay contracted pensions to *all* Northwest retirees *including* their *pilots*! CEO Anderson doesn't appear to regret, nor apologize for, the fact that, of all the various retiree groups, there is simply no money to pay retirements to Delta's *own* pilots! The logic, or justification, for this clearly gross injustice escapes my understanding. It will apparently remain a mystery as no explanation is forthcoming from Anderson. He appears to be on this path for no better reason than that he *can*.

Greed? You be the judge.

Chapter 32 | Some Thoughts on Deregulation

Simply put, deregulation has been a disaster. What? Don't you believe in free enterprise? Are you a socialist or something? No, I believe in free enterprise and the capitalist principle. The problem is, those principles cannot be applied fairly to the airline business. Why?

I recall Alfred Kahn, an economics professor, preaching for deregulation. Looking like the undertaker had done a lousy job on him, old Al stood before the cameras and preached all the benefits to be gained. Small cities would get better and cheaper service. Of course, old Al had never run a business and met a payroll, but he did have lots of economic models.

His models didn't tell him that big airlines served small cities at a loss to feed passengers into their main routes where the losses were recouped. Nor did his models tell him that freedom to fly anywhere would not create a laissez-faire system. Why? Because all the airports are owned by cities, counties, or states and they have a finite capacity for landings and loading facilities. These facilities, being government owned, put everybody right back into politics to obtain space, therefore, *re-regulation*!

Nor did his models tell him that all the newcomers were not going to jump headfirst into the thin small town market. He didn't see that they would cherry pick highly lucrative main routes and start fare wars. Well, that's good, isn't it? Lower prices would result, right? Yes, but there's a Catch 22 in that.

The airline business has always been a balancing act between safety and economics. Safety and profits always work against each other. You can only have *both* when returns are stable. Safety costs money! That's money for salaries for competent people, for overhaul and maintenance of a fleet, and for upgrading equipment and training.

I flew for the old Capitol Airways. I saw firsthand how they shaved corners and how they nibbled away little pieces of safety margins. The pilots who flew the Pan Am interchange, alternating between our DC-8s and theirs, knew early on that Pan Am would fail. We would pick up their DC-8s in New York to continue same-plane service westward. They always had long lists of "deferred maintenance" items and looked like trash. Too often we were forced to substitute one of our DC-8s. Our crews simply would not fly some of the "rambling wrecks" that Pan Am operated.

The public thinks that those fare wars and cut-rate prices benefit them. The public shops for discount airfares the same way they shop for discount furniture. There's a small difference there, however. A sofa which falls apart in five years instead of lasting ten may still be a bargain. An airline ticket is a contract with some people to move you from point A to point B and get you there alive!

The inescapable truth is that skinny profits equate to skinny safety margins. Pre-deregulation airfares were constantly decreasing in terms of real dollars. In the late 1930s, airfare coast to coast was the price of a new Ford. The seat mile costs constantly came down as aircraft capacity and speed increased. This was all a natural result of increasing aircraft productive capacity. Today's airline market is causing some results which make me cringe and happy to be out of it.

Aircraft size and speed have always been dependent upon engine developments. You can fly anything if you have enough power. Howard Hughes put eight Wright R-4360s radials on his Spruce Goose. The Wright R-3350 made the L-1049 Constellation and the DC-7 possible. The JT8-D jet engine made the B-707 and DC-8 possible. Development of engines producing fifty-thousand pounds of thrust offered us the B-747, L-1011, and DC-10. Such large aircraft needed three or four of these engines. Safety and redundancy were well served. If one failed, you still had other good ones to carry on.

However, a new development has come along—a class of engines that produce one-hundred-thousand pounds of thrust. Two of them will power an aircraft as big as the B-747 that now carries four engines. They offer somewhat better economy and half the maintenance time of two smaller engines. That sounds great to the airline bean counters, but there's a hidden cost attached about which the bean counters prefer not to talk.

Forget the vast Pacific Ocean for now. Let's talk about the shorter North Atlantic Ocean routes. Out in the middle of the Atlantic lies Iceland. If it's weathered in, the closest airports are Stornoway, Ireland, to the east, Nova Scotia or Newfoundland to the west. Either direction is hours away. I've been out in the middle of that route with a failed engine on both the L-1049 Constellation and the C-135 jet. On *both* occasions, Keflavick, Iceland, was closed by weather.

Did the crew and I sweat? Not too much. We still had three healthy engines, so we only lost a bit of cruise speed. How would I like to repeat the failed engine event and have only *one* still running? I don't even want to think about it! That remaining engine is going to have to carry on at a much higher output load.

Statisticians tell us that better engine reliability has reduced the odds of losing two to astronomical proportions. They hope that we will interpret "astronomical" to mean "never happen." Not so. When engineers develop a two-hundred-thousand pound class of engine, will the bean counters agitate to fly a *single engine* jumbo jet across the Atlantic?

Why do you think pilots of four-engine jets practice landing with two engines out on one side? They do it because it can *and has* happened. A jet engine is a very efficient vacuum cleaner. It will suck up anything put in front of it, including shrapnel from a disintegrating engine mounted on the wing next to it. Does it happen frequently? Nope. *Can* it happen? Yep.

Another technological development is the computer-driven, fly-by-wire system. With this system, the pilot inputs his commands to controls and throttles fed through a computer, which then sends electrical signals to servos to move these controls. This saves the weight of cables and pulleys, etc.

Pilot suspicions of that technology began with the crash of a new Airbus A-320 at the Paris Air Show. The airplane made a low pass down the full length of a runway and into the trees at the far end. A computer fault didn't allow the pilot simply to add power and all on board were killed.

As I edited my earlier work on this chapterk, a new event hit the news. U. S. Airways Captain "Sully" Sullenberger made an emergency landing of his stricken Airbus A-320 into the Hudson River and he did a magnificent job of it. That event shed light on the question of fly-by-wire controls and also on the smaller number of (larger) engines on big jets. The A-320 is comparable in size (150 passengers) to the original DC-8. The DC-8 had four engines. The A-320 has two bigger and ostensibly more efficient ones. The DC-8 could lose two engines and still fly. The A-320 can afford to lose only *one*.

Captain Sullenberger reported hitting a flock of geese on his climb out from La Guardia. The encounter cost him *both* engines. With his machine suddenly converted into a very large glider, he did the only thing he could do—find a flat place to land. He did what a professional should do and did a great job of it.

Consider for a moment the lucky side of the event. He had a flat river, not an open ocean with seas running, and was able to get to it. In addition, it was not a summer day with pleasure boats all over the river, so he had a clear space in which to set down. He also landed near a ferry crossing and boats arrived to help almost immediately.

Now consider the unlucky (or poorly engineered) aspects of an air emergency. I once had a bird-damaged engine on a B-727. The engine was still running, but I shut it down because it was vibrating. I still had two good engines. What were the odds of my losing the other two (or losing all four on a DC-8 for that matter)? While big birds, or a lot of small ones, will damage an engine, the odds are it will still be capable of running long enough for a safe landing. If Captain Sullenberger had lost only one engine, he could have returned to La Guardia on the other one. How could he be unlucky enough to have two engines actually *fail*? Yet, he was and they did.

Chapter 33 | Some Pointers on Security Procedures

Back during my DC-9 days, the era of "Take us to Cuba." hijackings produced some horrible events. Unarmed crews were sitting ducks. I flew a DC-9 from Miami through Orlando to Chicago one night and, on an approach to Orlando, we were put into a holding pattern. There was a hijacking in progress on the ground. Southern Airways Captain Billy Haas was dealing with hijackers on his DC-9. At one point, those maniacs tried to get Billy to dive into Fort Knox while en route. Billy kept cool and finally negotiated a fuel stop in Orlando. There the crazies decided that they wanted to go to Cuba. So far so good.

We were able to follow some of the action on the Ground Control frequency. The plane had been refueled. Then FBI agents ordered a fuel truck to park in front of the plane and block it. Hijackers responded by shooting Billy's copilot dead.

Billy's language ordering the truck out of the way was scathing and unprintable. As he taxied, the FBI marksmen shot all four main tires flat. With crazies screaming that they would kill passengers if he stopped, Billy made an incredible takeoff on four flat tires. His radio comments about the FBI were not complimentary. Upon landing in Cuba, police removed the hijackers, who expected to be greeted as heroes, and locked them up. The plane was repaired and released to fly back to the U. S.

This incident prompted some serious dialogue between the Airline Pilots Association and the FBI. The outcome was an agreement upon a group of signals which guaranteed Captains ultimate control over any decision forcibly to terminate a flight. The security procedures post 9-11 are really crippling to the airlines. We, of course, need security, but first let me talk about one of the results.

I pulled two examples from my logbook to discuss. In 1964, a flight between Atlanta and Chicago in a DC-7, powered by four reciprocating engines and props, took three hours, twelve minutes. In 1979, the same flight took one hour, fifty-eight minutes in a B-727. The jet age saved our passengers an hour and fourteen minutes. Today's security screening procedures have eaten up that hour and a quarter and then some. Effective travel times have *regressed* over forty years.

Dotty and I have discovered that if we start the clock leaving our home and stop it upon leaving the building with bags in hand, we can fly our old Piper Aztec from mid-

Florida to Denver in about 30 minutes less time than it takes to ride on the airlines. It's just ridiculous that a twin engine Aztec, cruising at 165 knots, and making two fuel stops, can get us to Denver faster than the airlines can.

Now, let's speak about the actual screening security process. I'm going to be very un-PC here, so be advised. The PC approach to avoid offending any Arab Muslims treats everyone as a potential threat. Never mind that all the embassy bombings, ship bombings and aircraft attacks have been made by male Arab Muslims between the ages of 17 and 45.

Here are just a few examples I have witnessed:

1. A beautiful young woman wearing open sandals, thin short shorts (no panties), a thin halter top (no bra), being wanded over her bare arms and legs when a dime in her pocket would have shown through.

2. A grammar school wrestling team (12 boys, ages 8 - 10), wearing team jackets, forced to remove shoes, belts and jackets to be wanded.

3. A man behind me arguing over a small pair of nail clippers which were being confiscated. They had no blade, only an inch-long file with dull point to clean under fingernails. Had he pointed them at me and demanded my wallet, I would have been laughing too hard to stand up. To help him prevent his arrest, I asked him if he had a dollar and five cents.

"Yes. Why?" he asked.

"Give the man your rusty clippers," I said, "and go fifty feet over to the magazine stand and buy a new one for ninety-nine cents, plus tax."

The security guard took the clippers and turned to the next in line, as the man walked directly to the newsstand.

4. A security guard in Dallas wanted to take my little pocketknife. A gift from my wife, it had a one-inch long blade and a nail file, useful for opening envelopes and sharpening pencils. I was in uniform. I told the man that I wanted it returned and that I wanted him to follow procedure for that. I waited patiently about ten minutes for a supervisor to show up. He produced an envelope. I put my name on it and he sealed the knife inside. He asked what flight I was on and then we walked to the gate check-in counter. There, he handed the envelope to our gate agent who then handed it to the captain of that flight—*me*. I ripped open the envelope and put the knife in my pocket. There was no objection from the security supervisor. He had followed "procedure."

5. Security in Atlanta once confiscated my two aluminum Maglite three-cell flashlights. Again, I was in uniform and the flashlights were in my flight bag. I was told they could be used as weapons. I did not argue. I went directly to my Chief Pilot's office.

"I can't legally operate my scheduled flight today," I said.

"Why?" he asked.

"Because I don't have all my legally required equipment," I answered.

"What don't you have?"

"I don't have my two required flashlights."

"Why not?"

"Because security confiscated them as potential weapons."

"*What the hell!*" he roared.

Phone calls to Corporate Security followed, etc., etc. A very red-faced security supervisor, out of breath, delivered the two flashlights to my cockpit about three minutes before departure.

What's my point here? Well, first, you cannot have security by employing ex-Burger King employees at minimum wage and tell them to "look for things." I have been through Customs in many countries hundreds of times. These trained and experienced people do not look at stuff. They look at people. They use profiling, body language, and other cues to "make" you for a good or bad guy and they are damned good at it.

All sorts of off-the-shelf technology exists to identify people properly. Hundreds of security sensitive government facilities are accessed daily by workers using these tools. I have a Concealed Weapons Permit. It required training, an FBI background check and fingerprints on file with the FBI. I think the fee was fifty dollars for the background check. Business travelers, who have deserted the airlines in herds in favor of charter flights, would gladly pay a fee for such a check. A holographic photo ID could carry computer data on iris scan or fingerprint data. The technology exists. Swipe the card, look into the lenses, and *Beep!* you're cleared. In fact, twenty years into the process, the TSA has now come up with TSA-Pre, similar to a concealed-carry card (and its security checks), where travelers can shorten the check-in process. Security people could then monitor *people*. X-ray machines, or the people watching them, cannot detect many types of weapons. In case you're wondering, I'm not going to give a seminar on how to get deadly weapons past the X-ray. Our enemies already know how.

Guns in the cockpit. During the days of the "Take me to Cuba." hijackings, I carried a 9-mm pistol in my flight bag. Then the FAA decided that pilots should go through weapons screening, too as if I needed anything more than my fingertips to kill three-hundred people! Pilot security training classes (annually) used to be presented by an FBI Special Agent named Leon Blakeny. Hijackings were discussed. He once posed a question.

"What would you do if you were told, on your intercom, that a hijacker had a knife at the throat of a flight attendant and demanded entry to your cockpit?"

Silence followed, as everyone pondered the problem. Sam Bass, one of the pilots, mumbled from the back of the room.

"Tell him no, see if he's serious enough to cut her throat."

336

Some nervous laughs followed Sam's sick humor, but Blakeny nodded.

"That's the right answer, because once you let him in your cockpit, all bets are off."

An armed crew does not need to play SWAT team up and down the aisles. They need only to prevent someone from coming through a two-foot wide door. So long as the crew have control of the cockpit, survival is possible. What about bombs? Well, if they are suicidal and have a big enough bomb, they could destroy a plane, but destruction is certain if it goes off in the cockpit. Detonation elsewhere becomes iffy. Airplanes are a lot tougher than many think. Many have landed safely with appalling damage. While an armed crew is not the total answer, a gun trumps a box cutter every time.

The flying public has never been told *why* crews are not armed. One reason is corporate lawyers. You see, if an armed crew killed a group of hijackers and saved a planeload of passengers that would be okay, but if, in doing so, they accidentally shot "grandma," then corporate liability enters the equation. On the other hand, if hijackers destroy the plane and all aboard it, corporate liability for crew actions will not attach. Sound thinking—from a *legal* point of view. The few pilots who have been certified to carry guns have been forced to go through many obstacles and hurdles. This serves to discourage many from attempting the process.

Two days after the 9-11 horrors, I spoke with the Director of the NRA Police Training department. The NRA (National Rifle Association) provides training to hundreds of police

337

departments which may be too small to support an independent program. He informed me that he had sent a letter to the head of FAA Security, in which the NRA offered to train pilots at *no cost* as a public service. There was no response. Eventually a program was created.

Any pilots desiring to carry a weapon must first submit to an invasive psychiatric exam, this even though they have already been evaluated as sane enough to be entrusted with an airplane full of people! Then, the pilots must travel to Albuquerque at their own expense and many more miles to a remote site in New Mexico for the training. They also pay for their own rooms and board during the week of training.

I'm going to exercise my First Amendment rights and do a bit of preaching at this point. I've been a proud Life Member of the NRA for over four decades. It's not about guns, folks, it's about freedom. An armed, law-abiding person is a citizen. Forcibly disarmed, he's only a *subject*. Every dictatorship in history proves this fact. Since the NRA defends the First Amendment equally with the Second, you are free to stand up and loudly disagree with me. Just remember that your right to do so was paid for, *in blood*, by citizens with guns!

Few realize that the security problems today's crews face are just *one* part of a worldwide battle. We're quite literally in the midst of World War IV. We won WWI, II, and III (the Cold War). This one is about Militant Islam and its rabid drive to capture the world and return it to a Tenth Century caliphate.

"The actions of terrorists don't reflect the Koran," we are told. "Most Muslims don't agree with what these people are doing."

Oh, really? How many times have you seen a Muslim Imam stand up in public and denounce terrorism? How many terrorists have been denied sanctuary by Muslim countries? How many of us saw the TV interview of children in a Muslim school in New York? Asked if they thought it was okay to fly a plane into a building to make a point, they all smiled and nodded, "Yes!" The interview caused such an uproar from the public that the TV crew later went back to the school for another "take." By then, the children had all been coached to answer "No." to the question.

Muslims are taught that they have the only true religion. All others are infidels, worthy only of death. Therefore, the fact that they live in the Tenth Century cannot be their fault. It must therefore be the work of the Great Satan. The irony sails over their heads that they must obtain weapons from the modern world because they are too backward to make their own.

Our incredible penchant for political correctness and our reluctance to hurt anyone's feelings are weapons used against us. Many Americans clamor to grant all the Constitutional protections and Civil Rights to captured terrorists as if they were American citizens accused of robbing a bank. They are *not* citizens accused of a crime. They are enemy combatants engaged in the effort to kill Americans (including women and children). If we persist in stuffing our heads in the sand (or elsewhere), they will win! These people do not treat Americans in their care by any Geneva Convention standards, but if we declared war on them, we could use the Geneva Convention code. Enemy combatants, captured out of uniform may be shot as spies.

Wake up Americans!

Late-breaking news: Homeland Security, the agency which the Federal government cobbled together to "protect" us, keeps coming up with *brilliant* new ideas.

A few years ago I got a phone call from a Bahamian friend. He asked that I fly to Nassau to fly back to Ft. Lauderdale with him. His airplane was part of his business and he had flown to and from the U. S. for years. I asked why he needed me with him. He explained that Homeland Security had just decreed that *all* flights to the U. S. would have to be on IFR (Instrument Flight Rules). As a VFR (Visual Flight Rules) pilot, he could no longer fly here. I hopped a flight to Nassau and filed IFR for him, flying back with him.

The next day, I called Homeland Security and was finally transferred to a supervisor. His explanation for the new rule was that it would put all arriving flights under "positive radar control." He was totally *unaware* that *all* international flight plans (IFR *or* VFR) were *already* required to be radar identified and given an *individual* transponder "squawk code" before crossing the U. S. ADIZ (Air Defense Identification Zone) Line. Failure to do so would *already* result in an Air Force fighter plane on your tail and an *armed* greeting team

340

upon arrival! Homeland Security *did not know the existing rules* before issuing their brilliant new rule. It was soon dropped.

Now they are currently planning another *"new"* rule. They're proposing the idea that *electronic* (e-mail) notification to Homeland Security be sent *before* a flight. Passengers will be checked against a no-fly list and they will electronically send eventual permission to take off. Many airstrips in the Bahamas have *no buildings*, let alone e-mail facilities. A cell phone call to Customs at a U. S. destination airport will no longer suffice. What possible purpose can this serve? Customs at *all* U. S. International Arrival airports *already* have access, by computer, to the no-fly list!

Another new proposal in the works would require airline type screening for people wishing to buy a "dollar ride" on one of the few remaining WWII aircraft at any *air show!* The handful of these old planes that remain are flying *history.* They are maintained by volunteer groups and small foundations, mostly with *donated* money. Forcing them to pay for Airline type screening systems and operators will simply *put them out of business.* No more historic aircraft for people to marvel over at the next air show. What *purpose* can that serve?

I hate to mention it, but will their next idea be airline type security at our little grass airport community? Will I need to be wanded and strip-searched before I can fly my Aztec solo for a sightseeing hop?

Until they can stop millions of bodies and tons of drugs from being *walked* across our borders, all the rest of their proposed "rules" are just another bad joke and a harassment of us citizens. Find a way to seal our borders and search the *millions* of containers coming into our ports before doing stupid things to *destroy* our general aviation industry.

Chapter 34 | Looking Back...

I have now been retired for twenty-three years. I have amassed some twenty-six-thousand hours of flying time, now. Most of my extracurricular flying has never been logged. I was advised, early on, not to provide any evidence the FAA might use to accuse me of exceeding various flight time limits. Looking back, I'm sorry I didn't keep a separate logbook as I can only recall Aero club flying, Cessna 310 trips for pay and other casual flying, from memory, now, not that it really matters.

Dotty and I flew our Aztec to and from the Bahamas and an annual run to Colorado and Wyoming. With my marriage to Dotty, I gained a stepson, Rob and a stepdaughter, Kristen. Both are now married, Rob to Patricia and Kristen to David. Living in Colorado, Kristen and David have a wonderful life, coaching other folks and writing computer programs. Rob and Patricia, in Wyoming, are busy with two precious grandsons and flying. We were very blessed. We made an annual trek out west to visit them, combining it with a reunion of USAF Academy classmates.

I look back over a career which started over fifty-six years ago and I feel very satisfied with what I did. It's gratifying to have done something useful and productive in life. All my passengers were delivered without a scratch or bruise and mostly on time and I damaged *no* aircraft. There were plenty of opportunities to do so. I have always felt fairly lucky, but luck only goes so far. Pure dumb-luck cannot run continuously for a third of a century, so it follows that some skill and good judgment played a part in my success and I take a certain amount of pride in it.

I believe that my career spanned the best years of the airline business. I flew the old piston-powered birds and the new jets. I worked for, and with, some great old timers who started and built businesses. The truths they taught and practiced have not changed.

The moral duty owed to paying passengers can never change. The equipment may change, become more modern and, perhaps, more reliable. Operating systems will improve. With all this modern 'gee-whiz' stuff, however, it still falls upon the shoulders of the Captain and his crew to operate it safely.

Some developments help, while others only add to the burden. Corporate managers still try to pound round pegs into square holes. They still try to substitute rigid "systems and procedures" for freethinking sound crew judgment.

344

Managers who have never sat in the left seat of a plane, full of people on a nasty night of bad weather can never be made to grasp what the job requires. You would have more success explaining brain surgery to a chimp.

The career of an airline captain is very unique. There are more lawyers and doctors in dozens of big cities than Airline Captains in the whole country. Lawyers do not deal directly with life and death daily. Doctors do, but they walk away from their mistakes. The Airline Captain operates in a uniquely hostile environment. Flying is not an inherently safe thing to do. The incredible safety record of the airlines is due primarily to the performance of professional crews over decades. Safe operations require a framework of procedures and systems. Beyond a certain point, making this framework ever more rigid is counterproductive. Pilots need a wide latitude of discretion in their operational environment.

Pat "Mother" Malone used to say at the opening of her Operations Specifications classes, "Darlings, I'm not here to teach you how to operate safely – you all know that already. I'm here to teach you what's *legal* to do, and there's a big difference between legal and safe." The point she was trying to make is that something which is legal to do may not be a *safe* thing to do today. There are also situations where the safe thing to do may not be *legal*. It is there where one may need to know how to CYA.

There can simply be too many variables in an emergency, or weather situation, ever to create hard-and-fast rules, which will always offer the safest options. No computer program will ever be able to sort out these variables and produce the correct answer. No computer will ever develop a sense of self-preservation. Only an experienced pilot can sort out the options in a given situation and he may have to do so in seconds. It's a fascinating, rewarding and challenging world in which the professional pilot operates.

Would I recommend the airline world to a young pilot? That's a tough question. Today's airline world is a lot different from mine. Today's managers and personnel departments try constantly to hire and then stamp pilots into a compliant corporate mold. Free thinkers and mavericks are shunned, even though they are often superb pilots. College degrees are required, even though they have no bearing on whether a future captain can make solid decisions.

Here's a sketch of what a good Captain must have:

- Good hand-eye coordination and sense of spatial orientation. That covers the stick and rudder part of the business.
- The ability to make rational decisions from masses of information—often in seconds—and often when you have every reason to be scared witless. You cannot freeze and you cannot panic, at least not more than once.
- A solid understanding of a complex machine and the limits of its capabilities.
- A firm confidence in your own abilities. Macho daring will only get you dead. Confidence must be balanced

with judgment about what one can, and cannot, do. As Clint Eastwood said, "A man's gotta know his limitations."

To any young men, or women, who honestly believe they have these characteristics, I would say, "Go for it!" It's a very rewarding feeling to drive home tired after a day which demanded four or five approaches to minimums in crappy weather and knowing you did everything smoothly and safely like a *professional* and your passengers had all been delivered safely. You'll be a part of a very small number of people who have the skill to do these things and no stadiums will be filled by our numbers.

I look back with pride at the huge number of people I delivered safely. I never had to sit in an office cubicle looking at a pile of paper. I never had to pound on doors to sell someone something people did not want or need. My world offered a great view of something new every day. I'm sure I could have made more money, but I would do it all over if offered the chance.

Delta Chief Pilot, Atlanta, Cliff Johnson Presenting Capt. Jerry with his
retirement from Delta Airlines award.

Airline Pilots Association Chairman & Capt. Jerry

Capt. Jerry (Left Seat) and Wife, Capt. Dotty

Capt. Dotty (Left Seat) and Husband, Capt. Jerry

2nd Officer Steve Fry, Capt. Jerry and 1st Officer Bruce Olmstead w/ Framed L-1011 Photograph (Capt. Jerry's Last Airliner)

Captains Dotty and Jerry at His Retirement

Captains Jerry and Dotty in Uniform

Bruce Olmstead, Steve Fry & Capt. Jerry (in hats)
Last Flight, First Leg, with the Atlanta Crew

Bruce Olmstead, Capt. Jerry & Steve Fry (in hats)
Last Flight, Second Leg, with the Ft. Lauderdale Crew

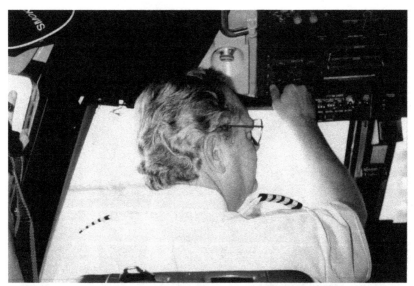

An Engineer's View of Capt. Jerry

Captain Dotty Westby in Her "Office" on her B-727, Having More Fun than the Law Allows!

Ready for 1st Line Flight | DC-6 Flight Engineer | Aug. 1963

First Capt.'s Rating, DC-6 | Apr. 6, 1966 (27-Yrs.-Old)
Jerry, FAA Inspector Marvin Thornton, Instructor Don Ellers

Last Piston Engine Flight on Delta, April 25, 1970
Jerry, Wanda Cornet, Charles Winstead

Jerry Making His Final Landing in a L-1011

Jerry Receiving Last Flight Water Cannon Salute from Airport Fire Trucks

The Planes Capt. Jerry Flew

L-1049 Constellation. Another Kelly Johnson, Lockheed
"Skunkworks" Masterpiece

DC-7 | Jerry Spent More Time Ferrying DC-6 & -7s
on 3 than on 4 Engines

DC-8-61 | Delta was First to Put in Service

DC-9-32 | Delta First to Put in Service | Jerry's First Captain's Slot

B-727 | Jerry Spent One Year in the Left Seat (8700+Hrs.)

Convair 340, the Last Piston-engine Airliner in Service

Lockheed L-1011 TriStar | Kelly Johnson's Last Masterpiece

Sick Engine – DC-7 3-Engine Ferry Flight

Captain Dick Gillette and Me

Me with Cessna 310

USAF Trainer T-37 1960

Lockheed L-100 Freighter Military called it C-130

The Master Captain, Walter Lee Mc Bride

Wife, Captain Dotty Westby's J-3 Piper Cub

Engineer Panel L-1011

Printed in the USA
CPSIA information can be obtained
at www.ICGtesting.com
LVHW090302081223
765818LV00054B/844